THE ETERNAL JOURNEY
Meditations on the Jewish Year

THE ETERNAL JOURNEY

Meditations on the Jewish Year

Jonathan Wittenberg

AVIV PRESS

NEW YORK

Aviv Press
The Rabbinical Assembly
3080 Broadway
New York, NY 10027

This book was originally published by Joseph's Bookstore, London, in 2001.

Cover designed by Adrianne Onderdonk Dudden

Printed in the United States of America
10   9   8   7   6   5   4   3   2   1   2003

This book is printed on acid-free paper with recycled content.

Library of Congress Cataloging-in-Publication Data
Wittenberg, Jonathan.
     The eternal journey : meditations on the Jewish year / Jonathan Wittenberg.
       p. cm.
     Includes bibliographical references.
     ISBN 0-916219-25-9
     1. Fasts and feasts—Judaism—Meditations.   I. Title.

BM690.W58   2003
296.4'3—dc22   2003063032

*To Mossy, Libbi and Kadya
and to Giga and Dani.
May love be carried safely from
generation to generation.*

Preface to the American Edition

There are circumstances so close to us that they become part of our souls. I love the gardens and woodlands, the streams and mountains of England and Scotland. The smell of the leaves and the sight of the snowdrops is as much a measure of the flow of my life as the melody of the great Kaddish and the opening blessings on the morning of the New Year. But I am aware that my favorite trees and flowers are northern European. I scarcely know any of the forests of North America or the colors of the maple leaves in the fall, which will one day, I hope, be a discovery for me.

I trust therefore that, though it is set in a different climate, this book, which is a search for the heart and for God, will cross the ocean safely and find a receptive home. For beneath the different leaves, the quest is surely the same.

This book is also set in a different time; it was written in the world as it felt before September 11. There are new things to ponder, and fear; but this book has already been its own journey and every journey begs its continuation.

I am extremely grateful to Aviv Press for adopting *The Eternal Journey* as one of its very first publications. I want to thank Rabbi Martin Cohen for introducing me to Aviv and the editorial board for accepting my work. I appreciate the effort Michael Joseph has made, not only for bringing out my book with so much care in England, but also for helping to see it through publication in the States as well.

Tzipora Sofare has been an excellent copyeditor. She has patiently and painstakingly helped me clarify many points, particularly among the references. Amy Gottlieb has been a kind, sensitive, and supportive editor; and I am thankful to her for the beautiful way this book has been produced. I appreciate Adrianne Dudden's inspiration and care in creating a beautiful cover for this edition.

I hope that this American edition of my book will bring new energy to the journey, both for myself and for many others.

JONATHAN WITTENBERG
London
Heshvan 5764–November 2003

Foreword

I'm sure my grandfather did speak of it, but I had quite forgotten that his mother wrote poetry. That was until one day last year, when in her beautiful flat my aunt Ruth handed me a slim volume and said she was giving me a collection of my great-grandmother's poems. I was thrilled with the gift and put the book carefully into my bag. Back at home, I began to read it. On the first page was a handwritten dedication to my grandfather and a list of contents. The book contained a cycle of poems about the Jewish year. I was overwhelmed. Three generations and almost exactly a century later, here was I, struggling to explore the very same themes.

I have been motivated to write this book by a love of the Jewish year, its seasons, songs, and symbols, which was given me in childhood and which seems as natural as life itself. I am equally compelled by an appreciation of the beauty, tenderness, and incomprehensibility of life. I am haunted by the sense of an almost secret spirit which, amidst the many encounters of existence, may, if I am not unworthy, for some rare seconds cross the threshold of the soul and be revealed. This is what makes me return again and again to the challenge of trying to find in the wisdom of Judaism a key to the joy and confusion, the frustration and mystery, of every day.

This book is dedicated to the journey of the past into the future. I hope that what follows is faithful to the spirit in which I was raised, to the tolerant and deeply rooted Judaism of my family, to the love of literature of my late mother, and to the affection and devotion of my father and Isca. I met Nicky, my wife, through our love of Jewish living, gardening, and animals. Together, and with our children, we have grown more appreciative of the world; through her I affirm life far more deeply.

I hope that the following reflections are loyal to these values and to the beauty and sanctity of life which they seek to honor.

This is not an academic work. It is intended rather to be a companion through the seasons of the year, whose sequence it follows, from Elul, the month of preparation for the High Holidays in the autumn, to the Fast of Av and the weeks of consolation in the summer. I hope that readers will find in it echoes of their own thoughts and that it will lead them to meditations of their own.

JONATHAN WITTENBERG

Pesaḥ 5761 – April 2001

IN ACKNOWLEDGMENT AND APPRECIATION OF

My father, who has always been there for me, who nurtured my love of traditional Judaism, and whose loyalty and humility I deeply respect;

Isca, my mother's younger sister who became my second mother, without whose love and insight I would never have reached the point where I could write this book;

Nicky, my wife, without whose love and companionship I could not think of my life, and whose help and advice I seek in everything I undertake;

The members of the New North London Masorti Synagogue, my community, for challenging me, inspiring me, and helping me, to discover what is set out below;

The North London Hospice, from whose spirit of welcome, dedication, and reverence I have been privileged to learn;

My teacher Dr. Joanna Weinberg, for her friendship, wisdom, and support;

John Schlapobersky, for his fellowship and inspiration;

Bette Rabie, for her warmth and solidarity;

Michael Joseph, for taking on this project when I was hesitating, for developing it so thoughtfully, and for giving me so much encouragement;

David Elliot, for being such an excellent editor, finding just the right balance between enthusiasm and insightful criticism;

The Jewish Chronicle and Masorti Publications, for allowing me to reprint articles first published there.

Unless otherwise stated, all translations of poetry are my own.

Notes

Unless otherwise noted, all Bible, Mishnah, Talmud, and Midrash translations are those of the author.

Mishnah references read as follows: M. Rosh Hashanah 1:2 (First chapter, second verse of the tractate Rosh Hashanah). All talmudic references are to the Babylonian Talmud, and citations are rendered as follows: B. Rosh Hashanah 18a (page 18a of tractate Rosh Hashanah).

Spellings and Hebrew transliterations in this American edition of *The Eternal Journey* conform to American publishing standards and to those of Aviv Press. Transliteration guidelines:

ʿ	=	ע	ʾ	=	א
tz	=	צ	ḥ	=	ח
ei	=	ֵ	kh	=	כ
ai	=	ַ			

Contents

You, who've been my lover always,
Whose love bears my ignoring every hour,
Who, constant, knock
While yet my heart, too noisy, does not hear;
I shall yield in silence
For I feel your power.

J. T. W.

ELUL — THE MONTH OF PREPARATION

A Glimpse of Wild Deer

One thing have I asked of God, that do I seek:
to dwell in the house of the Lord all the days of my life . . .

from Ps. 27:4, said evening and
morning from the first of Elul

It was at the edge of the old forest below Box Hill in Surrey, where the woods rise up from the field which runs along the bottom of the valley, that my wife and I caught a glimpse of them. Half visible at twilight, two deer ran swiftly across the ploughed land and off into the trees. We stood totally still after they had disappeared, as if we had seen another world.

For some moments we waited by the side of the field, encircled by the shrinking ring of dusk, gazing at the midpoint of the fading light where the animals had been. Then we walked on, carrying within us the awareness of our transformation. It happened more than ten years ago, but I still live that moment now. I still feel the power, both humbling and quickening, of the revelation of a vitality of such extent and penetration as to permeate the valley and the woodland, the horizon and the darkness all about.

Sometimes, everything seems closed off. Life, for sure, is there all about us, but between ourselves and its vitality, between us and its mystery, is a thick barrier. Nothing of life's beauty penetrates. It is only our own consciousness, of course, which is sealed, untouched either by wonder or trepidation. This is the state that the Ḥasidim described as *katnut moḥin*, littleness of mind. Then all at once something happens. Wild deer flee up the valley to the woodland; we are drawn after them and the world round about and the world within are suddenly filled with life.

I recall feeling sad after the deer had gone. Awe was followed by sorrow. Thinking about it now, I believe it was the same mourning as is often provoked by moments of great intensity. They make the rest of life appear half-lit and half-lived. It is as if they visit us only to render more apparent the loss of some elusive spirit that could have made life more simple and more sacred. As Rabindranath Tagore put it:

If it is not my portion to meet thee in this my life, then let me ever feel that I have missed thy sight — let me carry the pangs of this sorrow in my dreams and in my wakeful hours.[1]

I think of the experience differently now; I no longer mourn for it because it has not gone. In the world of the spirit nothing is irredeemable. There may be much forgetting, a constant losing, but there are also many moments of illumination and opportunities for rediscovery. They come in the ice on the branch of a tree, the smell of the earth in spring, the unfurling of a wave in a cove. For all the earth is full of God's glory and the heart does not sleep forever. Therefore thank God for the renewal of life!

Elul is the month of wakefulness. We are roused with the sound of the shofar, stirred by the words of its special psalm:

One thing have I asked of God, that do I seek: to dwell in the house of the Lord all the days of my life . . .

When I first read this verse I thought that what its author wanted was never to leave the sanctuary in Jerusalem. Perhaps he was, in modern parlance, "suffering from the pressure." He was hoping for the ancient equivalent of an early retirement, leaving him time to frequent the silence of sacred places. Now I read the words differently. What the psalmist wants to change is not the outer state of where he is but the inner state of how he perceives. What he really desires is the gift of understanding that he is in the house of the Lord wherever he may be. He wants to see God wherever he is.

Presumably, though, like the rest of us, he has to make do with sometimes. But "sometimes" can be sufficient, and the occasional glimpse of wild deer enough to change a life.

God?

God, you are my God; I seek you at dawn;
My soul thirsts for you, my flesh longs for you
In a parched and weary land with no water.

Ps. 63:2

We cannot explore our own spirit, let alone a religion, without encountering the word "God." For some people it is natural to speak of God. But for others it is extremely difficult. Stirred by beauty, awe, companionship, and love, the soul nevertheless remains uneasy with the notion of God. It seems, perhaps, too definitive, too personal, to imply too much belief, to draw too many concepts in its wake. Despite being committed to the practice of a formal religion, I share that discomfort and often feel more at home with those who experience it than with people who speak of God with the appearance of much confidence. So I want to ask: What does it mean to say "God"?

There are many names for God. Just within Judaism God is spoken of as the Lord, the Almighty, the Holy One, the All Present, I Am that I Am, the *Shekhinah*, the Source of Blessing, and many further appellations. Other faiths address God by countless different names. Whoever we are, all our words for God are only names. But they present the danger that language will divide us, Jew from Christian and Moslem, "believer" from "nonbeliever," those comfortable with saying "God," from those who do not feel the same.

That is why it is so important to acknowledge that whatever we say about God is always provisional, always inadequate. Language is tentative. Its use is in itself part of the search for what we can never quite express but are compelled to name, if only in order to try to explain our experience to ourselves. God is not a shorthand for certainties, a cipher for dogmas and fixed beliefs. It is only a syllable, a sound, which, if it indicates anything, points to a quest; a searching that is at once as intimate as our own soul and as vast as the universe, and that takes as many forms as there are moods in a lifetime. "God," therefore, ends up being used as shorthand for sometimes knowing, sometimes longing, sometimes hoping, often doubting, that there is some ultimate being, some presence that encompasses everything.

Far more therefore than our different faiths divide us, I believe that our common needs unite us — to question the purpose of our life, to find values and meanings which are not subject to death, to open ourselves to the presence of whatever it may be that, for want of another word, religion calls God.

These considerations govern everything to be said in all of what follows.

I believe in God the Creator. This has nothing to do with theories about the origin of the world. Rather, it is based on an intuitive sense of the presence of God within every living being. Some days I sit at my desk, looking out at the garden and am overtaken by the awareness that all life, every bird, each squirrel on the grass, my own self, all share the presence of the same consciousness. The same invisible flame burns within us all. Sometimes this intuition expresses itself as a tumultuousness of being, like the mighty freedom of the sea. Sometimes it is articulate in silence, as in the deep stillness when a lamp burns by a person who has died. Sometimes it surrounds us with a cheerful ease. The other day on the way to the synagogue a friend stopped me and said, "Look at that spider's web, see the sun shine through it." This is what it means to speak of all the earth being full of God's glory.

I believe in God who knows and judges. I don't mean that God judges in any way comparable to human judgment. I can't understand God in such personal terms. Yet the experience of God's judgment is palpable nevertheless. It is a feeling of being known; the sense of something around me and inside me which challenges who I am. Perhaps it is the very sense of awe or wonder that illumines the conscience like a great light, so that I know myself with a clarity I cannot deny. At that moment, far from being afraid, I am glad to be known, as if that in itself were a privilege, and truth were an act of love.

I believe in God who teaches. God teaches through beauty, wonder, companionship, and love, through shame and remorse. These feelings draw me closer, make me want the barrier of selfishness between myself and life to go away.

I believe in God who loves. Love is the vital force that animates the heart. When my heart is closed, I do not know God. When my heart is open, in a small way perhaps I sometimes do. God is the heart's inspiration, and the heart's love is manifest in all life's paths, in the delight of a child, in the everyday affection of held hands, in the encouragement of a teacher, in the ministrations of a nurse. Such love survives death; it draws the spirits of the living and the dead together in a single bond.

I believe in God who is eternal. I do not think that life is swallowed up in nothingness, whatever the fate of our particular being. For we live and die in the presence of life's enduring source. We depart amidst the constant generation of new life, and the stars, the trees and the leaves, and animals and children have the power to reconcile us with our fate.

I believe in God high above what we can know and deep beneath what we can say. For all our words are tentative; they cannot match the reach of our thoughts, and our thoughts themselves are only intimations. Our words represent only a kind of searching, an endeavor to capture merely a moment of meaning.

I do not believe that God is fair, at least not in any way we can recognize on this earth. I don't believe we can use God to square the circle, as if the right theological answer would take away all the issues of life's pain. Life is frequently unjust. God, the liturgy says, "cuts [the length] of life for all who live." God appears to do it unfairly. Some have plenty and some go hungry; some are at ease and some undergo torments others couldn't even begin to imagine. That is why I will not go to a sick person and explain why God has sent such affliction, or to the bereaved and explain God's secret reasons for taking away the person they love.

Consequently, I don't believe in a God who intervenes in the outer course of our life in any obvious and consistent manner. There are countless situations in which we want to cry out, "God, stop this!" But there is no satisfactory answer as to why God doesn't. Belief in God is no insurance against terrible and unjust things occurring, as well we know. When bad things happen, we pray and hope; but if we don't get what we want it doesn't mean that God said no. There are laws of nature; there are accidents. There are also cruelty, carelessness, and indifference. There are things which are our fault, things which are the fault of other people and things which are nobody's fault at all. How, and if, life's tragedies express God's will is inscrutable.

I cannot therefore believe in an "it's-all-okay" God. There are people who say, "If you had more faith you would know that there is a reason for everything." A friend of mine, whose brother died, was told his grief betrayed a lack of faith that what God does is for the best. But I cannot believe it's right to use God as a panacea to take away the questions and the pain. God is not the ultimate placebo. The search for faith, the life of trust in God, are deeply rewarding, but they neither resolve all issues nor remove all suffering. We want a heart open to God's being, not hard with God's answers.

There are things it is wrong to believe about God. It is wrong to use God to deny the humanity of another person. The Torah asserts at the outset that every human being of whatever race or faith is created in God's image.

It is perverse to use God to incite hatred, to claim that God invariably supports any one land, religion, or party. God favors righteousness everywhere. It is cruel to use God to justify the unjustifiable. Such behavior makes religion evil. It makes me understand the humanist who argues that religion is responsible for more bloodshed than any other cause. Often I think it is not the atheist but the believer who has to answer for their case.

Yet at the same time I believe in a God who creates, teaches, loves, cares, and endures for evermore.

It seems, therefore, that we are left inhabiting a contradictory and para-doxical world, compounded of God's presence and God's absence, of what God does and does not do. We are left struggling. We are left searching, morally and spiritually.

We search spiritually for all the resources God can possibly give. God may not prevent painful things from happening to me, but God may be with me through them. Therefore I want to make myself available to won-der and accessible to awe. I want to seek out what is good and loving, to be inspired and learn from it. I want to be taught, purified, and guided. I want to make time for the spirit. I want to learn to pray open to its pres-ence, because, in the words of Gale Warner: "Prayer is a call to partner-ship, a conscious placing of our spirits and intentions in alignment with the creative spirit. This call to partnership is always answered."[2]

We are left struggling with our moral responsibilities. Abraham Joshua Heschel, rooted in Judaism's mystical tradition, described God as a stranger in today's world. Our task, he taught, is to bring God home.[3] God is in exile. Sparks of divinity are scattered in broken fragments, and God entrusts us with making the world whole once again. God, too, is vulnerable. We use our lives either to wound or to heal, to draw God near or to drive God farther away, and that decision is ours.

That is the challenge. Each of us carries a fragment of ultimate responsibility. The Mishnah describes us as passing before God on the New Year like the children of Maron. Puzzling over this phrase, the Talmud notes that Maron is the name of a mountain in the Galilee. The ascent is precipitous and narrow; no two people can travel side by side.[4] There is a level of existence at which, however gregarious, however popular we are, we remain alone. It is there in our aloneness that we make our moral and spiritual choices, there that we face the challenge of seeking God. Gale Warner, wrestling with a fatal illness, yet determined to meet her destiny with courage, described it thus: "We must walk out to meet our fate. We must walk to the edge of the canyon, the top of the mountain, into the cold waters of the ocean." There, she writes, we encounter "what has been labelled 'God's will.' The unseen dance partner of our will, whose steps we can only deduce."[5]

It's a hard journey; yet what a partner to dance with, whose breath is the soul of all life and whose word is the inarticulate wind.

Three Gifts

> On your behalf does my heart say,
> "Seek my face."
>
> Ps. 27:8

Three gifts — three faculties — are given us to draw us toward God. Our conscience knows right from wrong. Our heart feels love. Our soul makes us susceptible to wonder and awe.

In a remarkable poem the thirteenth-century mystic, Naḥmanides, describes the faculties with which each human being is endowed as the soul travels down to enter the body at birth:

> I am woven out of dust, yet your spirit is breathed in me . . .
>
> You place a light by my foothold, along my path,
> You search all the chambers of my being with the spirit given me.
> When I departed from before You, You warned me, saying:
> "Fear the Lord, my child, the King."
>
> You set the scales of justice in the jurisdiction of the heart . . .[6]

For many people the very mention of the word conscience evokes feelings of guilt. Like Lady Macbeth, haunted night after night by the impossibility of ever again having clean hands, they too feel that their conscience must always be dirty. How can that faculty ever be our friend?

Judaism does not teach that we are born guilty. Rather, to be human is to be granted moral opportunity and the capacity to distinguish between right and wrong. The conscience is where we weigh the nature of our words and actions, the place where we come to know our moral nature better. We test our conduct in our conscience, asking ourselves: "Was what I did generous or selfish? Were my words really kind, or did I secretly mean to be hurtful?" When we have done wrong, it is here that we recognize it, here that we feel shame and remorse. That is why it takes courage to listen to our conscience. But if we fail to do so, we ignore the voice of truth within us.

Our conscience desires to be clean. This is the true meaning of *viddui*, or confession — the process by which we return to moral integrity, the willing acknowledgment of what we have done wrong in order to regain our inner purity. The shame we feel when we know we have behaved badly is not a punishment, but rather, the way we register an internal cleansing process. This inner cleaning may be painful, but it isn't punitive. Rather, it is motivated by the longing of the conscience to be at one with its place of origin. Ultimately, therefore, confession is not something that we are made to do, but that we want to do in order to feel pure and close to God. Thus the season of atonement is less a time of reckoning and reprisal than a time of longing and return.

The heart knows love and sorrow. "The Holy One desires the heart," teaches the Talmud, but the converse is equally true — that the heart seeks God.[7] The *Shulḥan Arukh,* a key code of Jewish law, rules that the person who leads the services over the High Holidays should not be younger than thirty so that he is capable of having a *lev nishbar venidkeh,* a broken and humbled heart (Ps. 51:19). Prayers from such a heart reach God.

That is why the High Holiday liturgy is so full of images of tenderness: Rachel weeping for her children as she witnesses their exile; Jeremiah bearing God's words to the people of Jerusalem, "I remember the faithfulness of your youth, the love of your bridal days, how you followed after me through the desert, through an unsown land"; God recalling Ephraim, the child of his delight, for whom his inner being yearns.

But nothing so affects the heart as the love we actually know. In fact, one of the purposes of liturgy is to evoke our own experience of the feelings it describes. A friend told the following story at the seder table. She was a *Kindertransport* child and had been sent from Prague to England as a small girl. Her parents had sent her away, and she had never seen them again. Despite her awareness at an intellectual level of what it must have cost them to part from their daughter, she still felt hurt by what they had done. Irrational as she knew it to be, she felt rejected. But after the war she was invited to visit old friends in Holland. They gave her a parcel that her parents had entrusted to them, asking them to give it to their daughter should the opportunity ever arise. It contained their wedding rings. It was only then, when she received this gift, that she understood how truly her parents had loved her and quite what that love had meant.

The spirit brings us a sense of wonder and beauty. Without wonder or beauty, I doubt if we are fully human. For beauty stirs the soul, and the soul guides us toward beauty. That is why all of the *Seliḥot* — forgiveness — prayers that mark this season open with a meditation on the work of creation and the natural beauty of the world:

> To you belongs day, to you also night,
> You fashioned the luminaries and the sun.[8]
>
> In (your) hand are the hidden depths of the earth
> And the heights of the mountains . . .[9]

We are reminded that we belong to a wider plane of existence, that we are connected to the creative power that unites all being, through our participation in which — if only momentarily — our mortal nature is transcended and we are joined to immortal life.

Our conscience, heart and soul connect us to God.

But if we are not heedful, the conscience can grow dull, become acquiescent, go dormant. The heart becomes impermeable. An emotional membrane isolates it from sensitizing influences and it becomes unfeeling and uncaring. The soul, deprived of nourishment, forgets its God, and our mind soon confirms that we have no precise knowledge anyway of so vague and unascertainable a dimension of experience.

That is why Judaism offers us these days of judgment, mercy and awe. Their purpose is to alert the conscience, to awaken the heart, and to restore the soul.

Who We Are

> Who am I and what is my life . . .
> Ignorant of knowledge and devoid of skill?
>
> > Rabbi Shimeon ben Yitzhak Abun,
> > prayer for Rosh Hashanah[10]

In Elul, month of preparation and petition, we begin to ask the personal questions that predominate over the High Holidays, which are shortly to come.

A "Who am I?" question comes in two parts: There is, "Who am I in the eyes of other people? What do I look like to them?" And there is simply, "Who am I? Who am I before God?" These two kinds of questions lead us to different facets of our life.

Judaism teaches that it matters how other people perceive our conduct. We live in a network of communal relationships and responsibilities. What we do affects everyone around us. We cannot therefore avoid considering what other people think about us; this would be selfish. Judaism also teaches us to learn from other people so that we can grow in compassion, understanding, and wisdom. Most importantly, we learn from our interaction with others to know ourselves as we are, rather than as we might wish or fantasize ourselves to be.

The danger is that we can easily become haunted by the estimations of others and trapped by their judgments, real or imagined. Some people feel judged from the beginning. "I was the wrong music, / The wrong guest for you," wrote the poet Olive Fraser, who, despite her brilliance, always felt herself a failure and located the cause of it in her very birth.[11] Many children feel acutely aware that they don't achieve what their parents expect of them; half a lifetime later they still harbor primitive wounds in their self worth. Sometimes judgments emerge in our closest relationships; a person carries a humiliating consciousness of not living up to the man or woman their partner had wanted them to be. Sometimes we feel judged and wanting because of relationships we don't have. All of us are aware at times of such hurts — and inflict them on others.

In our work-lives many of us experience the effects of the ever more competitive marketplace. In these days when everything and everyone is assessed, we are conscious of being evaluated for our performance virtually all the time. What Michael Dell, founder of the computer corporation which bears his name, has to say about his field applies to much of modern life:

> In our business, the product cycle is six months, and if you miss the product cycle, you've missed the opportunity. In this kind of business, there are two kinds of people, really: the quick and the dead.[12]

Many people who considered themselves to belong to independent professions now feel the hot breath of the inspector at the back of their necks. Even the spirit is subject to audit; churches and synagogues are conscious of the marketplace and their leaders speak in terms of assessment and performance.

It is certainly good for us to consider what we can learn and to listen to advice and criticism. But we can also become persecuted by comparisons and end up compromising our creativity and forgetting our spirit in the struggle to satisfy the expectations of others.

The question "Who am I before God?" is of a different order. Judaism teaches us to keep it before us always, but in the High Holiday prayers it recurs with the frequency of a refrain:

> Who are we?
> What is our life? . . .
> What is our salvation, what is our strength?

For, important as the estimation of others may be, it is not that which defines our essential nature. Were it to do so, we would be no more than the sum of our desire to conform, as moral, or immoral, as the will to which we bend. Who we ultimately are is a matter between ourselves and God.

Different people have different needs. For me nature provides an essential context for this return to the basic question of who I am. It is often there that I feel closest to God. The process by which the heart sifts its experiences and turns them into nourishment is inspired and assisted by rivers, forest, sea, desert, and the company of birds. In cities we think of what our place is and who we are in the competitive network of human estimation; it is almost impossible to be free of constant rush and constant worry. God is there; God is always potentially there in people. But God may be harder to find. However, when we have sufficient space another kind of consciousness can return, an inner process different not so much because of the objects of its thought, as because of the nature of the thinking subject. The heart becomes aware of itself and the soul cognizant of its own existence. They speak to us on God's behalf, saying, "Seek my face." Then the question, "Who am I?" emerges in an altogether different dimension. Who am I to have the privilege of life, to feel the wind with the forest, to breathe together with the animals, to look upon a view of water and of sky? Osip Mandelstam wrote:

> A body is given to me — what am I to make
> From this thing that is my own and is unique?
> Tell me who it is I must thank for giving
> The quiet joy of breathing and of living?[13]

When Moses reluctantly accepts the mission of telling Pharaoh to let the Children of Israel go, he asks to know God's name. "I am that I am," says God. It may be that in our best moments we too have a portion in that divine name. We shed our given names and duties, and all the expectations that invariably accompany them, in order to be what we are. Engaged with the wonder of being, part of eternal life in its ever changing manifestations, we are what we are and, nameless before God, participate in life. Such an experience may only last a few seconds, but it transforms our consciousness, cleans us and restores our soul.

It would be tempting to say that the second "Who am I?" is the only one that matters. Who cares about anything else? But we do care, and rightly so. Judaism requires us to commit ourselves to relationships and work within society. We need the deeper sense of who we are, not so as to evade our tasks, but to sustain us in fulfilling them. The awareness that we live before God, nurtured and replenished by God's spirit, sharing life with all other beings, privileged to participate in this experience full of wonder, gives us a deep resilience and vitality. That is the source of our love, the inspiration for any goodness we may have, and our true strength.

ROSH HASHANAH

A Good Year?

"It's been a very full year, but a good year," I've heard myself saying several times recently. What I mean is that I am grateful for my good fortune. But then the deeper question goes through my mind, "Have I, for my part, lived the year well?" That isn't such an easy question to answer. How can I know? How do we assess the years of our life?

Sometimes the answer to the question, "What kind of year have you had?" is obvious; only a forgetful or insensitive person would ask it. Maybe joys have been dominant, the blossoming of a relationship, the passing of exams, the birth of a child, a special anniversary. Or perhaps it has been a year of difficulty, sorrow, and loss. Maybe someone is even dying over the High Holiday period itself. Then the very words, *"leshanah tovah* — A Good Year," are impossible to say and, pain being inevitable, all we can do is hope for the strength to face it and keep faith with life.

But many of our years are more humdrum; they are not marked by dramatic events. Is there any means by which we can measure them and know for ourselves whether they have been good or bad, whether they represent time squandered or time well used?

Ben Zoma lived in the first part of the second century, during the period of Roman persecutions between the destruction of the second Temple and the crushing of the Bar Kokhba revolt. He died young, before achieving rabbinic ordination, but was nonetheless mourned as an outstanding teacher of Torah. Yet he is best known for a simple but penetrating series of questions through which he guides us to look within, at what kind of person we are.[1]

His first question is: "Who is wise?" He answers: "The person who learns from everybody." Hasidic folklore is full of stories about how the great rebbes followed this counsel. Rebbe Zusya of Anipoli used to say that he learned three things from babies: always to keep busy, to cry out when you want something, and to be satisfied when your basic needs are met. Rebbe Elimelekh of Lizhensk used to tell how he overheard the wife of his neighbor, who was a furrier, chastising her husband, "Don't go to sleep just because it's late; skin the animal while the candle's still burning."[2] From this charming practice he learned that so long as the soul's candle was alight one should never neglect one's tasks.

Real learning, however, is not easy; it always requires a certain inner readiness. Even in the formal setting of a classroom one has to be prepared not to know. But to learn from others in the wide arena of all life's encounters requires real humility. Have I allowed people to be my teachers or have I been too proud, too prejudiced, or too blind? Perhaps my attitude has been, "I know it all already." Then what I might have gained by thinking about how kindly the man in the queue in front of me spoke, or how my friend managed her troubles, or what my wife said to me, has been squandered. Perhaps I have made myself too busy to learn Torah; perhaps I have been too judgmental to value the insights of a different culture and another kind of wisdom. Am I more open or more closed as a result of my year? Do I listen, with head and heart, or have I no time for such things?

How we learn from life is a true measure of who we are. A tree has a ring for every year of its existence; is my life marked by new discoveries and developments? Or am I always going to remain the same old person with the same old limitations?

Ben Zoma's second question is: "Who is strong?" He responds: "The person who overcomes his/her inclination." We tend to measure strength by our ability to control external phenomena, our possessions, our body, our fortunes, and of course, other people. Ben Zoma sees strength as the ability to manage ourselves, to rule our passions and our fears. Paradoxically, we often seek to control what we cannot and, as a result, feel weak. Yet frequently we abdicate our capacity to govern our inner self, which may be a source of strength even at times when there is nothing we can do about our outer fate. Perhaps life's ultimate challenge is how we manage our own thoughts and feelings, how we affect the quality of our own consciousness.

Have we tried to understand ourselves, to know what it is that makes us fearful or angry? Or will a similar scenario find us just as little in control in ten years' time? Are we using our good characteristics as generously as we can? Are we feeding, or poisoning, our capacity for compassion, our feeling for beauty, our sensitivity to others? Have we been strong or weak this year in understanding and developing our inner selves?

Ben Zoma's third question is: "Who is rich?" He replies: "The person who rejoices in his/her portion." In the West, most of society is materially richer than any previous generation. Yet according to Ben Zoma's definition we are among the poorest people ever to have lived. We have created a culture of constant dissatisfaction. Our very economy depends on the manufacture of ever more and diverse kinds of want, and is driven by the "fulfillment" of constantly generated "needs." As a result we find it particularly hard to rejoice in our portion and live with too little gratitude. One of the secrets of unhappiness is to want *something else,* or to want to be *somewhere else,* or to want to be *someone else,* all the time.

Have we run away from our true wealth? Have we walked past our own riches, taking for granted friends or family, ignoring all kinds of treasure just because we have it already? Are we really poor, in feeling or fortune, or do we only feel so because we have absented ourselves from our actual wealth?

Ben Zoma's final question is: "Who is honored?" He answers: "The person who honors [all] beings." Very few of us can manage without the approval of others. As children we seek it in the form of praise and prizes; as adults many of us do exactly the same. There is nothing wrong with this, up to a point. But it can easily become a form of idolatry in which what we really worship are our own attributes. Ben Zoma teaches us not to behave like that. Let honor take care of itself; respect will come naturally to those who cherish and care for all living beings. That is real honor, and that is all that matters. Ben Zoma is not being naïve. We have all met people, often older people, who are held in esteem because they have time for everyone, because they are compassionate, because they are honest, because they listen well. Such people feel themselves honored by their very contact with other people, sometimes even with animals too. To be close to life's heart is to receive real honor. The rest really doesn't matter.

The Evil of the Decree

Bosnia 1996: "Where are the children?
I told you not to lose sight of the children!
Who's taken the children?"

heard on a news report

Life is the most precious gift we have. Sometimes when I hear of terrible things, of people waiting with quiet courage for the bullets of their persecutors, of sudden disappearances and murders, I go into the room where my children are sleeping and sit there watching them breathe. In this simple act, I recognize a privilege which millions of people would give all their wealth to share.

This truth, that life is the most precious gift we have, is at the heart of the most difficult, most feared passage in the whole High Holiday liturgy, the *Unetaneh Tokef* prayer:

> On Rosh Hashanah it is written and on Yom Kippur it is sealed, how many shall pass away and how many shall be born; who shall live and who shall die; who by fire and who by water . . .

We may be moved to awe by this prayer. We may be terrified by the reminder of selections, war, and disaster. But we cannot easily ignore it.

It is hard to know whether the author meant us to take his words literally. The Talmud, from which he draws them, probably did not intend to teach that our fate is sealed by God over the High Holidays in as irrevocable a manner as the *Unetaneh Tokef* seems to suggest. The prayer may also reflect historical reality as much as its literary sources. It may come from a period, perhaps toward the end of the Dark Ages in Europe, when death by sword or wild beast, famine, fire, or plague, was not so much a punitive act of God as a regular feature of everyday life.

Unetaneh Tokef is a meditation on life's most frightening eventualities. These have changed in character, but they haven't gone away. The prayer expresses a basic fact familiar to all: no one knows what lies round the corner. We are ignorant of what destiny has in store, and none of us can be sure whether we ourselves will be here this time next year or whether death will take away our nearest and dearest.

The story is told of a man lost in a deep forest. Eventually he finds a hut through the dusty windows of which glimmer a multitude of small flames. He enters and sees countless candles burning, some in beautiful lanterns, some in rusty metal holders, some with much oil left and some with almost none. An old man appears and, in answer to his question, tells the traveller that each flame is a life. "Then which," he asks, "is mine?"[3] We might well have asked the same question. But would we want to know the answer?

However, the prayer is more than a meditation on our destiny. It tells us that we don't stand helpless before our fate, that we have the power to do something about it.

> *Teshuvah, tefillah* and *tzedakah* —
> Repentance, prayer, and charity,
> avert the evil of the decree.

The question is: what are repentance, prayer, and charity; and how do they "avert the evil of the decree"?

Teshuvah, "repentance" or "return," is generally understood as return to religion, but it can be thought of more generally as return to the good within us, to the best of which we are capable. That best is surely love.

I learned much about love at a funeral I once attended. After the eulogy the wife of the deceased asked to read a few words she had written for her husband. She spoke of how she remembered the day she met him as if it were yesterday. She described his charm, piety, modesty, and kindness. Then she looked up from her script and, struggling to speak, said that in spite of her pain, she felt grateful for their twenty years of love — love with all that meant: support, companionship, intensity, and partnership of spirit.

Few of us are as mindful of those we love as we should be. There are good reasons; we have to live with the everyday, with strife and disappointments. Even so, how good it would be for us to return regularly to the place within ourselves that knows how to give and appreciate love. My children have a CD-Rom game called *The Logical Journey of the Zoombinis.* The little creatures have to be taken on a journey, but — unless the player is very skillful — many of them get lost along the way in caves, fall off precipices or into the jaws of animals. By the end there are generally far less zoombinis than at the start. The heart is like that. Parts of it get lost in life, frozen or dehydrated, atrophied through disuse or closed off by pain. If only we could enable our hearts to grow rather than shrink. What joy this would bring us and what capacity for love!

After repentance comes prayer. Prayer is hard. There are so many words and so many prayers that we can forget what praying is. For prayer is not mainly about asking or even telling God anything. Prayer is the desire for, and the experience of, participating in the deepest realms of life. In the words of Rachel Naomi Remen:

> When we pray we stop trying to control life and remember that we belong to life. [Prayer] is an opportunity to experience humility and recognize grace . . . Prayer is a movement from mastery to mystery.[4]

Where do we find God in prayer? A pilgrim, weary on his way to Mecca, lay down to sleep by the side of the road. Angry worshipers shook him awake and told him off for lying with his feet pointing toward the nearby shrine. Unperturbed, he asked them to set him down in such a way that his feet would not be directed toward his maker.

God is all about us. The purpose of prayer is to humble us in God's presence, to comfort and include us in a greater life, to nourish and inspire us and to remind our spirit of the flame of which it is part. For prayer we therefore need stillness. Like a child holding a jar of clear water to which drops of color have been added, life shakes us up till all the many tints are dispersed to every corner of our being and everything is opaque. Only inner quiet, meditation, and prayer have the power to restore clarity to our being. In that clarity we experience once more the capacity for love — and the desire to give.

"Charity" is a poor translation of *tzedakah*. *Tzedakah* means doing what is right; it expresses the desire to contribute to life. We are inspired to do what is right through our sense of justice and our feelings of compassion. Justice teaches us not to stand by and see wrong done. At some point we must say, "I'm going to do what I can to stop this happening again." Compassion leads us to involve ourselves in life because our heart cannot bear to do otherwise. A woman once told me that she had "failed" professionally in her work with suffering children because she couldn't stop herself from giving them affection.

This may be what repentance, prayer, and charity are, but how do they "avert the evil of the decree"? There are those who take the words literally and believe that good conduct can win us a reprieve from our maker. I am uncomfortable with this view. I don't believe God works like that and I don't believe life is fair in that way. Perhaps that is why Rabbi Nehemiah Nobel observed that the prayer doesn't say our conduct will change the decree, only that it will help us *overcome the evil* and bitterness of that decree whenever fate does strike.

I sometimes think of the *decree* as the basic fact of our mortality. We are susceptible to sickness and pain, we suffer and die, we witness others doing the same. The *decree* is not a punishment; it is simply how life is. We *avert its evil* by living our life to the best of our ability. When death comes, it isn't God's punishment. God does judge us, but through our conscience, which teaches us to live better. Living as best we can is our most worthy response to our mortality, to our ignorance of what lies round the corner.

The mother of a family whom I know well died suddenly and young. During the days of mourning a close relative said:

> Her death was untimely and the number of her years incomplete. But she left no unfinished business: we knew that she loved us and she regularly said so; she knew that we loved her and we told her frequently.

The *evil of the decree* cannot be avoided; it is to this that we are born. But it can be transcended through the way we live — through returning to our capacity for love, through prayer, which nourishes and inspires us, and through doing what is compassionate and just.

Passing before God

On Rosh Hashanah all who enter the world
pass before God like sheep in a flock

M. Rosh Hashanah 1:2

What it means to pass before God is a mystery. Even Moses, in his greatest moment, was told that he could not see God's face and live; he was placed in a cleft of the rock while God's glory passed by. So how can we possibly "pass before God"? Unsure of what this really means, we can only rely on our tradition, and the intimations of our own spiritual sensitivity.

Of course, one could take a negative view and ask why it matters so very much. After all, presumably the omniscient God, if there is a God, knows us, whether we are aware of it and whether we care about it or not. But unless we wish to live our lives blindly, it is not a real option to be dismissive about our side of the relationship with God. It would be as if we didn't mind when people said to us, as happens from time to time, "I know you; don't you remember me?" I always feel mortified when I realize that I ought to have known the person concerned. Just as it shames me when a human encounter fails, so I would be pained to feel that I had gone through my life with God saying to me, as it were, "I know you, but you don't recognize or care about me!" Furthermore, in having some sense of knowing and being known by the spirit, however vague and however fleeting, may lie one of life's greatest opportunities both for gaining self-knowledge and for discovering something of the vitality that is the expression of God's presence in the world.

There are moments in life which disclose a deeper sense of being. They may occur in all sorts of circumstances but they are in essence moments of prayer. To sit beside a stream while the mind is emptied by the rush and plunge of water over the ledge of rocks; to listen at night to the sound of the wind in the trees; to become conscious of one particular tree, its sap, its wakefulness; to ponder the words of a poem and sense the company of all the people who have mused over the same image; to sit with the sick and learn from their speech and their silence what lies at the doors of mortality — in all these ways God enters our consciousness. These experiences calm the preoccupied mind, wake the dormant soul, and open us to the sheer power and depth of life.

At such moments there may come upon us a simultaneous realization of both our smallness and our greatness. Our smallness lies in the awareness that life and its beauty remain while we will pass away. We are a fragment of consciousness, set in a form of flesh and bound by the limitations of time, and all we know is virtually nothing. Our greatness lies in the appreciation that we are nevertheless not entirely ignorant, that we are given the opportunity to be a conscious and, albeit to a very limited degree, comprehending part of the infinite life. The challenge of our existence is to be inspired by that knowledge and to use it as the source for creativity in all our relationships, with people and nature, with words and music, wood and clay. Touched, each in our own way, by the eternal presence, we strive to "sing God a new song."

But there is another aspect to the encounter with God. Judaism speaks not just of God as the maker who creates and inspires, but also as the judge who searches and knows, who "examines the kidneys and the heart." We are taught that God is not only outside us but that God also knows us from within. God, too, "holds . . . the mirror up to nature," and, compelled to perceive the image, I cannot but see myself as I am. And, careless, mistaken or short tempered, I am often far from the person I like to think of myself as being.

I have learned something about this from my children. Frank and spontaneous, they haven't yet acquired the art of knowing what not to say. "Why are you speaking to us in that voice, daddy? That isn't your nice voice; nor is it the loud voice that you use in shul for sermons — and I don't like it!"

Our children have to suffer us in ways that even God may not know much about. They're certainly more direct in saying what they think of us. But God's knowing can be real enough too, conveyed through the conscience in moments of recognition and feelings of shame and regret. I cannot meet God without also encountering myself. Some of us were taught to be afraid at the thought that God should know us. Yet we should be willing to be known, in spite of the anxiety and fear of guilt that this may bring. Who wants to go through life with the same faults, learning nothing, caught up in the same pattern of mistakes and missed opportunities? Who wants to proceed through life unknown and unproved? Isn't it better to learn and change, to use life as fully as possible for goodness and growth? Therefore we also have to welcome moments of shame, though with the hope that they will come in small doses, in private and without humiliation, that, like the salt that stings but heals, they will be for our cure and purification. For just as a sense of unworthiness often accompanies deep feelings of love, so a feeling of sorrow for what we have done wrong may be part of our closeness to God.

Still, such feelings should not be exaggerated; they are part, but only part, of the relationship. God's chastening presence is only an expression of God's love. Thus in our moments of deepest understanding we realize that the awareness of our faults is for our growth, and that remorse arises within us to cleanse us and prepare us for living a deeper life. We should not therefore be afraid.

The Shofar's Question

> And when Elijah heard it, he wrapped his face in his mantle and went out, and stood in the entrance to the cave. And behold there came to him a voice and said: "What are you doing here, Elijah?"
>
> 1 Kings 19:12–13

One of my colleagues had the custom of holding up his shofar to show that it was in the shape of a question mark. I often blow the shofar on Rosh Hashanah, but mine would have to be twisted considerably before it would look the same. Still, I agree that the shofar presents a question. This is true even at the most basic level. If one strikes the keyboard of a piano, it produces a note. But if one blows into the shofar, even though one has some skill and has blown successfully on a dozen previous occasions, there is always a doubt. Responding to the atmosphere in the synagogue, or the spirit of the service, or some hidden facet of the blower's state of being, the shofar may simply refuse to produce any sound at all. There is always a mystery, always a question.

To whom is this question addressed? Jewish law provides a clear answer. Everyone has to hear the sound of the shofar. The very blessing that the blower recites tells us that the commandment is not to make, but to listen to, the sound. Just to overhear it is not enough. If one passes a building and happens to catch the sound of the notes, that is not considered proper listening. There has to be a partnership between blower and hearer, a shared attentiveness. For the shofar addresses each person individually. Its question cannot be heard by proxy or by the outer ear only; we have to listen to it in the fullness of our own being.

What is the shofar's question? There is an important clue in the story of Elijah, who journeyed for forty days to reach the mountain of the Lord and entered the very same cave where God was revealed to Moses. There he heard the terrifying sounds of earthquakes, fire, and thunder. But they left him unmoved; he remained in his cave. When, however, he heard the voice of fine silence, he was struck by awe and understood that this was a summons he had to answer. Covering his face with his mantle, he came out to confront the ultimate question, "What are you doing here, Elijah?"

That same sound of fine silence is likened in the liturgy to the voice of the shofar, as it says: "The great shofar will be blown, and the voice of fine silence will be heard." So the question of the shofar is simply: What are we doing here, you and I? It is addressed to each of us and pursues us all our lives.

The question is first and foremost a personal one. Its tone varies; it need not always be serious. On the way back from synagogue the other day my son got stuck between a lamppost and a fence, and the inquiry, "What are you doing there, Mossy?" had a quality with which every parent will be familiar. But as we get older the issues become more pressing. In loneliness, in indecision, amidst trivial routines, the question, "What am I doing here?" penetrates the most intimate regions of self-doubt and despair with the power to evoke a seemingly irresolvable anguish. Yet there are also moments of joy, at night in the streets or in a garden, looking at the blue-black sky, hearing a late bird call sharply out, when the feeling, "What a privilege it is to be here!" and the questions, "What can I do and what can I give?" traverse the mind like a blessing.

Even at the close of life the shofar's question follows us. I remember a wedding for which the date was put forward because the groom's father was terminally ill. On the day itself he found a special strength, and the celebration was marked by a particular tenderness and joy. However, I was not surprised to receive a phone call twenty-four hours later telling me that he was dying. To my surprise, he wanted me to come and see him. By the time I got there, he could hardly talk. I leaned close to him, and he asked me, "What do I have to do now?" The question was pursuing him even then. He needed to hear that he had fulfilled his responsibilities on earth with dignity and love and that he was free to go in peace.

Thus the shofar's question, "What are you doing here?" follows us into our innermost being and until our final breath. But the shofar is also a specifically Jewish instrument and its sound traverses Jewish history. The ram's horn recalls the binding of Isaac and God's covenant with Abraham. It reminds us of the giving of the Torah at Mount Sinai, when the Jewish people entered into a bond with God. The shofar was to be blown every fiftieth year, to proclaim freedom to all the inhabitants of the land of Israel. And at the end of days when the exiles are gathered in, ". . . a great shofar shall be sounded and those lost in the land of Assyria and cast away in the land of Egypt shall come and worship the Lord on the holy mountain in Jerusalem" (Isa. 27:13).

Of these connections with history it is the association with the binding of Isaac that is most important on Rosh Hashanah. It is as if by blowing a ram's horn we are specifically reminding God of all that the Jewish people have sacrificed throughout the ages, in a protest and a declaration: "See what we have given for the sake of our relationship with you, God. Remember your side of the partnership and protect us with your love."

These themes, sacrifice and tenderness, were brought home to me in a picture by Ernest Neushul, which I saw at the house of a friend. It depicts, in warm colors and something of a cubist style, a young man and a ram. They will shortly be partners in sacrifice. The ram grazes placidly, showing its fine horns; the man, to the left of the picture, is reflective. The ram appears calm, but the man gazes out at the world. Who knows what he can see — the sacrifice to come, all the sacrifices of the Jewish people before the power of Greece and Rome, through the Dark Ages of the medieval world, during the Nazi persecutions? Yet at the same time the picture is peculiarly tender in its choice of colors — purples, pinks, and greys. It conveys the gentleness and wisdom of Judaism, the softness of its melodies, the riches of its spirit. Such associations reach us on the notes of the shofar and again ask a question: "What are you doing with all this wealth? How are you relating to it in your life?"

The sound of the shofar is also a universal call. Produced on a raw horn without the intervention of a mouthpiece, it is more primitive, deeper even, than a human sound. It is the voice of an ancient partnership, between man and beast, between creation and the spirit of creation. Sometimes, when I blow the shofar, I think of animals and birds, squirrels, foxes, wrens, trees, running water, wind, and storm; and I listen in the shofar for the expression of all this wild and teeming life. The shofar's question then comes on the very breath of existence: "Where are you, partner amongst us, in this moment of shared time?"

The Shofar's Story

> Rabbi Abbahu instituted [the following order for the blowing of the shofar] in Caesarea: A simple note, three broken notes, a weeping note, and a simple note.
>
> B. Rosh Hashanah 34a

On the mantelpiece, perhaps, or in a glass cupboard in the living room are the objects that tell the tale: old brass candlesticks brought out of Russia in the bottom of a trunk; or a spice box, now the only remnant of a grandparent's house, with a fragrance more of memory than of herbs. The shofar, too, tells a story, a simple tale, yet descriptive of the whole growth of the human heart. The story of the shofar has four chapters: the first *tekiah,* or simple note, containing all the naïveté of childhood; the *shevarim* in which that innocence is broken; the *teruah* of sorrow and weeping; and the *tekiah* at the end, representing a different kind of wholeness, a courageous integration.

The Rabbis called the first *tekiah* blown on the shofar the *peshutah lefanekhah,* the simple note that precedes the *shevarim* and the *teruah.* Is it only a myth fabricated by adults, or can childhood still be filled with simplicity and surprise? Last summer, as we were driving home through the darkness to a cottage in the middle of the forest, I finally asked the children a question which had long been on my mind. What did life feel like to them? Was it full of wonder, was there a sense of rubbing steam off winter windows to witness new mysteries, the first frost, the first snow of the season? Was there the excitement of discovery, the regular warmth of affection, the safety of discipline and learning? The children were half asleep, and I can't remember what they said. But the road was covered in a canopy of trees, and as we spoke, an owl flew just above the windscreen and a deer's eyes shone in the darkness ahead. Isaac Babel wrote: "My child's heart was rocked like a little ship upon enchanted waters." Would it were the same for all children!

As adults we often mourn the innocence and comfort we consider ourselves to have lost. No one tucks us up in bed or reads us a story or tidies everything up while we sleep. No one holds our hand when we cross a dangerous road. But childhood is not only a time of innocence, nor need adulthood be as deprived of it as we might think. It is there for the recapture. I have watched people sit in a garden or on a park bench and arise refreshed by that simple pleasure. Look at the partnership of grandparent and grandchild. Consider whose heart rejoices more in little things: a biscuit, a walk, a cuddle, a story.

The very name *shevarim* means broken pieces. "From where does pain, like a worm, enter the heart?" asked the poet Ḥayim Naḥman Bialik.[5] I remember a debate I had with a congregant a long time ago. We were planning to take a class of eleven-year-olds to the cemetery to bury old books and look at gravestones. This father declined to give permission for his child to come. "Childhood," he explained, "is brief enough; I want to protect my daughter from the knowledge of death for a little while longer." At the time I didn't have children of my own and couldn't understand. I do now.

Nevertheless, younger or older, there comes a time when we cannot, indeed must not, be protected. There is a point when it is no longer innocence but complacency if we fail to be affected by suffering. "You shall not stand idly by the blood of your neighbor," teaches the Torah (Lev. 19:16). We are not allowed to be bystanders; we are required to commit ourselves in the struggle against cruelty and pain. "Because of the brokenness of my people I am broken," cried Jeremiah when he witnessed the destruction of his city and the exile of his people. What happened to them happens to him; they are both shattered by the same *shever,* the same breaking apart. In a world that contains so much pain, there are times when it is inexcusable not to experience brokenness. Basic compassion commands us to hear the *shevarim* and to answer with our feelings and our deeds.

The Talmud relates the *teruah* note to the sound of weeping. A familiar Yiddish song describes how the rebbe teaches the children the *aleph-bet*. He tells them that they will soon learn how many tears lie in these letters.

Whether it is a good way to communicate enthusiasm for the Hebrew language may be debatable, but the observation itself is not. The dramatist S. Ansky described how he was sent after the First World War to the communities of Eastern Europe to document their suffering and distribute relief. While he was staying in some Galician town engaged in this impossible task, there appeared behind him a gaunt fiddler who had managed the impossible feat of procuring a violin. They both wept, recalled Ansky, the instrument and the man who played it. Till then he had thought that phrases like "drenched with tears" were exaggerations. Now he knew that they were the plain and simple truth.[6]

Half-hidden in the liturgy of Rosh Hashanah are many tears. Hannah weeps because she has no children. Hagar weeps because she and her son have been cast out and he lies dying in the desert. Rachel weeps for her children as they pass before her on their journey into exile. We weep, too. In the old prayer books it used to appear as an instruction: This is where one weeps. Most of all we weep for love, for a love that has been destroyed or a love that has never been found.

Sometimes I see people who cannot weep. Tears would be a relief, a release from the pressure of sorrow. Some people weep only in secret, because there is no one to share their misery or because they are afraid no one wants to see their tears. Some people weep precisely when they hear a kind voice and realize someone is listening.

The story of the shofar does not end in sorrow, however. There remains the *peshutah shel 'aharekhah,* the simple note afterward. That is, the note which closes the cycle. We need more than anguish and tears. We need to carry on; we need the courage and the confidence to keep going. When tragedy strikes, people often initially need a structure to support them, something to hold on to hour by hour, day by day. After a while their horizon begins to grow wider, thoughts of the future become less unbearable. Life continues. The "simple note afterward" marks the bravery of keeping going. Perhaps that is why the final sound of the entire sequence is the *tekiah gedolah,* the "great simple note"; long, drawn out, and full of strength, it represents the sustained effort of resilience and courage.

What qualities must we have in order to sound that note? First and foremost, we need hope. Hope is a basic necessity. I often hear the criticism, "He took my hope away." We need a sense that life is worthwhile. We need to know that there are values that are indestructible, even if we are not;

that there are things we can accomplish which death does not have the power to unravel or annul. I recently spoke to a man who was very ill. "Everything I've learned from my sickness," he said, "will be rendered useless if I die." While recognizing his pain at the prospect of dying, I sought to reassure him: "Time does not take away the love we share. What you have given those around you will be treasured and passed on to others." I believe we also need a sense of the indestructibility of the spirit. Hannah Senesh, whose life was all too short, understood this well when she composed her famous song:

> My God, my God, may these things never end;
> The sand, the sea and the sound of the water,
> The radiance of the sky
> And the prayers of man.[7]

What then is the difference between the simple note before and the simple note after? — Experience, understanding, courage, wisdom, and, if possible, the gift of laughing at ourselves.

The story of the shofar is an account of the development of the human heart. In life this story is probably not sequential. The different notes and moods often coincide, and even a day may well contain them all. But if there were no simple note at the beginning, if there were no plain, innocent joy, would life really be worth living? If we felt no brokenness, no empathy with suffering, would we be truly human? If our heart were incapable of weeping, could we feel close to one another, could we really love? And if there were no simple note afterward, how, with all the burden of distress to which we are constantly exposed, could any of us keep going? In a full life, in a good life, all the notes are sounded.

Trust

What does the Torah mean when it says: "Let us make man"?
God says to man, "Let us make man, you and I."

Rebbe Avraham Mordekhai of Ger[8]

How quickly the hours pass. Just now it was midnight — and already it's three in the morning. I had a visitor in my bed. Mendelek had a bad dream. He stroked my face and went to sleep.[9]

Thus runs the entry in the diary of Janusz Korczak, director of the orphanage in the Warsaw ghetto, for an unspecified night between May and July 1942. Mendelek woke up and screamed, thinking he was in his own bed. Korczak told him to lie back down and reassured him, "I'll be writing. If you're frightened, come back."[10] What an endeavor, to create a sense of security and trust in such a place.

Rosh Hashanah is the anniversary of the making of the world. Like all creation, it is an act of trust. Specifically, Rosh Hashanah is the anniversary of the fashioning of the first human being in the divine image, when God placed divine trust in us, partners in creation. Rosh Hashanah is also, according to rabbinic chronology, the day on which Adam and Eve were separated out from one another, parted down the shared back that held them bound like Siamese twins, and given to each other face to face in mutual trust. Rosh Hashanah is, finally, the day when the two of them were placed in Eden, entrusted with the tending of God's world. Thus, if Rosh Hashanah is a day of judgment, it is surely a judgment on how well we have borne that trust, toward each other, toward the world and toward God.

Yet it is apparent that the world is full of trust's abuse. I remember a story in the newspaper about a dog handler who hung his young Alsatian up by the collar and beat it to death; he took it down and the animal licked his hands while it died. Some years ago, I saw a film which showed a man returning to the village in Poland where his father and brother had been murdered while trying to find a hiding place from the Nazis. The man went from place to place and house to house till he found a peasant who was prepared to tell him what had happened: "Your brother was a beautiful boy," he recalled. "They said to him, 'Go round there into the yard and we'll play with you.' As the little boy was walking in front of them, they shot him in the back of his head." Our world is full of such horrors.

My heroes, on the other hand, are those who use their lives to create and foster trust. Janusz Korczak lived and died doing exactly that. It is said that, until the end, he was offered many opportunities to escape from the ghetto and the death camps. But he refused because he did not want to desert the children whose faith in humanity had already been undermined so often. He chose to die upholding the trust he had created through the way he lived. It is no small thing to comfort a child who wakes in the night terrified, to run an institution where children feel safe amidst terrors, and to encourage and console them when they know they are about to die. It takes only seconds to destroy trust. To rebuild it takes years and the utmost effort, courage, patience, and love.

Mercifully, most of us in the West are not presently exposed to the horror of war, though the recent battles in Bosnia and Kosovo warn us that it is never far away. But trust is lost, and regained, all around us in a host of smaller ways that are simply part of what life can do to any of us at any time.

We lose our confidence in life when someone close to us dies. Death can make the very ground we tread on feel unsure. When a parent dies, people often say that there is no one out there in front anymore. The person who protected us has gone and we are next in line. We have only to think of the familiar image of an adult hand holding the little child's hand that reaches up to it in fear. Now take the big hand away. However grown-up we are supposed to be, in some part of ourselves our hands always remain small; we still need comfort and reassurance. When other relatives die, people suffer differently and often even more. The Talmud says that when a man loses the wife of his youth his steps become smaller and his counsel fails.

Illness can undermine our trust in our own body. I learned a great deal from my brief experience of food poisoning one summer, when, instead of enjoying my holiday walking the Scottish hills, I spent it attached to a drip in the Aberdeen Royal Infirmary. I had been used to telling my body, "do this," and it would. Now it simply couldn't. I had been accustomed to controlling my bodily functions as one assumes every adult can. It was humiliating to have to ask the ambulance to stop three times on the way to hospital so that I could do what I had to do — and with another person present. All this drama occurred because of something minor, almost trivial. How shocking it must be really to feel betrayed by one's body, to realize that one's legs may never hold one upright again, to know that inside the fatal tumor is growing.

The breakdown of a relationship can shatter our confidence in life and in ourselves. Even a petty incident can rupture our sense of security. I know of several people who, when confronted by some sudden outburst of hatred in the street, responded not with fear or anger, but with shock and dismay: "Have I done something to deserve this? Am I really filth or scum?" More profoundly, a feeling of failure may invade us through the falling apart of an important relationship — with a best friend, partner, or spouse. A corrosive sense of doubt begins to eat at our own self-worth, and anxiety starts to haunt the spaces between ourselves and others.

Often we lose confidence simply because our life does not seem to be running along the same path as that of everyone else. Everyone else is working twice as hard as ever and we have been made redundant. Our children haven't achieved the good results that everyone else's seem to have. One of the children has periods of mental illness. We cannot show our face because everyone's doing fine and we are not.

But if we were all aware of the number of people who have such feelings, we would be unlikely to feel so isolated. It would be obvious that we all have our wounds and that we all need each other. For none of us feels confident more than part of the time, at best. The essential question, then, is: what can we do to strengthen and restore trust? For we either build trust or destroy it; we either give each other confidence or strip each other's confidence away; we either foster or erode faith in people and in life.

There is much that we can do. First and foremost, we can strive to be just and fair in all our dealings. "Justice, justice shall you pursue," teaches the Torah (Deut. 16:20). Anything else undermines the basis of human interaction. A member of my community once showed me a letter his father was given by representatives of the local population during his wartime service as a doctor in the British Army in India. "The bearer is a good man," it said simply. "You can trust him." It is no small matter to merit such a letter.

Secondly, we can go further than being fair and try always to be kind. Kindness is an affirmation of the dignity and value of the other person. We all know how easy it is to tell whether a nurse or doctor has a kind touch when they take blood. We can all tell kindness in the tone of a teacher. I remember the deputy head of a school where I used to teach. It was an old Victorian building in a poor area, and many of the children came from homes where there was a great deal of distress. In the mornings, before the children came in, one could almost touch the sense of neediness; it felt as if it clung to the very walls. Then this teacher would pass by the classroom. I don't know quite what quality it was that she possessed, but she would simply say, "Good-morning," and everyone felt better. She had perfect command of the children though she never raised her voice; she spread around her a carpet of kindness on which they sat content.

Thirdly, we can avoid crossing the road. People who have suffered tragedies sometimes tell me that their acquaintances cross the road when they approach. We may think that we would never even dream of behaving in such a manner, but there are many and subtle ways of crossing roads. We can stay on the same side of the street but indicate by the tone of our "hello" that we have no interest in a proper conversation. We can stop inviting people round. Women who have been divorced often say that their friends stop asking them over because they are, to put it bluntly, no longer packaged in a socially convenient manner. We can give people our time while refusing them our heart. How often do we silently tell someone not to cry because we don't want to be burdened by their weeping?

Fourthly, we can try not to prejudge and alienate those who may well feel like pariahs already. For when something in our life becomes painful and the ground begins to rock under our feet, we start to feel like an outsider, and we don't need anyone else to reinforce the sensation. Callous judgments and careless remarks magnify such sensitivities and make us feel even more rejected.

The building of trust draws primarily on our human qualities, but faith in God can help us find them. I would understand such faith to be more of a challenge than a promise. For I do not believe in a God who is fair in any manner we can readily justify or perceive. I do not believe in a God who protects us from all harm. But I do believe in a God whose image and dignity rest in every human being. I do believe in a God who challenges us to act at all times in harmony with the value, beauty, and sanctity which inhere in life by virtue of its character and source. It is surely, therefore, no accident that many of the greatest builders of trust have been people of faith. For the recognition of the dignity bestowed on us by God challenges and inspires us to live in accord with its demands.

Rosh Hashanah is the beginning of the time of judgment. According to the Talmud, the first question we are asked in judgment is, *Nassatah venattatah be'emunah?*[11] This is usually translated as, "Have you dealt in good faith? Have you behaved honestly and decently in all your transactions?" But the words can be made to yield a different meaning. *Nassatah be'emunah*: Have you borne and been worthy of the trust invested in you? *Nattatah be'emunah*: Have you given, spread, and fostered trust in all your undertakings?

THE TEN DAYS OF RETURN

Human Nature and Moral Growth

Rabbi Ḥama, son of Rabbi Ḥanina said:
"Great is repentance for it brings healing to the world."

B. Yoma 86a

Judaism is neither sweetly naïve nor sweepingly negative about the human character. It looks upon us and our capacity for good and evil with incisive realism, while maintaining an outlook of confidence and hope. We do right and trust that one good deed will lead to another. We do wrong, and though bad may lead to worse, we may be able to learn. While recognizing our capacity for evil, Judaism teaches us never to lose faith in our ability to do good and in the efficacy of repentance and return.

Judaism regards human nature as neither intrinsically bad nor necessarily good. We are born with great potential. The Jewish mystics would agree with Wordsworth that we come here trailing clouds of glory from God, who is our home. But we are also born into a situation of moral vulnerability. Thus, according to one strand of rabbinic interpretation, God's admonishment to Cain that "sin crouches at the door" refers to the *yetzer hara,* or evil inclination, which is considered to enter every human being as soon as they pass through the portals of birth. "Evil inclination" is an unhappy, if familiar, phrase, because the *yetzer hara* is not in and of itself evil. Rather, it is undirected energy and refers to those drives which, if used wisely, lead us to build homes, have families, and live creative lives. If, however, they are left ungoverned, they lead us straight into temptation. That is why the Rabbis liken it to the yeast in the dough: without it the bread won't rise, but on its own, it's sour.

Therefore Judaism believes strongly in the need for moral education. This may come both from within and from without. From within shines the light of conscience, the lamp of the Lord, which is the soul of every person and which searches all the chambers of our being (Prov. 20:27). It is part of our human endowment that God sets the scales of justice in our heart so that we may know right from wrong.

However, we cannot rely only on our inner moral sense. Judaism rejects the romantic notion of the noble savage who, if only civilization left him alone, would live in perfect harmony with nature and God. Of course, the wrong "education" may also corrupt. Jews have generally been clear about the social influences from which they want to protect their children. But wise education, both in its formal sense of learning, and in its wider meaning of moral training, is essential. With its comprehensive array of structures, strictures, and wisdom, Judaism seeks to refine and discipline us. It endeavors to protect us not only from the wrongs that may be done to us, but most especially from the evils that we may ourselves perpetrate unless we are guided toward the best in our nature through knowledge, example, and discipline.

Judaism may be realistic, but it is certainly not cynical. It maintains its faith in the capacity for goodness and self-sacrifice, which lies within each person. When a child is born we pray that he or she will grow up to study Torah and do good deeds. Each month, on the Shabbat before the new moon, we ask God to put into our hearts the love of Torah and the feeling of awe before heaven. The Jewish journey has as its goal the attainment of a vision of peace and justice, and each of us is capable of sharing the dream and contributing toward its realization. Furthermore, as we grow up, our *yetzer hatov,* or good inclination, matures. For unlike the "evil" inclination, which is held to enter us at birth, the good inclination does not, according to the rabbinic view, fully awaken in us until we reach bar or bat mitzvah. This puzzling distinction should not be taken to imply that children have no conscience or are incapable of deep concern for others. Experience shows us that this is not so; on the contrary, children are generally naturally loving and can learn from good role models right from the start of their lives. What it probably means is that we need a measure of self-knowledge and self-discipline — traditionally gained through following the teachings of the Torah — before we can fully achieve the best of which we are capable.

Judaism thus believes not only in our capacity for goodness but also in our ability to grow and learn. Nowhere is this made clearer than in the teaching of *teshuvah,* repentance or return. Nothing is too terrible for remorse; never is it too late for regret. Indeed, the power of repentance is so great that, according to the Talmud, our former "deliberate sins" may not only come to be looked upon as mere "errors," but can even be turned into merits.[1] How can this be? No doubt the statement is intended to startle and encourage us, but how can our faults become good deeds? The Rabbis of the Talmud were certainly not blind to the fact that there are many things we do, with which, however much we may later regret them, we still have to live. The consequences of some of our actions may haunt us till our final hour. Furthermore, though it is never too late for remorse, it may well be too late to tell another person what we now desperately wish we had said. So perhaps what the Talmud means is that remorse can lead us truly to understand how mistaken we were in what we once thought right. Thus our "deliberate sins" become "errors" because we now realize that the better part of our nature did not really want to do them. Furthermore, deep regret has the power to make us determine to change our lives — perhaps, for example, to care for others in ways we wouldn't have thought about before. If that is so, then the wrongs done in one part of our lives can become our teachers for the rest, causing an awakening of our conscience and acting as a spur to compassion and commitment.

Teshuvah may have a profound effect not only on our character but also on our relationships. Very often in life, mistakes and misunderstandings lead to distance and distance leads, in turn, to distrust. We drift on, and the years drift away. But a fresh understanding of ourselves leads us to see others from a different perspective, and the consciousness of our own mistakes generally makes us more forgiving. Even after many years, people can be released from the mental manacles in which we bind them, and our relationship with them can find a new freedom.

Teshuvah thus brings a threefold opportunity for return — to the potential for good in ourselves, to restored trust and rediscovered affection for others, and to a new closeness to God. We can't necessarily change other people, or how they see us, and we can't alter the established facts of our lives. But as we stand before our own conscience and God, we can come to perceive life differently and thereby rehabilitate the past.

It Was Not Someone Else

> This thing of darkness I acknowledge mine.
>
> Shakespeare, *The Tempest*[2]

As a little boy I loved to watch the children's television program, *The Magic Roundabout*. All the characters were charming, but it was Zebedee who captured my imagination. This must have been because whenever he was summoned he would appear instantly, landing on his single springy leg with a great big bounce.

Some people regard repentance in that way, as one long leap straight into the lap of God. Sometimes, though rarely, that is a person's actual experience. But more often there is a journey, and a long journey at that, which includes both the fuller discovery of our own self and the deeper awareness of other people. Therefore, in considering the prophet Hosea's injunction, "Return, O Israel, to the Lord your God" (14:2), it is important to emphasize the seemingly insignificant word *ad* — "to," or, more literally translated, "as far as" — and to focus on the travel as well as the destination.

The journey begins with acknowledging who we are and what we have done. Children often say, "The table hit me." Ask how the vase broke and you discover that "it happened," the child's proximity at the time of the accident being a totally irrelevant detail. We were doubtless just the same when we were small. We have to concede that it was I, not someone else, who was responsible, who did, said, thought, and felt not nice things. When I was four years old, I fell in the school playground and cut my knee. Even now I can recall how much I hated having to say the words, "I fell." It wasn't because of my knee that I was upset, but because I hated the experience of feeling vulnerable in front of others. My self-image had been bruised and I didn't like it.

As adults we don't necessarily behave any differently. We have a rich range of ways of avoiding saying that it is we who did it. There are a number of familiar strategies. The subtlest are the circumlocutions: "Something came over me," or, "I don't know what got into me." Such paraphrases suggest that whatever we did was the responsibility of an "other" who temporarily displaced the real "me." Next comes reshaping. If we do own up to our role in an incident, we tend to retell the story a dozen times over, first to ourselves and then to others, gradually diminishing or mitigating our own responsibility for those elements that most upset our sense of who we would like to believe we are. All this applies, of course, only if we don't resort to simply blaming someone else. Would we be so brazen? Well, it's easy to forget how much we manage to forget.

These may all seem little things, but they are significant, and, if they become ingrained habits, dangerous. We run the risk not only of doing other people a constant injustice, but also of deceiving ourselves and making it impossible to do anything to make amends. For if it is always someone else, some alter ego, who is to blame, what can we possibly do to put things right?

The Talmud tells the story of Elisha ben Abuya, a contemporary of Rabbi Akiva and for a while his companion, who became disillusioned with Judaism, gave it up, and went to the bad. In an effort to persuade him to mend his ways, Rabbi Meir, the only disciple who maintained contact with him despite his apostasy, led him from synagogue to synagogue in the hope that he would hear something that would help him to repent. Wherever he went he asked the children what they were studying. In each case this turned out to be a verse about the opportunity God gives us to change our ways. But, as if pursued by a personal demon, Elisha invariably heard an accompanying voice append the words "except for *'aher*." Who was this "'*aher*"? *'Aher* means *other* and was the name by which Elisha had come to be known since he had begun to do wrong. In other words, *'aher* is the disavowed and disconnected part of the self, the part we cannot access unless we acknowledge that it too belongs to us. Depressed by what he kept on hearing, *'aher* eventually said to himself: "Since that person [i.e., *'aher*] has been driven out of that world [that is, the life of the world to come], he may as well do as he likes down here." He promptly set out in search of a prostitute, but the girl recognized him and exclaimed in surprise, "Aren't you Rabbi Elisha ben Abuya?" To prove that he was no longer the rabbi of that name, he pulled up a turnip, an action strictly forbidden on the Sabbath, and offered it to her as payment. Thereupon she observed, "He is indeed *'aher*" — he has become another person.[3]

In this story a man allows himself to become all bad, entirely *another,* by putting all the good in himself into his former identity and ascribing all the bad to his new name and persona. Rabbi Aharon Soloveitchik makes the profound observation that whereas *'aḥer* can't repent, Elisha ben Abuya surely could have done so, if only he had not disowned that part of himself.

The two parts of us, the good person and the bad, must be brought together. If we feel that we are all evil, who is there in us who has the power to effect change? If we believe that we are all good, what is there in us which we need to change? If we never own up to what we do wrong, if it is always *not myself* who is to blame, how can we bring our misdeeds under our control and begin to do something about them? It is in this context that we discover the real importance of *viddui,* a word usually rendered as *confession* but which might also be understood as *acknowledgment* of who we are and of what our responsibilities consist.

Maybe in our fear we say to ourselves, "If I admit to myself that I've been wrong, I'll feel totally bad. It'll be like putting red dye in clear water; the whole of me will become tainted." But we shouldn't be so afraid, for if we're not all good, we're not all bad either. That's why we find it painful to say, or even think, "I've done wrong," or, "What I said was hurtful." An incision in an anesthetized body isn't felt; it's because we are morally alive and experience shame that our admissions hurt and sting. Indeed, although we may not like it, we can nevertheless trust that unpleasant feeling. For shame is to the conscience as pain is to the body; it is the outrage of what is healthy in us as it confronts what is not.

This inner process of acknowledgment enables us to be fairer toward others. For the more honest we are with ourselves, the more just we will be in our assessment of other people. In the first place, we will find that we are less compelled to engage in the ugly business of projecting on to them whatever we dislike and disown in ourselves, a destructive activity indulged in by every society and almost every individual. One of the things bigotry does is to provide us with a legitimate target on whom to off-load our troubles. They can be located safely in someone else who may now be hated, "ethnically cleansed," and disposed of with a clear conscience. But once we have learned to perceive and acknowledge our own faults, it becomes harder to behave in this fashion. When we realize that there is within ourselves much that requires forbearance and tolerance, we are likely to become less critical, less persecuting, and more forgiving toward others. Albrecht Goes, a pastor in the German Protestant Church who devoted a large portion of his life's work to Christian-Jewish reconciliation, had the following to say to an audience in Hamburg:

I believe we all learned all over again what the countenance of a person who is truly able to help others looks like. It is a face from which stubbornness, cocksureness, the worshipping of success, rigidity, and a pedantic clinging to principles increasingly vanish to give way to other, greater, realities: astonishment, the ability to be frightened, defenselessness, reverence, awe, gratitude.[4]

It is easy to see why Albrecht Goes includes reverence and awe, but why does he mention defenselessness and the ability to be frightened? The answer must be that these qualities are the windows through which the needs and feelings of other people enter our souls. It is through our own sense of vulnerability and imperfection that we come to appreciate the strengths and weaknesses of others and to understand and value them more. And, as Kafka wrote, one can suppress one's fellow beings much better if one doesn't know them.

"Return, O Israel, to the Lord your God." The journey toward God is also a journey through ourselves. I'm suspicious of those whose fervor takes them directly to the Throne of Glory, if that journey circumvents the knowledge of themselves and the awareness of other people. I reject the strident values of those religious movements which believe only in their own great and often militant ideals, while ignoring the challenge of self-knowledge and the complexity of our relationships with others.

There is, in contrast, much truth in what Coleridge's Ancient Mariner learned in the course of his lonely and searching voyage:

> He prayeth best who loveth best
> All creatures great and small.[5]

Perhaps that is why Hosea, after emphasizing the word *ad* — "as far as" — speaks of "the Lord *your* God," using the possessive suffix in the singular form. It is to the God who helps each of us know ourselves that we have to return.

YOM KIPPUR

Atonement and Responsibility

> And he shall confess upon it all the iniquities of the children of
> Israel, and all their transgressions, even all their sins; and he shall
> put them upon the head of the goat, and shall send it away . . .
>
> Lev. 16:21

Three times during Yom Kippur, in a ritual known simply as the *Avodah*, or
Service, which constitutes the most ancient core of the atonement ritual,
the high priest makes confession. Each time, there are subtle differences in
how and for whom he does so. Strange and distant as the sacrificial worship in the Temple is to us, we can nevertheless learn much about the
nature of responsibility from the conduct of the High Priest as prescribed
by the Torah and transmitted to us in the liturgy, almost verbatim, from
ancient rabbinic accounts.

The High Priest confesses first for himself and his family, then for himself and the tribe of Levi, and finally for the sins of the whole house of
Israel. On the first two occasions the high priest makes confession over his
own bullock, acquired from his own funds, before slaughtering it and
sprinkling its blood upon the seat of mercy above the Ark of the Covenant
in the Holy of Holies. Only the third confession is made over the scapegoat, chosen to be sent to a forsaken place where, driven over the edge of a
cliff to its death, it carries the sins of the people into oblivion.

First the High Priest confesses his sins and those of his family. The
Torah actually says that he should make atonement *ba'ado uve'ad beito*, literally "for himself and for his house." The ancient Aramaic translation by
Onkelos understands this to refer to the sins of all his household, whereas
Rabbi Yehudah takes it to mean only those of his wife.[1] In any event, before
he can atone for others, he must do so for himself and his close family. For
all of us, the acknowledgment of wrong must begin at home. It is easy to
look at the sins of society and condemn what is wrong in the world, while
remaining blind, or paying lip service only, to what we do wrong in our
own lives. Furthermore, the process of reflection should include our clos-

est relationships, ourselves and our household — that is, ourselves as we behave toward those in our household. No one sees us from such close quarters as our partner, parent or child, our brother, sister, or very close friend. No man is a hero to his butler.

After entering the Holy of Holies to burn the incense, the High Priest returns to the same animal to confess again, this time on behalf of himself, his household, and "the children of Aaron, your holy people."[2] Why does the High Priest again include himself in this confession, when he has already sought atonement? We learn from this that no one can separate himself from the group to which he belongs, especially not a leader. To think of oneself as morally insulated from one's community is to misunderstand the nature of responsibility. We are, in the terms of a famous rabbinic saying, as responsible as the sphere of our influence. This does not mean that we are personally guilty for every wrong that a host of other people may commit. But it does mean that we are answerable for the wider impact of our behavior on society, as well as for the impact it might have had were we to have found the wisdom and the courage to conduct ourselves otherwise. Anyone can lay blame, anyone can throw up her hands and say, "What are you expecting me to do about it?!" That, we learn, isn't good enough.

Only now, on the third occasion, does the High Priest turn to the scapegoat. He lays his hands firmly on its head and asks atonement for "your people, the house of Israel." This time he does three things differently: he does not refer to himself, he invokes God's attachment, and he places the sins on the goat to be sent away. One might have thought that he would still include himself, to show that while responsibility begins at home it extends to the farthest horizons, as in the environmentalist saying, "Think globally, act locally." But this may reflect the modern phenomenon of the worldwide market where our actions sometimes really do make an impact at the far ends of the earth. In any event, the High Priest now invokes a different relationship, the bond between God and the children of Israel. They are, he says, your people, God; therefore, pardon them.

"Scapegoat" has become a dirty word and rightly so. However, it should be noted that while the contemporary usage still reflects the biblical concept of laying sins on the head of another, there are crucial differences. The High Priest used an animal; we use other people. The High Priest — and all Israel — were conscious of the process that was being enacted and understood that the animal was a symbol. We scapegoat unaware. The High Priest blamed no one, nor could anyone imagine the goat to be guilty. We blame and we hold guilty.

When we are angry or indignant and perceive no connection between ourselves and the cause of our outrage, we indulge in blaming. We label and condemn: "Look at what those people do!" "See them, they don't behave like us." Where our sense of responsibility ends, prejudice usually begins. The High Priest speaks differently. He does his personal best; he makes atonement for himself and all those to whom he is bound by the close ties of responsibility. Only then does he invoke God. "The children of Israel are your people," he says. "Whatever they have done, you are still bound by your covenant and they are still made in your image; therefore be merciful to them."

Judaism has put animal sacrifice behind it. It belongs, as Maimonides already explained eight hundred years ago, to the practices of an earlier age. But that does not mean that we should ignore the very real sensitivities which may be expressed within its alien forms. In certain respects, indeed, ours is the crueller age. Certainly, the *Avodah* service on Yom Kippur articulates an attitude of responsibility and compassion, which, without the beasts and blood, we might do well to emulate today.

Between Memory and Forgiveness

> For all these things, God of forgiveness, forgive us,
> pardon us and grant us atonement.
>
> from the confessional prayers of Yom Kippur

In an address to the Polish Parliament in 1990, Vaclav Havel, then President of Czechoslovakia, declared that his program was:

> To bring spirituality, moral responsibility, humaneness, and humility into politics, and, in that way, to make clear that there is something higher above us, that our deeds do not disappear into the black hole of time but are recorded somewhere and judged . . .[3]

It is a view which Jews find familiar and appropriate. We are a people profoundly conscious of memory; the daily prayer book is a chronicle, the ritual year a history, and every family a living testament to our past. We know, furthermore, the risks of amnesia, both at the personal and national levels. The evidence of events from without and of the conscience from within teaches us to refute those who seek to wipe from the record whatever is too uncomfortable or too inconvenient to remember.

To remember and celebrate positive events is easy, but what do we do with recollections that are painful and bitter, with memories of wrongs done to us and wrongs we have done? How do we heal the wounds? How do we forgive others, ourselves, life, and God? Do we even want to heal and forgive? If we don't, the result will be bitterness, and bitterness, however justifiable, in the end only poisons the person who harbors it. Like a fruit in vinegar, the heart gets pickled, and who wants to have a sour heart? So what do we do, caught between the need to remember and the necessity to let go?

For this dilemma Judaism prescribes a process culminating in the Day of Atonement, with its goal of reconciliation with God, our fellow human beings, and ourselves. During the course of this day, as we again and again confess our sins, we say the following prayer, which effectively serves as a chorus: "For all these things, God of forgiveness, forgive us, pardon us and grant us atonement." Each of the three phrases: *selah lanu* — forgive us, *mehal lanu* — pardon us, and *kapper lanu* — grant us atonement, denotes a different aspect of the inner work required to come to terms with the past, its pain and its mistakes.

Selihah, forgiveness, belongs to God. Although in modern Hebrew the word simply means "sorry" and is often used with as little genuine feeling as in any other language, in the biblical context *selihah* refers to the forgiveness that comes from God alone. The implications of this were made poignantly apparent in an article by Rabbi Dr. Albert Friedlander, published in the *London Times*. Rabbi Friedlander fled Germany as a child, and has devoted much of his life's work to understanding and reconciliation. The article was commissioned just before President Reagan's ill-advised visit to the Bitburg cemetery, where, as it emerged to his embarrassment, members of the SS were buried among the other German war dead. Rabbi Friedlander wrote of how he was approached by two people after a talk he had given during a church conference in Germany. The first was a young girl who said to him, "Rabbi, I wasn't there, but can you forgive me?" They embraced and wept together. The second was a camp guard. To his request for forgiveness, Rabbi Friedlander responded as follows:

> It is not the function of rabbis to give absolution, to be pardoners. In Judaism there is a ten-day period of Penitence, between the New Year and the Day of Atonement, when we try to go to any person we have wronged and ask forgiveness. But you cannot go to the six million. They are dead and I cannot speak for them. Nor can I speak for God. But you are here at a church conference. God's forgiving grace may touch you . . .[4]

In the course of the bitter debate which ensued in the columns of the newspaper, the regrettable comment was made that "failure to forgive . . . dehumanizes the victims in a way the oppressors could never on their own achieve."[5] This misses the point. It is not a question of willfully withholding forgiveness; it is rather that we are not empowered to give pardon for wrongs done to other people, or to do so in the name of God. But if Rabbi Friedlander was right, so was the guard. He spoke his truth and this is where the process of seeking forgiveness must always begin. We can ask God to forgive us only after we have acknowledged our faults.

What, then, is it like to be honest before God? It is easy to see the sins of others but hard to contemplate our own. Perhaps we can imagine this difficult process as having the film of our life played back. Nothing is missing, no scene ostensibly forgotten is absent in the relentless memory of conscience. We sit in our heart and watch; maybe God sits there with us and watches too. In those painful moments of fuller understanding, perceptions we repressed at the time and effects on others we never noticed become apparent and sting. And again we have a choice. Again we can say, "It wasn't my fault!" Again we can find excuses and shift the blame, except that now we may be filled with a desire for truth so overwhelming that we willingly acknowledge everything we have done and wish only that we could go back and do it better. For at the same time as we perceive our faults we become aware of all the best and most beautiful things in our life. A great tenderness floods through us and we seek not to make excuses, but only to be worthy of such privilege. Then, for the sake of everything we love, we find ourselves desiring not evasion but responsibility, and remorse and healing begin to do their work upon our soul.

What does God's forgiveness mean? Some have said that it is the wiping away of the record of our failures from some hidden book. Others have suggested that it is being helped never to do these same wrongs again. Or perhaps forgiveness is the remorse itself, that scourer of the soul.

This stage is the beginning of the process of atonement, but not the end. How could it be? We cannot turn to God without also turning to those we have wronged. To confess to God while avoiding the people we've hurt is both an evasion and a dangerous form of self-delusion. Forgiveness must therefore be followed by pardon. Unlike *seliḥah,* the word *meḥilah,* or pardon, is not a biblical, but a rabbinic term. It describes not divine, but human interaction and means the remission of a debt, the readiness to forego one's due. Hence the idiomatic phrase *moḥel kevodo,* which indicates the readiness to forego the claims of honor and station. This concept is very important in the context of Yom Kippur: both as seekers and as givers of pardon we must be ready to give up something of ourselves. As petitioners for pardon we must be prepared to be mistaken, in the wrong, responsible, guilty — concessions most of us loathe to make and feelings most of us hate to acknowledge. As givers of pardon we must forego the desire to stand upon our right, feed our grievance, or keep the moral high ground for ourselves. In either case, we both lose and gain, lose in pride and gain in humanity.

It is rarely easy to apologize. Many of us will doubtless remember how we were told when we were children: "Go to your room and think about your behavior. Don't come back until you're ready to say you're sorry." If it felt hard when we were children, it probably feels even harder now that we are adults. After all, it's acceptable for a child to do something wrong. But for a "grown up"? The higher our station, the harder it may be to admit that we are still fallible and remain subject to our weaknesses. It takes humility, courage and honesty to own up to our faults.

It is just as hard to pardon the faults of others. To do so does not mean that we have to abandon the pursuit of truth and right. History has repeatedly shown that justice cannot leave the protection of the oppressed to the gentle powers of mercy alone. Truth and justice are undermined by facile forgiveness for the sake of making everything sweet and pleasant. Nor ought we necessarily to exempt the other person from striving to make good. But to be foregoing does mean making the effort to let go of offenses and the resentment they may engender in our hearts. However impossible this may sometimes feel, we need to strive to reach a position of understanding and acceptance. This is for our own good as much as for that of others and applies not only to the wrongs done to us by other people, but to the hurts delivered us by life itself. Tragedy can be devastating. Tragedy can rob a person of all that made the past worthwhile, fill the present with anguish, and leave a future of heartache and creeping loneliness. Only the capacity for *mehilah* can save us from the fate of Lot's wife, who, petrified by her tears, is trapped forever in a ceaseless looking back.

The third term, *kapparah,* means atonement. In Temple times it referred to the ritual sacrifice by which such atonement was obtained from God. With the destruction of the second Temple, it acquired a new application; our *kapparah* was no longer an offering on the altar in Jerusalem, but what we offered on the altar of our own table by way of food to wayfarers and the needy.[6] By extension, *kapparah* therefore refers to our ability to give, to make good, and to use the learning born of our mistakes and failures to make a contribution to other people. Often we gain a special sensitivity through our awareness of our weaknesses and in our sorrows. There are many people who, in the long struggle to understand their own pain, choose to make themselves available to others who may be suffering in similar ways.

The simple confession of the dying is: "May my death be an atonement for all my sins." Perhaps the living should say, "May my life be an atonement for all my sins."

Thus the often repeated prayer that punctuates the confession, "And for all these, God of forgiveness, forgive us, pardon us, and grant us atonement," marks the process toward reconciliation. What motivates us to embark on such a journey? Sometimes it is the finger pointing at us from without, the charge of injustice, cruelty, or carelessness that forces us to reconsider our ways. But on the Day of Atonement the motivating force generally comes from within. What is it? Guilt, remorse, inadequacy, a sense of sin? All these may be relevant factors, but we should not forget the simple power of love. In our struggle to find forgiveness, pardon, and atonement, we do best if we take with us the thoughts of those who have loved us, from our ancestors to those who surround us in the present, so that love can give us the strength to face the wrongs we have done and the hurts we have received in a spirit of humility, courage, and generosity.

With Everlasting Love

With everlasting love have I loved you;
Therefore have I drawn you after me in tenderness.

Jer. 31:2

Yom Kippur is the touchstone; it has the power to restore to us the consciousness of what matters most. Of course, it is a day of atonement and reconciliation, when we determine to make good the past and do better in the future. But more than anything else, Yom Kippur is a day about love. When we seek the core and wellspring of our own self; when we reach out to others and make ourselves available for others to reach us, when we call to God and God calls to us to draw close — what else is at the heart of this, if not love?

By speaking of love, I do not, of course, have in mind the stereotypical scenes that make their way onto posters in underground stations. I mean, rather, the kind of love that passes between grandparent and grandchild; the kind of love that, if we are lucky, day by day and year by year as children, adolescents, spouses, we both rely on and provide, give and take for granted; the kind of love that is bashful in word and resolute in deed; the kind of love that animates a nurse's hands as she changes the dressing of a sick and anxious patient. I mean the kind of love that bites its lips and controls its heart, that enabled parents to send their children out from Nazi persecution to unfamiliar lands in the knowledge that they would almost certainly never see them again; the kind of love that, as the records of the Nuremberg trials testify, enabled a grandmother to tickle the baby's chin and make her smile, and a father to hold his little son's hand and point at the sky, even as they stood naked by the death pits. What I mean is the kind of love that, whether spoken or silent, whether angry with too much concern or tender in encouragement, can never ever stomach cruelty. What I mean is love unto death, be its actions as banal as putting on the kettle or as courageous as saying the final goodbye. I think of how Gerda Weissmann Klein, then a girl of eighteen, remembered how her parents spoke through the final hours before their deportation:

And so they talked on through the night, animated and happy. They faced what the morning would bring with the only weapon they had — their love for each other. Love is great, love is the foundation of nobility, it conquers obstacles and is a deep well of truth and strength. After hearing my parents talk that night I began to understand the greatness of their love. Their courage ignited within me a spark that continued to glow through the years of misery and defeat . . .[7]

Such love is surely part of the love of God through the love of God's creation, and especially through the love of people, created in God's image. Such love reflects God's love to us in giving us the capacity to have a receptive, though at times an aching, heart.

Why this theme should so predominate on Yom Kippur may simply be because, on a holy and tender day, love is the most holy and tender thing we know. But there are other reasons, more obviously rooted in the liturgy and traditions of Yom Kippur, though together they add up to that reason beyond reason.

First and foremost, love is connected to the capacity for forgiveness. There are, of course, many aspects to forgiveness. According to Jewish teaching there is an ultimate forgiveness that can be effected only by God; but I refer to the very human struggle to forego recriminations, rebuild relationships, and carry on with life. Lines like "forgiven and forgotten" make it sound as though it were easy, but the ability to manage such matters is not to be estimated lightly. If we are honest, most of us will acknowledge that, on a bad morning, our minds will throw up even a trivial incident from ten years ago and still be full of fury. How much more so do most of us remember and rehearse the deeper hurts we consider ourselves unjustly to have received? It takes a great deal of generosity and forbearance to let go of our wounded feelings and carry on with life without them.

There is the challenge of forgiving other people for what they have done to us. This can be enormously difficult. How do you forgive a person who cheated you out of a fortune or slandered you out of your job? How do you pardon the betrayal of love? How can anyone forgive terminal neglect, as when a parent disappears from a child's life, or when, for decades, a man shows no appreciation for the devotion of his wife?

There is the further challenge of forgiving life itself. Life is not fair. Life lets the unthinkable happen. It makes some people desperately ill and others the victims of war. It brings accidents which leave vital men and women unable to walk, speak, or think. Life lets children die. What, as we acknowledge in the frightening *Unetaneh Tokef* prayer, do we know about our own future: "Who shall live and who shall die . . . who by fire and who by water"? One of the most terrible aspects of tragedy is that if we cannot forgive life, we suffer doubly, not only from the dreadful events themselves, but also from our bitterness over them. Here the poet Rachel Bluwstein struggles with just this question during her long, slow decline with tuberculosis:

> In my great loneliness, loneliness of a wounded animal,
> Hour on hour I lie, keep silence.
> Fate has gleaned my vineyard, left not a grape behind;
> But the heart, subdued, has forgiven.
> If these days are the last of my days —
> Let me be calm,
> Lest I cloud with my bitterness the calm blue
> Of the sky — my companion of old.[8]

What is there strong enough to absorb the anger, fierce enough to neutralize the acidity of bitterness, if not love? What else is there, when destiny is truly harsh, to help one move from rage to reconciliation? If we are to forgive, we need all the love and gratitude we can muster, for other people, for life itself, for the clear blue sky, and for God.

There is a second part of the Yom Kippur liturgy which relates just as powerfully to love and can help us draw on our deepest resources of it — the *Yizkor*, or memorial service. *Yizkor* entered the liturgy after the Crusades and is therefore less ancient than the confessional prayers, but in the minds of most people it is no less essential to what the day is about. During *Yizkor* we remember, in the presence of God, those we have loved. Traditionally it was recited as a means by which, together with the giving of charity, the living might assist the dead on their journey. But nowadays most of us say it as a focus for our memories, as well, perhaps, as in the hope that the spirits of the dead will be with us, the living, and help us through our travails.

I was recently asked by a young woman to pray with her husband, who was dying. They had a nine-year-old boy. "Say a prayer about the world and how beautiful it is," the man asked me. I thought for a moment and said a line in praise of creation from the morning service. The couple responded with assent, recalling the places they had visited, the walks they had shared and the joy they had found in one another. "Now," he said, looking tenderly at his wife, "say a prayer to help me part from life, because I've loved it." I do not believe that such generosity and grace simply die. In ways which cannot be foreseen they will be communicated to the heart of the little boy so that in five, ten, or twenty years' time, there will be days when he will look out at life full of joy and say, "My father is speaking to me now." During the *Yizkor* prayers it is possible for our synagogues to be filled with a palpable sense of that very connectedness of life, a testament to the continued presence in us of the past that makes us and the love that forms us. We need every bit of it we can muster in our struggle to be forgiving and forgiven, and so that we too can give love to others for the future.

Thirdly, and perhaps most forcefully of all, the very awareness of life's transience, which so many of the High Holiday prayers evoke, awakes in us the recognition of how precious life is, how full of beauty it is, how privileged, and how short. Our body is, as the liturgy reminds us, "like a pot that breaks . . . a flower that fades, a shadow that passes, a cloud that disappears." Yet our prayers tell us that it is precisely from creatures such as us that the great and everlasting God desires praise. I am moved by the juxtaposition and the contrast, our smallness and our greatness side by side. We are mortal; yet we have the capacity to perceive beauty, to feel wonder, to experience awe, to be grateful, to create, to sing, and to be silent with a full heart. Of such things, in its brief interval of consciousness between birth and death, the human heart is capable.

In the flood of such feelings, the desire fills me overwhelmingly to cherish life, to love it only more. Naomi Shemer was right in her song: *'Od lo 'ahavti dai — I have not loved enough.* The deep green leaves of the beech tree, the sound of the rain on its canopy, the children sheltering underneath, the wise words of an old woman, books of poetry, the vitality of Torah — all these we have not loved enough. We pray for strength to love them more!

In such moments, when one sees according to this God-given light, the desire to love extends as far as we are capable of perceiving it. We recognize something of the immense need for tenderness in the world. It seems then as if the three great love commandments — love of our neighbor, love of the stranger, and love of God — flow from the very spring of being and

61

sing in their course of the need for a deep and tender respect for life in all its forms. Of course it is essential, if our love is real and unselfish and not a romantic and self-aggrandizing delusion, that insight be followed by resolve. We are, after all, commanded not just to dream about love, but to conduct ourselves according to its laws. For love is, at best, patient, persistent, tenacious, unselfish, and wise.

"I have not loved enough" — how quickly one forgets. We know that our perspective will shrink, our heart harden, and our imagination fail. But while the sacred day of Yom Kippur lasts, growing more and more intense toward its final proclamations, we have at least the opportunity to remember what it is that matters most.

Love's Journey

And the Lord passed by before him, and proclaimed:
"The Lord, the Lord, God merciful and gracious . . ."

Ex. 34:6

Different kinds of adversity can make love's journey arduous. Sometimes it is life itself that puts the obstacles in the way — vast distances, wars, the very brevity of time that tears people from one another's arms. But often it is the difficulties within ourselves that create the distances and provoke the battles; then love's journey, if we have the will and the courage to make it, becomes a voyage toward others through the very heart and substance of who we are. It is this route that Yom Kippur, with its demand that we make peace with one another before we turn to God for pardon, requires us to take.

I once heard someone say to a member of his family after the fast: "You've been in synagogue for hours and prayed the whole day through. But from everything you've said since you've been home, it's obviously made no difference at all. You're exactly the same person you were before." Fair or unfair, this is a powerful criticism. What a waste to squander the opportunities that Yom Kippur provides by carrying on precisely the same as before. Yet if we want to be different when we come home, we have to make love's journey and travel through our faults, our limitations, and our mistakes. We have to do so not because we are bad, but because we are human and because it's through acknowledging the strengths and weaknesses of our nature that we develop and learn.

It is God who sets the example for this journey. For half-hidden within the liturgy of Yom Kippur is a divine journey down to make a declaration of forgiveness and love. According to rabbinic calculation, it is on this day that God, at Moses' behest, descends to stand with him on the mountain and proclaim the sacred attributes, "The Lord, the Lord, God merciful and gracious, long-suffering, and great in love and truth" (Ex. 34:6). These words, sung repeatedly on Yom Kippur, are in fact its key and core motif. As soon as he hears them, Moses petitions God for pardon and it is granted.

The first stage of the journey is implied by the words, "God came down . . . and stood there with him." If we wish to be close to other people we have to come down, or come back, from whatever distance separates us and "stand there with them" together. We have to ask not just what they seem like to us, as we naturally do, but more importantly what we look like to them. In this way we learn to see ourselves more truly and to understand our relationships with others more clearly.

What do parents look like to their children? One day when my son was about eight months old, I had to dress him in a hurry. It was one of those mornings when arms and sleeves simply wouldn't go together and I was impatient. I didn't allow myself to say anything cross but my mood was angry and he began to cry. He must have sensed the fading of the customary love; my behavior toward him was impatient and rough. I'm sure I'm not the only father who worries about how his children see him. A friend told me he fears his son will think of him as the "Not now, I'll play with you later" daddy. These are small matters, part of every parent/child relationship. But they are also the beginnings out of which a cold and isolating distance can easily develop, a sense of failing and having been failed. Where does that apartness come from that often breaks the bond between child and parent? I think again of the frightening lines in which Olive Fraser describes her parents' attitude to her:

I was the wrong music
The wrong guest for you . . .
Summon'd though unwanted,
Hated tho' true . . .[9]

Children must sometimes look at their parents and read rejection on their faces: "You're not the child I wanted, not pretty, not clever, not gifted, not graceful enough." Parents must sometimes look at their children and experience a silent condemnation: "You're not good enough, trendy enough, understanding enough, for me."

What we look like to our closest friends, partners, spouses may be just as disturbing. I recently got caught in the middle of a quarrel between a newly married couple. Words were flung viciously back and forth. I thought, "Why don't you try to understand one another instead of throwing ammunition across the room? Take a step back and give each other some space!" But am I myself a person who gives space, or a person who sometimes throws words like javelins? A famous and much-loved rabbi, Aryeh Levin, was once asked by a bridegroom for advice about marriage. The questioner no doubt expected some profound Torah insight, but all the rabbi said was, "When you go to bed don't leave your clothes on the floor for your wife to tidy away." Do those closest to us sometimes say, "I know he's been here because of the dirty dishes on the table"?

How do we look through the eyes of our colleagues? I overheard a conversation in which a man complained, "I can't possibly work with him anymore. He never consults. He goes right on ahead and leaves me feeling totally on my own." The reply was, "Yes, but have you ever considered how lonely you might be making him feel?" The truth is that most of us don't think enough about how we make others feel. Once in Jerusalem I was accosted by a man begging on the pavement. It transpired that his son needed transplant surgery, but no one in the family could afford to pay. I sat with him in the street for a while and watched the constant march of legs going past. It was then that I realized how absolutely and utterly indifferent the world must so often appear to so many.

These glimpses of ourselves through the eyes of others lead to difficult questions: Am I a giver or a taker? Am I a person who fills the fridge or one who expects to find it full? Do I take it for granted that my socks will be paired and rolled up in my drawer, or do I pick socks up and put them together and leave them in the right place for others? Am I the sort of person who, if a relative is ill, phones and visits and takes round a meal, or do I believe that these things ought to be done, but by someone else?

Am I an encourager or a detractor? Do I try, like many wonderful teachers and people who have the gift of nurturing others, to say just those words in just that tone that give confidence and a sense of well-being? Or do I pick on people's faults and leave those around me feeling inadequate and small? Nathaniel Hawthorne wrote a story about a beautiful woman who had a birthmark. Her husband adored her, but became increasingly fixated with her one small blemish until it became all he ever saw in her. Eventually she underwent an operation to have it removed. Now she was perfect in his eyes. But unfortunately the mark proved to be connected to the very essence of who she was, and she faded away and died.[10] Do we behave like that? Do we build others up or make them fade away?

Am I grateful or greedy? Can I ever be like the old man I once knew who used to say, "I've only got ten percent of my eyesight left, but thank God I can see. I'm ancient and walk very slowly, but thank God I can still get around. I'm not what I used to be, but thank God I have a wonderful wife who looks after me." Or am I always wanting something else; do I live with a list of all the things I haven't got but imagine others have?

Am I possessive? Do I need to get all the attention, affection, and praise? Or can I let go of my wants and be generous to others? Can I rejoice in their good fortune and help them toward their own future without seeking anything more for myself than the blessing of their wellbeing? In C. Day Lewis's words:

> . . . Selfhood begins with the walking away,
> And love [is] proved in the letting go.[11]

And there are many, and painful, kinds of letting go, as everyone well knows.

God does not only come down and stand with Moses on the mountain; God then proclaims, "The Lord, the Lord, merciful and gracious . . ." It is an eternal declaration of love. It reminds us of the force of love that exists in the world and teaches us how much greater that force might yet be. For, unless we have been deeply wronged by life, we are, to some degree at least, witnesses to love.

We witness love in the lives of other people. I often think of the letter Vera Gissing received from her parents after their death. She and her sister were sent from Czechoslovakia to England on the *Kindertransport*. After the war it emerged that their parents had not survived, but they had left a letter for their daughters with a friend. Vera's mother wrote:

> And now, my dear children, on behalf of your father and myself, I wish you — not only for the new year, not only for Eva's birthday, but for the rest of your life . . . Be happy, be brave . . . We gave you love, we gave you the foundations of life . . . Remember your home and us, but do not grieve . . .[12]

One can only wonder at such generosity.

We witness the power of love in great beauty. For there is a presence in beauty, a plenitude in harmony, a resonance in all things fashioned or conducted with good grace, which comes from the same source and overflows with the same spirit as love.

We witness the power of love in the recognition of what we ourselves have been given. Perhaps that, in the end, is the meaning of the memorial prayers we say on Yom Kippur — that love is indeed stronger than death. For love is not bound by time, and a child may feel supported forever by the affection of a parent who has died.

Above all, we know love from our own heart and soul. We may sometimes not feel it as deeply as we would wish; its flow may often be weak and its manifestation stymied. But in the end our greatest understanding of love comes from within ourselves. For we are able not only to receive but also to give love, and the words "merciful and gracious . . . and great in love" should be understood not just as a description of God's nature, but also of the potential in our own.

Two kinds of realization therefore meet and struggle within us: the awareness of who we actually are, with all our faults and failings, and the thought of who we might, and long to, be. Truth and love confront each other in our heart, but the heart is not a simple or a comfortable place.

Every heart has wounds, a chamber that is sealed, a room we do not want to open. Here life's tragedies are stored, and here wounds still feel fresh.

Yet the heart often says, "I want to be better and cleaner! I want to love more!" When that happens, when we recognize both who we are and who we might be, then we are on love's journey. Then there is hope of pardon, atonement, and growth. We can forgive without deceiving ourselves because it is our firm commitment to live more generously and wisely. We can forego — at least some of — our vexations with others, because we have tried to look at life from their point of view. We can turn to them, because nothing is ever only one person's fault, and say, "I'm sorry that I hurt you!"

Of course, there is no obliteration of memory; that would be moral oblivion. But there is a commitment to the future, to life, to love, and to partnership. There is a commitment to the journey.

Dying and the Spirit:
Reflections before the Memorial Service

> And when it will please thee to take us from
> earth, be thou with us . . .
>
> from the Memorial Service

We have to trust that, when the time comes, God, who helps us know how to live, will help us know how to die. We must hope that God, who privileges us with the capacity to know justice, share love, and experience beauty, will also grant us generosity, humility, and wisdom, so that we can both live and let go of life well.

Death must not be romanticized. People die in very different ways. I recently spoke with two friends, a man whose father died instantly of a heart attack in front of him and his small child, and a woman whose father died painfully of cancer. These two different confrontations with death are a chastening reminder never to generalize about dying. Also, the person dying and the family members around him or her may travel very different emotional and spiritual paths. I think of her husband's words at the close of Ruth Picardie's testament, *Before I Say Goodbye:* "The lump not only grew within her, but between us, spreading, as inexorably as the cancer itself did."[13]

With this caution, I would like to reflect on two moments in particular people's experiences, one which I shared and one about which I read, which moved me. I would describe each of these moments as deeply spiritual, although neither has any connection with anything religious in a formal sense, or even, overtly, with God.

I remember a woman with whom I spoke many times over the course of her slow decline. She was a warm, welcoming person who had been a teacher and caregiver. She was also good at drawing. One day I found her copying a photograph of a mother elephant with a baby. The illness had affected her hand control, and she was struggling to complete the picture. "It's not right," she said, as she carefully redid the baby. "It's important to get it right." I have often asked myself since why this apparently trivial scene stuck in my mind. I think it's because the lady communicated such a loving commitment to nurture, to mother and baby, and so showed, despite her own rapidly waning strength, a great generosity toward life. This expression of the spirit exemplifies the grace that I have sometimes seen in the dying, the ability to appreciate the breadth of life and, in that knowledge, to part humbly from the world.

The second moment is taken from Rachel Naomi Remen's book, *Kitchen Table Wisdom.* The writer recollects how she was taken as a little girl of three to visit her godfather, who was dying. Her mother had just put her on the bed next to the emaciated man when she was unexpectedly called out of the room. Rachel remembers how, while she and her godfather were alone together:

> In a voice that was barely a whisper he called me by my name . . . I was very young then but I knew that whispers meant secrets, so I leaned toward him to hear. He smiled at me, a beautiful smile, and said, "I've been waiting for you." My family were intellectual, formal, well-mannered people who were not openly affectionate or demonstrative. My godfather's eyes and his smile were full of a great love and appreciation. For the first time I felt a deep sense of welcome, of mattering to someone. His hands were resting on the covers and, still smiling, he slid one a little toward me. Then

he closed his eyes. After a short while he sighed deeply and was still again.[14]

Rachel's mother was horrified when she returned to find her little daughter alone with the dead man. It was many years before the child was able to explain to the parent quite how profoundly those moments had affected her.

I could think of other examples. On one of the last days of his life, my friend's father was leafing through a book in a desultory fashion, and no one could understand what he was looking for or even if his activity had any real purpose. But then he found the passage he had treasured all his life. It spoke of the gratitude of a fugitive prisoner of war toward the peasants who had harbored him and his friend and who, though having the sparsest of material goods, had a love and sensitivity to all living, growing things that made them rich.

What, if anything, do these experiences have in common? They share, I believe, a humble and generous recognition of life beyond the self, beyond indeed the human, and beyond the present, of life which will go on without us. Such recognition may be indicated in as many ways as there are people. These may sound most ordinary from the outside. But, as my friend recently said to me after his father died, "When such activities are the last expression of the human, will they acquire a sanctity and dignity all of their own."

It is not easy to keep company with the dying. We face not only their fears, but often — and more acutely — our own. Yet such companionship also offers us a particular blessing, pushing our heart toward the deepest and most universal consciousness within us. We are led all the more directly to the awareness of the sheer breadth and depth of experience and helped to acknowledge the *not knowing,* which is so important if we are to be sensitive to the presence of the spirit. For if we are attentive and accepting of speech, or inference, or silence, we may be led to the threshold of the sacred, whatever particular form it may take.

To say what we mean by words like *sacred* or *spirit* is notoriously difficult. Rather than trying to define them, I would prefer to follow the negative path and remove constraints from what they may be. A sense of the spirit may, or may not, be experienced as a *religious* moment. It may, or may not, be brought to consciousness by ritual or prayer. It may, or may not, be experienced as connection with "God." It may, or may not, be

69

accompanied by a belief in the continuation of the individual life after death. It is perfectly possible to have a profound sense of the connectedness of all life and a forthright view of the raw and absolute nature of individual mortality. But I do believe that a sensitivity to the spirit will allow us to relate, in some form, to what Wordsworth described as:

> A sense sublime
> Of something far more deeply interfused . . .
> A motion and a spirit, that impels
> All thinking things, all objects of all thought,
> And rolls through all things.[15]

What can the consciousness of this dimension of being bring us? It makes an immensely important contribution to the process of dying, as it does to that of living. I believe that such contact with the spirit is always for blessing. It may nevertheless engender sorrow, with the awareness of the smallness of our own life and its imminent dissolution. It may herald joy in the appreciation of life going on. It may precipitate that sensation of simultaneous wonder and sadness that makes so many of those who work with the dying think over and over again how short but how precious life is. It has the power to bring reconciliation through the quiet and not necessarily spoken acknowledgment of past mistakes in the grace of a greater understanding. It can enable silent or misunderstood love to be acknowledged and renewed. It is always for our growth.

It would be wrong to romanticize the spiritual, as if it were an escape from the other moods that may be part of dying — pain, terror, anger, bitterness, and despair. These feelings are sometimes described as "spiritual pain," anguish over the emotional and existential questions, which, consciously or not, are bound to beset us: what are our life and relationships worth and what do they mean? Sometimes this anguish is so great that the moment's peace cannot arrive which might allow a glimpse of a greater life. I have sometimes witnessed such restlessness possess a dying person and found it deeply distressing. Anger, bitterness, and guilt call for help and understanding. They make it hard for a person to become in touch with their own spirit, but sadness and regret may lead us on into our own heart and soul.

Of course, nothing comes in discrete units; in dying, as in living, many people pass through moments of wider vision and narrower anguish interspersed. Moods change and change quickly; but it is the inaccessibility, not the presence, of the spirit, that brings real suffering.

For awareness of the spirit, though it may be chastening, is healing, a paradoxical healing, which is not rarely a gift from the dying to the living.

What We Really Lose

. . . as a blade of Your grass in a distant, wild field
Loses a seed in the lap of the earth
And dies away,
Sow in me Your living breath,
As You sow a seed in the earth.

Kadya Molodowsky[16]

A family friend of my parents' generation lost her husband very suddenly. They were an exceptionally close couple who had created a home full of warmth, grace, and welcome, and the loss was both shocking and immensely sad. Some months afterward, she spoke to me about what her husband's death had come to mean to her:

> What is it we really lose? His body is made of matter that becomes other forms and other life. His heart is not lost. His love doesn't disappear just because he died; it's with me, our children, grandchildren and all who knew him. It travels on to nurture other lives. As for his mind, I know his thoughts intimately and can say what he would think in almost every situation. The books he loved are all around me, I have letters and diaries he wrote. His spirit continues on its journey because the spirit never dies. What is it then that we really mourn? It is the presence of the person we love among us day by day. That is what we lose; but everything they have been travels on.

When the ultimate questions are asked — what we are and what our life is — I often think of her words. For everything is in transition, through our lives and beyond, and our existence is only a participation in that passage.

When Rabbi Yoḥanan went to visit his sick pupil Rabbi Elazar, he found him lying alone in a dark room. Rabbi Yoḥanan was a man of legendary and luminous good looks; he bared his arm, and the chamber is said to have filled with light. He noticed that his disciple was crying. "Why?" he asked, in a series of vain attempts to discover the reason, which elicited only the sound of further weeping. At length Rabbi Elazar responded, "I weep because beauty such as this must wither in the dust."[17] The body is indeed a thing of beauty, marvelously made. We often take for granted the basic joys it brings us; things like dipping one's feet in cool water after a long, hot walk, drinking a cup of tea at the end of a tiring day, or coming into the warmth after a freezing journey. There are the simple gestures of trust and affection; the embrace of old friends; grandparents arm in arm; fingers stroking a cheek. There is the joy of hearing a familiar voice, the longing for its sound. For all these things Rabbi Elazar weeps. He is right; our body will disintegrate, turn to ash or earth. Therefore we should be grateful for it while it it is healthy and use it to perform the commandments of the body — to reach out and give, to offer support, to be present where we can help.

Just as our body is composed from matter in transition, so our heart is formed of love on its long and complex migration from past to future. The love that makes us is fashioned, and foiled, through many generations. Once, when I was feeling very low, I met a favorite neighbor who said to me:

> Don't worry. Remember the strength that stands behind you. Think of your grandparents with their resilience and courage. Didn't your grandmother get the family out of Germany? Didn't your grandfather devote himself to his congregation until he was in his eighties? All that energy and love is with you; don't be afraid.

Often in the last few years I've wanted to say to mourners not, "I'm sure your loved one is with you," but, "I am sure their love is within you." We are nourished by the affections that reach us from the past. I often ask bar and bat mitzvah children to tell me about the most precious thing they own. Almost invariably they mention a necklace given by a great-aunt who had received it from her father when she was a little girl, or a ring inherited from a great-grandmother. They already know; it's the love that counts.

How far back does the chain of affection stretch? Thousands of people go on pilgrimages to family graves or the sites of massacres in Poland, Lithuania, the Ukraine, and beyond. I hope they find there more than just the place where their ancestors died; I hope such journeys help us to envisage our ancestors' lives. For it is their love that has reached us and formed our hearts. "My flesh and my heart faileth," says the psalm (73:26). My heart will disintegrate and the person I think of as "me" will perish, but the love I recognize and share will live on. So why not give it while I can? Why not keep the commandments of the heart — to love — to love our neighbor and the stranger for whom there may be no one else who cares?

The mind, too, receives its illumination from the past and has the capacity to refine and transmit knowledge to the future. Judaism regards the mind as a sacred faculty and the responsibility to fill it as a divine commandment. Knowledge of Torah is of course primary, but the pursuit of all knowledge can be seen as an attempt to understand and appreciate God's world.

Judaism has always stressed the chain of teaching, the importance of transmitting insights and opinions in the name of those who said them, and often in the name of that person's teacher as well. To study Torah is to engage with the company of the past. What this means became clearer to me when I bought my own copy of the Talmud. I hadn't wanted a new edition; I wanted to feel that others before me had pondered over the same pages. I wanted them to be with me when I studied. In the first shop I entered, I found a beautiful edition printed in Vilna in the 1860s. Whenever I open it, I think of the compositors working by candlelight to prepare the lines of minuscule lead letters for the commentaries, letters which were later used to make ammunition for the resistance fighters in the ghetto. I occasionally wonder who first bought the books and who, probably fleeing some pogrom, brought them to England. As for the commentaries, I used to be sceptical about the commentaries-upon-commentaries that form so significant a part of Jewish sacred writing. But now I feel otherwise. For each represents a mind, a generation, struggling with the same eternal questions, and the wisdom — and shortcomings — of yesterday's answers. They are at once a dialogue between each person and God, and a conversation between ancestors and children. This pattern fits the Islamic description of the poet who uses the language of the Koran as one who "lights a candle from a candle that is already lit." To learn Torah is to hold out one's own candle in the hope that the wick will take light; to teach Torah is to guide other hands holding candles to this same flame. While, therefore, our mind has the capacity to be illumined, we should perform the commandments of the mind — to study and teach Torah, to learn to appreciate God's world through the countless paths of knowledge and wisdom.

Then there is the spirit. "In order to give," taught Rebbe Moshe Leib of Sassov, "man must *be*." "A man who does not keep an hour a day for himself is not human."[18] We need time to nurture our spirit; otherwise, we lose it in the sheer pressure and confusion of everyday living. Perhaps that is why the dying sometimes experience, among all their painful feelings, a sense of freedom and release. Someone else will do the income-tax return, someone else will see to the dry rot. There are no expectations any more. The spirit can go free. For it is in our spirit that our ultimate freedom resides; here we are unassailable, at once alone and together with all life and God. As the simple words of the beautiful hymn *Adon Olam* say, "This is my God and my life's Redeemer." Sometimes life seems to be composed of nothing more than an endless series of petty tasks that grow in number more quickly than we can find the energy to dispatch them. Why am I doing this? What's the point of this dull, dead run of days? Then something happens, usually something small — a bird flits across the street, a flood of light fills the garden in a moment of radiance — and the spirit returns. Once again we live, our life has been redeemed. The soul is nourished once more. Why not then keep the commandments of the spirit while it dwells in us, to love and feel the awe of God, to expose ourselves to wonder and to beauty?

The *Ne'ilah* Service teaches us that the gate of life will close, but death is not the ultimate measure of what I am. For all that is now me has passed through life before. All I am is a coagulation of matter, a confluence of love, a formulation of knowledge, a manifestation of the spirit. All these forces will travel through me and move on. What matters is that I use them lovingly and richly while I am privileged to have life and that I pass them on, cherished, to others.

Sanctify Us with Your Commandments

And when I set out toward you, toward me I found you coming
And, amidst the wonders of your might, in holiness beheld you.

Yehudah Halevi[19]

Just as one can walk down the road one has lived on for years and see something never noticed before, so one can say prayers all one's life and still come across phrases which hold surprises, the meaning of which one has never before explored or which suddenly acquire a new immediacy. This is what happened to me with the familiar words *"kaddeshenu bemitzvotekha* — Make us holy through your commandments,"* over which I had never lingered before, and which have since come to express to me the essence of the Jewish approach to life. For in a world which prizes the useful above all — a world whose primary question is, "What can one do with it?" or, "What profit can I derive from it?" — Judaism maintains a very different ideal. It seeks to uncover the sacred, so that we should respect it and make time for it, but also in order that it should seep into us and turn us, at least to some small degree, into itself, as the words say, "Make *us* holy through your commandments."

What is holiness? The word has been variously interpreted. An ancient Aramaic translation renders it as "separate," but this does not satisfy me because holiness is also about togetherness. One modern English version uses the word "special," but that is unsatisfactory because many things are special. To say "sacred" is equally unhelpful because it substitutes one inexplicable term for another. I cannot therefore define the word "holy." I can give examples of what I mean by it, in small vignettes gleaned in moments of grace, which constitute my most treasured inner possessions.

The Torah is holy; I sensed this when we unrolled it once in the synagogue and a whole group of people who had never been that close to it before looked at the beauty of the letters and absorbed the love and care with which the Torah is written. I felt it when a woman told me of how she had wept on being called to read from the Torah for the first time.

Holiness is not limited to sacred objects; it extends throughout the human domain. I sensed this once when a nurse and I were called to attend to a dying man who was crying out in pain. The family was around the bed, loving, anxious. As the nurse bent over the sick man, I noticed how he did more than straighten the sheets and check that the flow of intravenous medication was proceeding correctly. I did not hear what he said because he spoke very softly, but at his words the man grew calm and the room filled with tenderness. The sacred had come palpably closer.

Nor is the holy limited to the human world. Recently I was in the garden when, hearing a sound like the tapping of a small hammer, I looked up and glimpsed in the neighbor's pear tree the black and white back and red head of a woodpecker. A shudder went through me, a sensation of awe at the sheer beauty of life. There lives in the midst of things an often invisible but not entirely imperceptible incandescence, which, like the bush in the Bible, burns but does not consume.

Judaism, however, doesn't just teach about the holy; it offers us a path which leads toward it. There are many steps along this path, but I believe they can be divided into four basic stages, corresponding to four aspects of our life.

The first is as simple as it is difficult: integrity in all our conduct. The Torah's injunction, "Be holy, for I, the Lord your God, am holy," is followed not by ritual but by ethical stipulations: Don't cheat, don't lie, don't be ugly in anything you say or do. The Mishnah teaches that however pious we may be, God is as close to us and as comfortable in our company as we are close to other people and make them comfortable in ours.[20] Unfortunately, religious zealotry often leads people to forget the sanctity of all life and the equality of all people. In every true spiritual discipline, justice and integrity are the basis of all service of God.

The next step involves those commandments that form the web of traditional Jewish life with its sacred seasons and their sounds, sights, and smells. I think of the kindling of lights; until I had a family I remained under the misapprehension that the Shabbat candles had to be lit in a mood of deep contemplation. But with three young children, I now know that shouts of "Mine first!", "I want to do the big ones!" and "When can I have my chocolate biscuit?" are all part of the atmosphere. Nevertheless I love to stare at the candles late at night when the household is still. They transport me to other lights: to the Ḥanukkah candles at my grandmother's home in the difficult years after my grandfather died, with memories of how she used to watch them and say, "How beautifully they burn!"; to the memorial light which draws other lives, other generations, into the luminous flame; to the everlasting light which stays burning when we leave the synagogue, when we leave the world. The commandments surround us with light. If we live with them sincerely, they have the power to transfer that light to our own actions and our own heart.

The third step, though some would say that this should come first of all, concerns our close relationships. Judaism calls the marriage bond *kiddushin,* the sacred "setting apart" of each partner by the other for a unique and singular relationship, but perhaps all our human relations can have an aspect of *kodesh,* of the holy. "She was supportive, encouraging, intelligent, artistic," said a congregant about her mother who had just died, "but her greatest gift was that she gave everyone her time. She always remembered exactly who everyone was and what mattered to them most." It's a wonderful tribute. If only in the rush and business of our existence we could treat people in this way, appreciating them for who they are, welcoming them, and giving them time, we would touch more lives with the sacred warmth of human contact, and they would touch ours too. More than anything else, I feel ashamed on the Day of Atonement of the panic and irritation that so often drive me and so frequently impel me to say even to my own children, through tone or gesture, "Out of the way! I haven't got the time!"

Finally, there is God. The prophet Zechariah declared: "God is in his sacred temple; let the whole earth be silent before his presence" (2:17). But where else would God be? The force of the verse must therefore lie in its second half, "Let all the earth be silent!" We fill the earth with our noisy presence and no longer notice that God is there. Pablo Casals is reputed to have said that he was blessed with wonderful music, a marvelous instrument, and an excellent bow. All he had to do was to keep himself out of the way. If the music is life and the instrument, the soul, then the bow must be our conduct every day. But how hard it is to keep ourselves out of the way.

We are therefore required to set aside time for the sacred: time for prayer every day, for the Shabbat each week, for atonement once a year. Perhaps then, in these interstices of silence, we may keep sufficiently out of the way so as not to conceal from ourselves that incandescence which, glowing in the heart of all things, burns but does not consume.

SUKKOT

From Yom Kippur to Sukkot

"This is my God, whom I will adorn."   Ex. 15:2

Rabbi Yishmael said: "Is it possible for a person to adorn their
Maker? Rather, let me adorn myself before God with *mitzvot,* let me
prepare a beautiful *lulav,* a beautiful *sukkah.*"

Mekhilta deRabbi Yishmael[1]

I love the transition from Yom Kippur to Sukkot. One goes home after the
fast, eats a little something, drinks a lot, and straight away begins to build
the *sukkah.* If Yom Kippur has gone well there can be no better way to
return to the banalities of life than by doing something as practical as ham-
mering nails into posts and planks. If it has gone badly, how much better it
is to hit a nail than a neighbor on the head!

Yom Kippur is a day on which we are deprived of the joys of the senses.
There is no eating, no drinking, no bathing, no anointing the flesh with
oils. Though pleasant smells are permitted, the olfactory being considered
the most spiritual of the senses, the scents of the day are in fact halitosis
and, for anyone who looks like fainting, the pungency of smelling salts,
possessing all the fragrance of an over-ripe camembert.

The meditation *Tefillah Zakah* by Abraham Danziger, which many say
before the commencement of *Kol Nidrei,* relates the affliction of the senses
to the meaning of the day. The prayer acknowledges that God gave us our
bodily faculties but that we have abused them; our eyes have looked on
what they should not, our ears listened to what they ought not, and our
mouths spoken things they must not. We meditate on the sins of heart,
hand, and tongue all day long.

We hope, though, that by the close of the fast a fresh innocence has been
granted us, and we return to rejoice in the world of the senses in all its purity and beauty. This is epitomized in the joys of touch and sound, sight,
smell, and taste, which we experience both in building and in rejoicing in
the *sukkah.* Here, then, are some of the pleasures of the senses on Sukkot.

81

Touch is the rough feel of unplaned wood used for the sides of the *sukkah* and the long struts that support the greenery on the roof. It is the smooth handle of the hammer and the uneven iron of galvanized nails. It is the bump against one's head because a marrow has been hung too low and the bash when a poorly tied fruit falls down. Above all, it is the feel of the weather, the slow drip down the back of the neck if it drizzles gently, the sodden saturation of rain. It is the growing sensation of seeping, insinuating cold.

The story is told among the Ḥasidim of Rebbe Shlomo Abba of Zichnin who refused, despite the persistent downpour, to stop teaching Torah in the *sukkah*. When the rain finally turned into a deluge and everything was awash, he stood up and declared in the words of the Song of Songs, "Mighty waters cannot extinguish love." "And I know what I'd have declared back to him if I'd been there!" said a friend of mine, shuddering at the very thought of such cold.

Though, if we're lucky, touch can also be the long, warm reach of the afternoon sun as it travels through the greenery of the *sukkah* to illumine the table with autumn brightness. However, it is to the sense of sight that most of the joys of the *sukkah* are directed. Jewish tradition speaks in general of *hiddur,* care and attention in keeping the commandments beautifully, but at no single mitzvah does it direct this injunction more clearly than that of the *sukkah*. In a deciduous land the *sukkah* may be adorned with all the colors of autumn leaves and fruits. I remember glorious hours in *sukkot* past, looking out at the brilliant reds of maples, the golds, greens, and yellows of all the other trees, delighting in the closing beauty of the year. We should teach our children to value such things, to be awake to the wonders of nature, and to strive to protect them wherever we are.

Our Rabbis, however, also warn us that beauty belongs not only in the outer manifestation, but with the inner intention of our actions. Generosity and hospitality are the beauties of the *sukkah* no less; without them our warmth goes no deeper than the colors on the wall.

The sounds of the *sukkah* are first and foremost its special melodies. We do not know whom we have to thank for creating *nusaḥ,* the special musical mode of the prayers, different for each festival, by which we can know from every *Amen* the season at which we stand. Without it our services would suffer a massive impoverishment, as if there were no seasons in the liturgy and all our prayers were one long monotonous summer.

Who can think of the joys of sound without the pleasures of conversation. If Jews talk even in the synagogue during the service, how much more so do we chatter and reminisce, recall, recount, and share words of Torah in the *sukkah!* Inevitably, *sukkot* present evoke the ghosts of *sukkot* past: "In our *sukkah* once in Stettin . . ."; "Where I grew up in Czechoslovakia . . ."; "In the Black Forest, near my parents' former home . . ." Thus the *sukkah* serves for recent times the very function ascribed to it by the Torah in relation to ancient days: it reminds us of our journey out of Egypt and of the journeyings of Jews throughout the ages. Apparently in warmer climates the conversation extends beyond the individual *sukkah* and is carried from rooftop to rooftop in greetings and stories told from booth to booth across the alleyways. In England one is often obliged to remember the authentic Jewish version of *Singin' in the Rain,* rushing through the Grace after Meals as the shower gets steadily heavier.

The smells of the *sukkah* are special, too. I think of the savor and flavor of autumn, the first frosty mornings, and the nights glowing with brisk cold; of the afternoons rich with brief warmth and the final fruitfulness of an Indian summer. There is the smell of flowers in the *sukkah*, the damp aroma of fresh greenery, the scent of ripe apples. Most important, there is the fragrance of the *etrog.* I have never forgotten how once I took my *etrog* with me to a hospice nearby. I offered it to a very sick man who, smelling it, began to recall the sights of the Poland of his youth; the scent reactivated the Jewish memories from which he had long been disassociated and which he had presumed irrelevant and forgotten. He kept that *etrog* by his pillow till he died.

Sukkot tastes vary from family to family. To my wife a tart apple provides the flavor of the season; what else would one expect of a girl from Kent? Cabbage rolls, piping hot, are my family's Sukkot favorite. Claudia Roden refers in her fascinating *Book of Jewish Food* to the custom of eating *kreplakh,* a kind of ravioli in which the meat filling is covered with a noodle-like dough, recalling how God's attribute of mercy surrounds the attribute of justice and holds it in. To me, a long-standing vegetarian, twenty minutes in the *sukkah* with a good cup of coffee and a book of poetry, the Talmud, or ḥasidic teachings, is a spell in heaven.

Is all this an indulgence? I think not! After all, on Yom Kippur we have declared that our days are like grass that withers and a dream that fades. We have remembered the dead and acknowledged that life can and will take from us our nearest and dearest. We have looked into our souls and admitted our faults. But right now we are here, and, in the interim, we are granted new life and fresh innocence. So why not enjoy them? Why not make the best of life? This can scarcely be called selfish. After all, a *sukkah* is nothing if not modest, and a meal there is never complete unless it is inclusive. For a joy shared is a joy doubled. So why not say, "*L'hayim! To Life! Come on in!*"?

Four Kinds of Joy

> Our feet shall stand inside your gates, O Jerusalem . . .
> Peace be within your walls, and prosperity within your palaces.
> For my brothers' and sisters' and companions' sakes,
> Let me say, Peace be within you.
>
> Ps. 122:2, 7–8

Sukkot is the festival of joy. The word *simhah* is not mentioned at all in the Torah specifically in connection with Pesah; the memory of slavery is too close behind. Joy is spoken of in relation to Shavuot, though only once; but it is referred to no less than three times in the description of Sukkot. Sukkot is *zeman simhatenu,* the season of our joy. The harvest is in, atonement is granted; now is the time to rejoice. And rejoice the Rabbis did, with processions, songs, dances, and juggling all night long. "All," declares the Mishnah, "who haven't seen the joy of the ceremony of water drawing, have never seen joy in their lives."[2] In this respect our generation (and all those for the last one thousand, nine hundred and thirty years) have been deprived, but we have other kinds of joy to make up for it. They are epitomized by Sukkot, but they spread their glow throughout the Jewish year and throughout Jewish life.

The first of these joys is simply *simhah shel mitzvah,* the joy of fulfilling the commandments. The Talmud teaches that God's presence dwells neither where there is melancholy, nor amidst heedless frivolity, but with *simhah shel mitzvah,* joy in the performance of the commandments. Such joy includes not only the spiritual but also the practical: the fun of making ḥallah, the bustle of baking one's own matzah, the green-fingered endeavor to grow one's own *etrog* (the pip we planted five years ago is now a plant with its first tiny fruit), and the clamber to hang an apple in the most awkward corner of the *sukkah*. Judaism is a "do-it-yourself" and a "do-it-with-joy" religion. This is a principle we should never allow ourselves to forget. Unlike the father who told his son that his favorite word in the Torah was *vayamot,* "And he died," we should be on the constant lookout for new ways of making our Judaism joyful, for we are sure to find them.

The second kind of joy is *simḥah shel rei'ah,* the joy of coming before God. Originally this referred specifically to the commandment to go up three times each year on the pilgrimage festivals to the Temple in Jerusalem, where the streets would be so packed with throngs of celebrants that it would be virtually impossible to find lodgings. Among these occasions Sukkot was unique. Imagine the stalls that must have lined the roads leading to Jerusalem in which merchants sold *etrogim;* myrtle, palm, and willow branches; and all kinds of materials for the *sukkah!* In the city itself the courtyards were illumined by candelabra seventy feet tall, and the people danced while the Rabbis juggled with torches. Meanwhile, at the base of the altar surrounded by willows, water libations were poured out amidst prayers for a fertile year.

Although we can no longer go up to the Temple, all is not lost today. On the contrary, every synagogue is a *mikdash me'at,* a small sanctuary, and a synagogue is created wherever the community meets to pray, celebrate, and invoke God's presence. This was the great democratizing achievement of the generations who lived after the destruction of the second Temple. They affirmed the significance of prayer, anywhere. In so doing they spread the focus of Jewish life outward from Jerusalem to wherever in the world Jews gather. That is why all our synagogues are adorned with the beauty of their own *sukkot* and have their own parades with *etrogim,* myrtles, willows, and palms. For there is a little piece of Jerusalem everywhere.

The third kind of joy is having a home, expressed in the rabbinic principle that one must bring one's family gifts to make them happy on the festival. Considering the rush in which most of us reach *yom tov,* this may be easier said than done. Yet squashed around the table in the *sukkah,* or more expansively at the seder, when family and friends meet, when those no longer alive have an unseen presence among us and we think of what they would have said or sung, then the joy of having a home, of belonging to a family and people with a spiritual home in history, becomes real. In a lonely and rootless world, we are privileged to belong.

It can sound insensitive to speak of the joy of family. What of those who have no home, no partner, or no children? Some years ago in our *sukkah* a woman asked to sit farther away from our baby, because she had no children of her own. My wife and I felt terrible. We have seen the anguish of the many who feel they "can't belong" because they don't fit the perfect image of the happy family. Of course, in one way or another, none of us do. The shoe presses somewhere for everyone. But many people face especially painful situations; there are all kinds of personal reality, among Jews as among every other group. What this requires of us is not to put aside the joys and values of community, family, and belonging, but to be inclusive and considerate. In so doing we follow in our own social context the Torah's command that we include in our celebrations the widow, the fatherless, the stranger, and the landless Levite who dwells among us. This is never more relevant than on Sukkot, when the booths remind us of the impermanence of our situation and the temporary nature of our relationship with all we imagine to be "ours."

The fourth, and most inward, kind of joy is the happiness of *yismaḥ lev*, of experiencing a joyful heart. According to Rabbi Eliezer, the *sukkah* represents God's protective presence, which was spread over the people like a canopy of cloud.[3] Rabbi Eliezer had in mind the journeyings of the Children of Israel after the Exodus from Egypt and the cloud of glory that sheltered them then, but we don't have to stretch the imagination far to appreciate the inner meaning of his image. The heart has its own weathers. Sometimes heavy clouds lie upon it, storms blow through it, feelings are swept over it that we can hardly describe or understand. But in precious moments we may sense there a spiritual presence, which, like a fine bright cloud in a pure sky, brings a deep and restoring wholeness. This is the inner joy of being both at one with self and in touch with others, of feeling that the *sukkat shalom*, the tabernacle of peace, is spread not only over us but within us. Prayer can bring that joy, the study of Torah can; so can beauty, compassion, and love. When we have it, we rediscover the goodness instilled within us and are reunited with the life that encompasses us all.

Autumn Grace

I remember the late summer when I climbed in the Moravian hills above Karlovy Vary in Czechoslovakia. The berries were bright red on the rowan trees, the leaves were beginning to fall, and I half-wondered and half-fantasized that it was along paths like these that my father's family used to walk to the synagogue when they lived in Eastern Europe well before the war. Every festival is a doorway into memory; memory in turn creates the requirements of the festival, without which it doesn't feel complete. My first recollection of going to *shul* is of holding my father's hand and walking through the fallen leaves on Sukkot. Sukkot is for me the festival of the autumn, of its colors, smells, and leaves.

It is at this time of year that I realize that I am a northern Jew, a Jew of deciduous lands. If someone were to tell me that I would never again celebrate Sukkot among the chestnuts and the red and yellow leaves, I would mourn for the booth as, for me, it really ought to be, and the part of myself I had lost.

In the part of London near Hampstead Heath where he lived, I cannot help but think of Keats's "Ode to Autumn" and his depiction of the season conspiring with the sun:

> To bend with apples the moss'd cottage-trees
> > And fill all fruit with ripeness to the core;
> > > To swell the gourd, and plump the hazel shells
> > With a sweet kernel;[4]

This mood of ripeness and fulfillment is captured exactly in Sukkot, *Ḥag Ha-asif,* the Festival of Gathering, which falls *bitekufat hashanah,* at the turning of the year. That description refers not only to the timing, but to the very soul and spirit of the festival. It is, of course, understood that we should keep all the traditions of the Torah thoughtfully and avoid a careless attitude. But our sources speak quite specifically of *noi sukkah,* the adornment of the booth; and the Talmud refers to the nuts, apricots, almonds, pomegranates, bunches of grapes, and crowns of woven grasses that were used to decorate the *sukkot* of those days.[5] The *sukkah* is the garner of the gains and natural glories of the year. It is a visible statement of gratitude to God for the tangible blessings bestowed.

It has always been my family's tradition to hang in the *sukkah* fruits and vegetables to which we have a personal attachment. This was reinforced when Nicky and I met and our two green-fingered hands were joined in matrimony. Olives, grapes, and such figs as the squirrels have left are saved from the biblical corner of our garden. One long marrow (if we managed to grow any at all that year) is reserved from the vegetable patch and left on its stalk for the festival. The melons we produce aren't much good to eat; they're far too small. But how wonderful to have them in the *sukkah* and to part from the summer with the hands-onpride and grateful heart that only the genuine grower can really know.

There is also a wilder side to the season, expressed in poetry and recorded in the laws of ancient Jewish practice. For autumn brings the gusts and tempests of which Shelley's great poem speaks:

> O Wild West Wind, thou breath of Autumn's being,
> Thou, from whose unseen presence the leaves dead
> Are driven, like ghosts from an enchanter fleeing,
>
> Yellow, and black, and pale, and hectic red . . .[6]

We may be all too aware of the power of such gales when we build our *sukkah,* which is required by law to be sufficiently strong to withstand an average wind, whatever that means. It would seem that the ideal *sukkah* should be firm enough to have a reasonable chance of serving out its eight days, but not so stable as to lose all appearance of its temporary nature. Many of us are chastened as we work by memories of years when the winds scattered the poles and branches of our ruined *sukkah* across the gardens and streets.

It is this aspect of the season which tells us that the autumn is a time for letting go. That is what makes its spectacular beauty also so poignant. This and the temporary nature of the *sukkah* lead us to consider that life may be measured no less by what we relinquish than by what we accrue. For from the very start, living involves letting go. None of us can know how great may be the sensation of loss for the child just born into a world of loud voices, rough textures, and violent light. When friends gather to study around the cradle on the first Friday night of a new baby's life, they eat the foods of mourning in sympathy for what it has foregone. Growing up, the child loses the closest intimacy with its mother when it is weaned. Perhaps the child, though feeling them instinctively, does not consciously mourn the little partings that come with every stage of growth — the first whole day at school, the first trip with friends — until he or she is a parent and watches the receding back of that other little boy or girl who is and always will be "my baby."

Adulthood, for all its gains, is a parting from the carefree times and the absence of responsibility with which we would wish each and every child-hood to be blessed. Even love, perhaps the most profound emotion which we are capable of knowing, has an aspect to it which requires us to let go and give something up. Follow love, teaches Kahlil Gibran, "Though his voice may shatter your dreams as the north wind lays waste the garden . . . Even as he is for your growth so is he for your pruning."[7]

Throughout life, the mind, too, must let go of its old thoughts if it is ever to open itself to the new. "Vanity of vanities, all is vanity," says Kohelet, whose book we read on this festival.[8] The root meaning of *hevel,* the word we translate as vanity, is "old [or used] breath," as if to tell us that this must first be breathed out before new breath, *neshimah,* meaning also life force and spirit, can be taken in.

In pondering these many partings that describe the course of our life, we find that we have a choice. We can understand them as painful only, as destructive, a slow unpicking of the fabric of ourselves, which we must resist, an intimation of the death that will, in time, undo us. But such a negative attitude does not really belong with the autumn, which, albeit an ending, is glorious, fruitful, and smells of the vigor of a new beginning. Autumn reveals the bud beneath the juncture from which the old leaf falls.

The message may rather be that if we want to grow, we also have to let go. Nobody gets old so quickly as the person who can never yield anything up. Of such people we say, "He isn't able to move on," or, "She lives in the past." Conversely, there is no greater antidote to age and internal mortality than the capacity for starting again, for relinquishing the past with good grace as part of the process of building anew. For the past, paradoxically, most nourishes the present when we allow it to be past. Perhaps, further-more, we infer too much from the finality of death that all our other earthly partings are a kind of dying. Maybe we should rather consider that, like those earlier experiences of letting go, even dying may be a kind of moving on into a new, though unknown, form of being. But these matters belong with the mysteries of God.

If Sukkot, set in the gateway to autumn, is related so closely to letting go, then the question arises: why have a festival about endings so soon after we have begun a new year? The answer to this paradox lies in appreciating that it is impossible to make a new beginning unless we are prepared to leave the old behind. That is why we hang the produce of the completed year in our *sukkah* — first to rejoice in it and then to part from it gratefully and with good grace.

Frail Home?

The *sukkah* is at once the weakest and the strongest thing we build, a fragile and temporary structure, yet representing the all-embracing protection of God. This paradox goes to the heart of what it means.

The Talmud teaches that a *sukkah* should be no less than ten hand-breadths high and refers in explanation to the Tabernacle which the Children of Israel built in the wilderness. Within it, in the Holy of Holies, was the Ark of the Covenant. Over its cover, formed of beaten gold, were two *keruvim,* their wings spread out ten hand-breadths above the Ark. Just as they represented the divine mercy, so the *sukkah* symbolizes the security of our spiritual home beneath the shelter of God's wings.[9]

Actually, the biblical evidence suggests that the *sukkah* was originally a practical structure, a canopy built at harvest time for shelter from the sun. Sukkot almost certainly began as an agricultural festival. On to this, the Torah grafted a historical meaning, teaching that we should live in booths for seven days because God caused the children of Israel to dwell in them on the journey out of Egypt (Lev. 23:43), but in rabbinic eyes the *sukkah* was primarily the representation of a spiritual reality. This is most obviously apparent in the kabbalistic name for the *sukkah, tzila de mehemanuta,* "The shade of the Faithful One." Thus the *sukkah* teaches us not to put our trust in houses or in anything which may, to our eyes, seem permanent, but to set our faith firmly in God on whose support alone we can truly rely. Without God's help we couldn't have survived either our journey through the desert some three thousand years ago or our many and hazardous flights and wanderings since. To dwell in the *sukkah* is to demonstrate our faith in the Divine. The *sukkah* represents God's protective power.

At the same time the *sukkah* evokes a totally different set of images that stand in contrast to pious tradition. For in leaving our houses for seven days, we are reminded of the countless partings that have compelled people to flee their homes throughout the ages. Sukkot is the festival of the refugee. Between its frail walls, beneath its leaking roof, we think of all those throughout history who have had to abandon their homes and seek whatever flimsy shelter they could find. We are reminded that no home is ever really permanent, that every abode is essentially provisional. Thus, when Jews came to what is now Bosnia following the expulsion from Spain in 1492, many brought with them the keys of their former houses. Signs of the hope of return, they became symbols of the reality of exile:

> Where is the key that was in the drawer
> My forefathers brought it here with great love
> They told their sons, this is the heart
> Of our home in Spain
> Dreams of Spain.[10]

So the *sukkah* brings to mind the immediate reality of homelessness — of makeshift protection against wind and rain, of helpless exposure to ice and snow.

> My darling [wrote Ida to her sister from a camp in Transnistria in 1941] the things and the money which you have sent me helped me greatly and arrived at the proper time. From the wool that you have sent me I have made a thick shawl for Vili's neck, because who knows how many days we will be on the way; at least, may God give us fine weather.

But God didn't give them fine weather, and Vili, whom his mother carried lovingly on her back, froze to death.[11]

How strange, then, that the *sukkah*, which is supposed to make us think about faith, should remind us of so many things that lead us to the opposite conclusion — persecution, flight, helplessness, abandonment, misery, the inability to save those dear to us, and the absence of protection. Where is the shade of the Faithful One now? Where is the shadow of the divine protection in all this?

Yet the very paradox is significant. In showing us what we cannot trust, the *sukkah* challenges us to ask in what we can put our faith. If our houses can be taken away from us and the protection of "civilized" society crumble, there has to be something firmer on which to base our lives. The *sukkah,* apparently weak and temporary, directs our attention to what is truly strong and sustaining: Is there anything we have which cannot be taken away?

My parents would often say to me when I was a child, "Everything can be taken away from you except what you have within." They knew what they were talking about. My mother escaped from Germany as a teenager with her family in 1939. My father and his family left earlier, in 1937. Following a tip-off that the Gestapo were going to arrest my grandfather, they simply packed and left that very night. What my parents meant was that our real strength lies in using, to the full, the capacity of our mind, heart, and soul.

What, then, are our ultimate resources? In times of trouble I hear so many people say: "If it weren't for family and friends I don't know where I'd be!" In times of crisis the question of what we have becomes the question of whom we have. Again and again I have witnessed the truth that there is no greater resource than a strong and supportive family. If we are not blessed with such a family, then close friends come a near second. Of course, those we love can be taken from us, too. Exile, for example, often means isolation as well, but in many of life's troubles the people we love are with us. If they cannot be close to us in external reality, they remain near to us in thought, sustaining an inner strength without which we couldn't survive.

The value of making close bonds with other people is epitomized in the *sukkah.* In the *sukkah* one does not sit alone; one invites family, friends, and strangers in as guests. The mystical tradition teaches us that when we do so, our ancestors — Abraham and Sarah, Rebecca and Isaac — come to our *sukkah,* too, and give us their blessing.

We find strength through our traditions. One can strip people of everything, one can take away all their material possessions, but one cannot so easily destroy the culture and principles by which they live. Such a culture enables them to reconstruct their existence out of the ashes. Force can erase neither the memory nor the love of their way of life. It cannot root out a person's or a nation's longing, or obliterate their yearning for the homes and customs from which they have come. It is precisely such love that has enabled the Jewish people to survive. For the fabric of our life is made not of bricks and girders, but of laws and customs cherished throughout many exiles and in innumerable lands.

The *sukkah,* with its multitude of rules about how to define a roof and what constitutes a side, may appear more fragile than other buildings. But in symbolizing the very need to build a structure and culture wherever destiny may lead us, it represents a power far stronger than the thickest walls. The *sukkah* is the physical manifestation of the undying creativity garnered in a beloved community and tradition. Year in, year out, we build the *sukkah;* indeed, to fulfil the requirements of the commandment, a *sukkah* must by definition be completed anew every year. Year in, year out, we rebuild our bond with those we love, with our tradition, and with our faith.

For above everything is the abiding strength of our connection with God. The relationship of the Jewish people to God has been the one fixed point from which we have steadfastly refused to be driven. For God, even when our fortunes have been low, when there was no resting place for the sole of our foot, has remained our challenge and our inspiration.

Kohelet

> Rebbe Avraham Mordekhai of Ger told the following story: "A certain Jew once defeated me. I was going into my room when a Jew came up to me and gave me a note. I said to him: 'Believe me, I have no time, not even a single moment.' He replied: 'I've had over twenty years of time to look after my sick daughter, and the Rebbe hasn't even a single moment for her?' "[12]

Hevel havalim — vanity of vanities; *hakol havel* — all is vanity. These are the key phrases, the leitmotif, of the Book of Ecclesiastes. Systematically the author examines life's experiences and with these words multiplies them all by nought. Whatever is, that also is vanity; it too can be reduced to nothing. The book's question is simple: Is there anything which can't be turned to nothing, is there anything worth doing at all?

Of course, we've all met people who are experts at finding reasons why not. There are "I wouldn't and I shouldn't" parents, "I'm bored and I can't be bothered" children, and simply plain, pain-in-the-neck, negative people. Most of us can be like that at times. In the wrong mood we can always find grounds for doing nothing, for dismissing everything, for having something negative to say about everyone, for being, in Oscar Wilde's words, the cynic who "knows the price of everything and the value of nothing."[13]

Such moods may descend on us for a number of reasons. We may simply be in a foul temper. Or we may be passing through a phase in which we find it hard to see any purpose in what we are doing. We may be overwhelmed by an experience that has shattered our confidence in our own worth. The death of a family member or close friend may leave us asking what life is for. Or we may be struggling with the issue of what in the world, if anything, has meaning. All these questions are reflected in Kohelet, a wry and challenging book.

I have always associated it with autumn, the season of falling leaves and encroaching darkness. The autumn certainly has its beauties; in this respect it is my favorite season. But it is also threatening. For many it heralds loneliness and doubt. What will the winter take from us? What will survive the darkness and cold? What lasts? These are the questions to which Kohelet turns.

The book is a vigorous stripping away, as the wind strips the leaves from the trees:

> What profit is there for a person from all the toil at which they labor under the sun? (1:3)
>
> All things are weary, a person cannot speak of them. (1:8)
>
> In the place of justice, there is wickedness. (3:16)
>
> That which happens to people and that which happens to cattle, it is the same thing that happens to them; as these die, so do those . . . (3:19)

These questions are not rhetorical. They are not intended as the preparation for preconceived answers. On the contrary, what the reader takes away from the book is the persistence of the challenge. The word *"hevel —* vanity" and the phrase *"hevel havalim —* vanity of vanities" recur tenaciously. All endeavor leads to the same question, "What was the point of that?" If there is nothing new under the sun, if, like the wind, everything blows round and round in circles, what purpose is there in anything we do? No wonder, "All things are weary" (1:8).

Yet beneath the probing questions there are affirmations, as the falling leaves expose the structure of the tree. Simple joys remain; indeed, they are all the more important because they pass away so quickly. The basic pleasures of life are not to be scorned; they are all we have: "Let a person eat and drink and see good come of their labor" (3:13). Human relationships matter, too; they are our only protection against our vulnerability: "Better are two than one, for if one falls, who will raise him up?" (4:9). Better still may be the group, because "the threefold cord is not easily broken" (4:12). We must rejoice in our youth and vigor while we have them, because soon time will take them away. It will not be long before, "Man goes to his eternal home, and the mourners go about the streets" (12:5). Transitoriness demands urgency. After all, "To everything there is a season, and a time to every purpose under the heaven" (3:1). If we miss it, as Rabbi Avraham Mordekhai of Ger believed he had missed his opportunity to show compassion for a sick girl, our life is wasted.

Kohelet also makes affirmations in the wider social context: darkness is better than light, justice better than corruption, honest speech than slander, activity than idleness. In the philosophical dimension, Kohelet's concern for wisdom outweighs his cynicism. "Of making many books there is no end" (12:12), but ultimately Kohelet prefers speech over silence and intelligence over folly. At least, "The wise person has eyes in their head, while the fool walks in darkness" (2:14).

For the essence of wisdom is not philosophizing, but the simple, ultimate concern: "Fear God and keep his commandments" (12:13). It has been argued that this verse is tacked on to the end of the book to make it "kosher," theologically acceptable, but I do not believe this. Kohelet is not cynical simply for the sake of it. His purpose in stripping away vanity with so little mercy is to lay bare what really matters in life. One of the essentials is joy, another is justice, another wisdom; the sum of them all is the fear of God. These things are a counterweight to life's brevity and apparent futility. To reinforce this message, the book has a profound sense of balance in both content and form. Nowhere is it more evident than in the famous "dance of time"; there is:

> A time to weep, and a time to laugh;
> A time to mourn, and a time to dance;
> A time to cast away stones, and a time to gather stones together;
> A time to embrace, and a time to refrain from embracing; (3:4–5)

Here is a rhythm — of birth and death, labor and pleasure, youth and age. The governance that maintains this balance belongs ultimately to God. God keeps the world in order, ordains and examines life's ebb and flow. One does not feel close to such a God; the God of love, the God for whom one can yearn, is absent. But the God of destiny is not.

"Vanity of vanities; all is vanity" (1:2). When all's said and done, this sentence remains the core and the key of the book. It brings all things into question. It derides their value, then reconsiders if this is just. But sometimes it is only when we are shown how much of life is vanity that we can see what actually matters. The answer may be chastening, but it is unlikely to be an illusion.

ḤANUKKAH

Hidden Light

Even the darkness is not too dark for Thee,
But the night shines as the day;
The darkness is even as the light.

Ps. 139:11–12

It is held that underneath the desert lie great reservoirs of water; this is why a spring may appear from nowhere and vanish just as suddenly back into the ground. Perhaps darkness is like that also, concealing an immensity of light that shines forth briefly and disappears. That may in part be what provoked the question of the Midrash: What did God do with the light of the six days of creation by which it was possible to see from one end of the world to the other? God concealed it.[1] God hid it beneath the material substance of this world, but it shines out in the Torah and will illumine the world to come. For, "A mitzvah is a candle, and Torah is light" (Prov. 6:23); that is why Jewish life can be measured out in lights.

The Shabbat begins with the lighting of candles for the sake of *shalom bayit,* a peaceful atmosphere in the home. It ends with the putting out of the *havdalah* candle, a sign of differentiation between sacred and ordinary, rush and repose. I like to extinguish the flame in whisky and watch the blue light dance above the spirit as if it were the soul of the Sabbath, till it ascends and disappears. There are all the lights of the festivals too, the candle by which we search every room before Pesaḥ, the ". . . light and joy, and happiness and honor" of the Jews on Purim (Esth. 8:16), the flames of hope and courage on Ḥanukkah.

As candles measure out the year, so they mark the passage of every life. Light, it is said, precedes our entrance into the world. "Who shall set me as in the months of old, as in the days when God watched over me, when his light burned radiant over my head?" pleaded Job in the midst of his misery (29:2–3). To what days and months can he be referring, asks the Talmud, if not to those spent by the unborn child inside the womb, when God's candle burns above her head and she learns the entire Torah by its light?[2]

When life is again transformed and someone dies, a second candle is lit by the person's head. On several occasions I have watched such a light burn, on a little table at the top of a bed cleared quickly of medicines and syringes, or on a shelf dangerously near to treasured books. This time it is an ordinary, material, visible light. Or is it? I have sometimes stood with the mourners for a while and watched as if it were the person's very spirit ascending and departing, hovering between attachment to the body that was its home and the power that summons it onward. Then the presence of the flame transforms the place from the scene of death into the focus of a mystery we are not entitled to understand.

Most of all, however, light is indicative of the presence of God. Once, to save a long walk home, I spent the night of Rosh Hashanah sleeping at the synagogue. Wanting something, I went upstairs at a late hour and found myself arrested by the *ner tamid,* the eternal light. I had known of course what that lamp symbolized, hung above the reader's desk before the ark, but had thought little of it by day. By night, however, it was different. The synagogue was radiant with its tranquil illumination, and a penetrating presence filled the empty room. I stood absolutely still, in awe. I had never felt such power here before. It was as if God were alone in solitary being and I had intruded on a consciousness which usually withdraws at the coming of the worshippers and the onset of ordinary light.

Since that time, the teaching that beyond the darkness lies light ines-timable has made increasingly more sense. For God's presence, the first source and ultimate goal of consciousness, is recognized as light, and the small and separated consciousness of every individual being is a fragment-ed portion of that same light, burning upward in concealment in the direc-tion of its source. The mystics teach that in the beginning the whole world was illumined by this light and that in it one could see from one end of the earth to the other, but when people began to sin, God hid it away. Some-times this light shines through even now, rendering itself perceptible to the soul. Often it is clothed in darkness and we see nothing, but it is present in the dark none the less. It is the vital, animating principle of all life and shall one day be recognized and set free.

Perhaps, therefore, all the different lights with which Judaism marks the passage of the year should be seen as signs and indications of that reality. Like the variously colored lamps on an airfield, they are beacons from one world to another. In each of them, a different quality shines through. The Shabbat candles bring the peace of the spiritual world into the rush and confusion of material existence. The Ḥanukkah candles burn with the steadfast faith that overpowers armies, their wicks emerging not so much from a miraculous supply of oil as from a world in which might and power are as nothing before the supreme reality of the spirit.

I have many happy memories of watching lights. I remember sitting with my grandmother while the candles burned softly in her olive wood *ḥanukiyah,* reflected in the bay windows that gave on to her garden. I remember Friday nights when I was the last to go up to bed and sat quietly for a few minutes on my own with the candles, drawn to an attentive stillness by their flame. I remember keeping company with the memorial candle as if through it I could talk to the person for whose *yahrzeit* it was lit. Like, I suspect, virtually everyone else, I love to watch the lights.

For light is generous, light is beautiful. Kindle a flame and the whole room flickers with the rays and shadows of illumination. There is not a festival in which Judaism does not in some form celebrate light, but what Judaism is really illumined by is the light that cannot be seen.

To Light, or Not to Light?

> For during those days the Menorah burned by virtue of the miracle
> of the very small quantity of oil they had; there is such a very small
> point in every person even now which belongs to God.
>
> Rebbe Yehudah Aryeh Lev of Ger, *Sefat Emet*[3]

If one lights the kind of oil the Maccabees lit, it will be sure to burn for longer than one day, for it contains the secret of inspiration and its radiance is God's light in the world.

The Maccabees were fighters. The early Maccabean leaders rose in revolt against the Seleucid tyranny and its Jewish collaborators who were turning Jerusalem into a Greek city, but the later leaders were no less power-seeking and corrupt than those whom their elders had made their reputation by defeating. For this and other reasons, they were little loved by the Rabbis, who accorded their victories hardly any space in the vast literature of the Talmud. But there remain three achievements to their credit. They had the vision to fight an impossible war and the courage to win. Once they had regained the Temple precincts, they had the persistence to search them until they found a vessel marked with the High Priest's seal. Then, although the oil they found was really far too little, they filled the lamps on the Menorah and set them alight, trusting in whatever would be. These three acts represent the essential stages of leadership and inspiration.

The Temple was defiled; Jerusalem, ruled by renegades, was in the grip of a foreign and antagonistic culture. But what the Maccabees saw was not defeat; they beheld the Temple as it would be — rebuilt. Look at the world in any age, in any place, and one has the same choice. One can either see only destruction and misery, the unending testimony of disappointment. Or one can see, together with and in defiance of it, striving, courage, and compassion, an ineradicable humanity in the humbling struggle to transform defeat into new hope. One can see only the ruins of the Temple, or one can see the rebuilding as well.

My friend, who works with victims of torture and persecution, shared with me a moving example of just this endeavor. An old peasant and a young man whose family had been killed for their political beliefs met in prison. One day the elderly man was brutally beaten. The young man comforted him, telling him that he would teach him to read, an opportunity his harsh fortunes had until then denied him. This, he said, would be their victory. By reading together they would make an affirmation of their common humanity. No amount of force could ever take that away.

It must have been a similar faith which led Anne Frank to write in her diary in July 1944:

> It's really a wonder that I haven't dropped all my ideals because they seem so absurd and impossible to carry out. Yet, I keep them, because in spite of everything I still believe that people are really good at heart . . . I see the world gradually being turned into a wilderness, I hear the ever-approaching thunder, which will destroy us too, I can feel the sufferings of millions and

yet, if I look up into the heavens I think it will all come right, that this cruelty too will end, and that peace and tranquillity will return again.[4]

Every moment of life presents us with a choice in how we perceive; do we see disappointment and defeat or opportunity and hope? I am filled with wonder by what people have managed to achieve. In situations of conflict it is often women who lead the way back to the appreciation that the enemy are people, too. Modern communications have enabled mothers to cross battle zones and find mothers on the other side who have also lost a husband or child. The common humanity they discover transcends the power of war. There are teachers who work with sick or maltreated children because they believe that the power of love will awaken the inborn creativity that lies within us all. There are caregivers who work with the dying because they trust that beyond pain and degradation lie acceptance and reconciliation. None of these people see only ruins; what they perceive is the human image, God's temple, restored.

Behind this lies an earlier question: what is it that gives us the capacity to look at the world in this way? Where is the oil that burns with the light that enables us to see the sacred everywhere? For, as the Sefat Emet taught over a century ago, "There is such a very small point in every person which even now belongs to God."[5] There is a vessel within each of us the contents of which are simply not susceptible to contamination, a part of us which remains eternally pure. It is there that we must go to seek the oil that burns with a pure and sacred flame. The difficulty is to find it. That is the inner meaning of the Maccabees' search among the ruins of the Temple for the one jar that was still intact, sealed with the High Priest's seal.

The Talmud, in recounting the brief story of how the Maccabees found and lit the oil, suggests that there were other jars. But they were not pure; the High Priest's seal was broken. In the same way, our lives contain many things that burn. Anger burns. Of course, righteous anger sometimes leads us to stand up against wrong, but even justified anger often simply consumes its victim. I have sometimes had to say to people who are angry that they may indeed be right — they have been exceedingly badly treated — but who has become the main victim of their anger if not themselves? It will devour them, a second kind of suffering, but it won't in the least affect the person who has wronged them. Greed also burns; in our society its flames are constantly fueled. We are lured by countless incitements into the heat of our own desires. We do not see clearly by the light of such fires.

Like the Maccabees we too must search the precincts of our inner self for what lies buried there. Then we may come to know by the testimony of our own heart that there is a part of us which nothing can contaminate. We have a certain purity of being that cannot be sullied. Light it, and it burns with a sacred radiance. Just as Midas's touch turned everything to gold, so the spirit has the power to reveal the spirit in everything that lives. But every day we have to struggle to find that flame; it is far more often lost than found. In silence, in beauty, in prayer, in the example of good people, we rediscover it and may be consoled by the reminder that, though hidden, it is never utterly or irretrievably lost.

Once they had regained the Temple and found their jar of oil, there remained for the Maccabees one more issue: To light, or not to light? It cannot have been a simple decision. They knew, after all, that it would take eight days to replenish their supply and that the contents of the single flask they had would suffice for only one. Should they light it, or should they wait? Perhaps they should wait. Till now, it had scarcely been their fault that the Menorah was extinguished; it was for this that they had fought. But if they were to light it now and then let it go out, wouldn't they be responsible? After all, the flame, once burning, had to be *tamid*, constant. The Maccabees lit the oil.

And light it one must. This is the essence of faith. We never know how long the flame that results from our deeds will last; but if the oil is pure, we must find the courage to use it. It is natural to think that we won't have the energy to see our plans through, to worry that our courage may not last, that our confidence, our spirits, our love or our faith may fail. These concerns are only human, but it would be wrong to let them prevent us from using what oil we have. We must trust that what we begin in truth we, and others, will be given the strength to continue. If we first have to know how everything will end, we will never undertake anything and our oil will go to waste.

Perhaps, it might be argued, the Maccabees were lucky. After all, God ordained a miracle and a single day's supply of fuel burned for eight; but to think like that is, I believe, to misunderstand the nature of such wonders. For it is a wonder, but true, that such oil always burns more brightly and for longer than we think. Start something with real spirit, and though we may not have the energy to see it through, others will come to replenish the fire and restore the flame. Thus one person's vision becomes the inspiration of many. Or sometimes it is the spirit itself that nurtures us. Then our hope, courage, and energy are replenished night by night as if by some invisible pipette, and we enter our day restored by powers we ourselves do not understand.

For where, whatever our vision, whatever our searching, whatever our courage to light the light, did the first fire come from if not from the One who set the spirit within us and made all life sacred, if only we could see?

Lights by Night

> Here do I take pen
> in this my cave of light,
> this cage of heaven and hell,
> in here unreel my life. I know
> what is inside this jail;
> this chapel my song is dawnlight;
> I must sing.

Nick Naydler[6]

Our parents gave my brother and me the lasting gift of many wonderful holidays. One of my most exciting memories is traveling by train through the night. Nothing in the whole holiday could ever quite equal the excitement of lying rocked by the rhythm of the wheels while pushing back the curtains to watch the lights fly by. There were the individual lights of farmhouses, rows of street lamps drawing nearer or slanting off at the edge of some field; there were the rushing, rocking lights of other trains, the bright lights of stations where I could see the men walking along the train and banging the wheels with their hammers, making them ring out. Watching, I felt uniquely alive, privileged to see the life of things at night.

This is a joy my wife and I have successfully communicated to our children — not that it was an especially difficult undertaking. Now they regularly play going to bed on the train, though unfortunately the highlight of the game concerns the little bags with toiletries and toothbrushes which the railways present to even the youngest passengers. For me, however, and I hope (or fear) they will follow suit, the excitement lay not in sleeping but in steadfastly refusing to do so. I could never comprehend why my parents insisted that I should "lie down properly" and close my eyes, but at that age it went well beyond my powers to explain to them that even for a little child there were moments of such wonder that it was inwardly essential to dispense with banalities like sleep. For already then, I believe, the contact with those lights had a spiritual value. There is nothing greater I would like to communicate to my own children.

To see through the darkness into the life of things is part of the special wonder of Hanukkah. The Talmud teaches that we kindle the lights for the sake of *pirsumei nisa* — the proclamation of the miracle. Officially, the miracle referred to is, of course, that of the single jar of oil which lasted eight times as long as it should. But in our actual experience of Jewish life through the generations, the miracle means much more. For there are many shades of darkness, requiring many kinds of light.

The depth of night is real enough in winter, when the sun sets early and dusk seals off the houses. Safe from the suffering that the chill and gloom impose on so many, I have always loved the long evenings that draw people together round the fire and light within. But the long nights symbolize other kinds of darkness as well, for with the death of nature comes the intimation of our own. Many elderly people hate the arrival of November, with its dark days bringing loneliness, anxiety, and cold. Night, too, is a spiritual state: the absence of hope, vision, inspiration. Night can mean the nemesis of good. Elie Wiesel chose *Night* as the title of the short and terrifying account of his families descent into Auschwitz.

There is all the more reason, therefore, to be grateful for light. For light expresses companionship, creativity, hope, and inspiration. Put on a candle in a dark room, and all at once the space has a center; everyone looks toward the flame as if the small, dancing fire had the power to unite our spirits and harmonize our thoughts. Even a small candle illumines a large area, even the littlest flame creates a community around it. Its radiance spreads out beyond the immediate circle. I love to watch the reflection of candles in a window. If the angles are right, one can sometimes see reflections within reflections in a diminishing perspective, as if one were travelling through time, backward down the generations. Lights shine to each other across the distances. Kindle a flame, and life speaks to life across the lands and years that cease to intervene and interfere. The one little candle by the windowsill relates to others, down the same street, across the same history, all the way back to the first dawn, when God said, "Let there be light!" This connectedness is also part of the miracle of Ḥanukkah. It is the radiance to which even a small candle, even an amount of oil sufficient only for one day, can allude and which it can provoke, enabling it to illumine an entire history.

It is said that everyone is ultimately alone. In the end, no one else can absolutely know the contours of our consciousness or share the pain where we are cut by the blades of experience. In the intimacy of mental suffering, no one but the person alone can put up the fight for each breath. Only our internal companions can sustain us, the small population of family and close friends which has over a lifetime come to inhabit our mind. Closed within that darkness we struggle for our most intimate and absolute quality, the sweetness or bitterness of our own consciousness.

Sometimes the physical world imposes on us in outward reality those same conditions that create internal loneliness — pain, isolation, cruelty, the absence of hope or relief. Sometimes the world is configured in a formulation of absolute night — hunger, torture, death camps, hell.

Yet perhaps, for all that, darkness and loneliness are not the final reality. Perhaps it would be truer to think of the materiality of our existence in general, and of evil and pain in particular, as if they were a vast tarpaulin dividing us from the warmth and brilliance of an infinite supply of light. That light is capable of piercing the fabric of the dark. Even within our restricted world of matter it glows in candles of courage and hope and creates about itself a radiance that transcends the limitations of space and time.

Those are the lights one sees as one travels through the swaying, rocking dark. Those are the lights, which once perceived, burn for longer than one day.

Ḥanukkah Memories

Und dann auch soll, wenn Enkel um uns trauern,
Zu ihrer Lust noch unsre Liebe dauern.

If grandchildren then should mourn for us
Our love shall last as long as they desire.
> one of my grandfather's favorite quotations from Goethe[7]

I looked up from the bus that was taking us north from Glasgow to Loch Lomond and realized that we were passing round the corner from the house where I was born. There are harbored most of the few memories I have of my mother: my mother showing me how to draw my first *aleph,* taking me to the shoe shop to have my feet measured, keeping me away while my father carved the chicken with a huge knife, paring down the Ḥanukkah candles so that they would fit into the small holders on my tiny *hanukiyah.* I was five and three months when my mother died. My son Mossy, sitting next to me in the bus, was already five and a half. The world had turned the cycle of a whole generation. How strange that it should all have happened in my mother's ignorance. She knew nothing of Mossy, or of my other children, or of my wife, or that I was a rabbi, or that I loved literature, poetry especially, as she had. There passed through my mind the discussion in the Talmud as to whether the dead are aware of the fate of the living, with its wry quotation from Job: "His children shall prosper and he shall not know" (14:21). Did my mother really not know anything about us, or was there some invisible path, a secret wavelength by which consciousness remained connected to its living progeny? Perhaps love could create such a path? Setting aside the matter of whether she was at this moment aware that her son and his children were passing round the corner from her former home, what was the link between my mother and myself, and between her and my children?

I trace my love of Scotland to these concerns. Of course, there are its natural wonders, mountains, rivers, forests, the sound of running water from falls and rills and drains, small pools where children and a dog can play, wet leaves, and the smell of clean, clear air. In Scotland are my first memories: the sight of a field from our bedroom window, horses, the blue trains that ran from Milngavie into Glasgow. But the power which draws me to the place dwells deeper, in the simultaneous presence and absence there of the source of my life and my early childhood years.

Yet I am far from being possessed, when I go to Scotland, by any sense of death. On the contrary, it is the strength of what is not extinguished that stirs me most, the residual presence of a vitality that time has made not weaker but more compelling. Something at once long familiar and quite fresh, old but regenerative, flows into my being and causes me to rejoice in the hills and by the waters. There is sunlight, many years after the valley of death.

There is something very special about celebrating a rededication. It can be moving to mark a beginning. But it is an altogether different experience to return to a place, to find its most precious light extinguished, to search for the remnants of the oil that once burned there freely, to find virtually none, but yet some, and to have the courage to light it. Such a light illumines far more than the contours of the everyday world. An ordinary lamp illumines nature; a lamp relit after many years bears witness to far more — to a deeper connection, to the survival of bonds that defy time, to an incandescence of spirit that cannot be extinguished even by death. It is to this that the Ḥanukkah candles testify. Time does not extinguish the light of a life in this world, not in twenty years or even a hundred, if there are those among the living who still seek to be nourished by the vitality it once expressed.

There then is my mother, on the second or third night of Ḥanukkah, carefully tapering down the ends of the big candles to fit into the tiny *ḥanukiyah* she had given me. I had complained that my brother had real Ḥanukkah candles while mine were only those miniature ones made for birthday cakes. I wanted the same as my brother — at least! That is one of my first, and few, memories of her — and it burns on.

This was the first time I had ever been asked about an inscription for a tombstone. It is always a privilege to search together with the family for the words that best evoke the life of the person they have loved. But this was the first time, when my uncle (two or three times removed, but close in the heart's affiliations) asked me, "Shall we put, 'Born on Ḥanukkah, she *was* a source of light,' or, 'Born on Ḥanukkah, she *is* a source of light'?"

She, his mother, was famed in youth as one of the best-dressed women in Basel and thought of in old age as one of the wisest in Jerusalem. When I met her she was in her eighties, very thin and already frail with her last illness. I spent six months living in her flat, accompanying her husband to synagogue every Shabbat because he couldn't walk there alone. I remember going slowly together along Ibn Shaprut Street toward the alleyways of Sha'arei Ḥesed and the Synagogue of the Vilna Gaon. The shofar sounded the coming of Shabbat, and the sadness of the weekdays seeped out of the stones and hung over the street. Twilight turned to dark while the rebbe taught Torah in Yiddish. When we came out of the synagogue after the evening service the streets were full of children and the atmosphere was gay as a song. I've missed all that ever since.

She wasn't undemanding. There were times when it was "Please do this" and "Please do that," and no sooner had one sat down than it would be "Please do" something else. But there was always a please, and there was no occasion when she didn't say thank you. I think her favorite word was the German, but highly personalized *goldig*, lovely, an adjective warm with affection and appreciation.

Once when she was lying in bed I noticed that her arms were so thin that one could count her veins. At the time I didn't understand why, and even thought it rather ridiculous that it still mattered to her to put on make-up every morning. Now, though, I can see that this was her refusal to give in, a commitment to life both generous and brave. It was the same spirit which enabled her, while herself feeling cold and weak, to make sure that everyone around her had their favorite flowers, their favorite chocolates, and their favorite books.

At one point she became so ill that she was taken to the Sharret wing of the Hadassah Hospital. I didn't think she'd ever come back. I had the sad task of taking her husband to see her. We prepared a bowl of semolina with jam, a favorite food which she was still able to digest, and put it on a tray in her lap. She couldn't hold it; it went tumbling over the floor. Alone at home, and as if preparing for the greater loneliness to come, her husband recounted his memories — how he had been a medic in the First World War ("They put me on a horse, I'd hardly looked at a horse before . . ."), how he first came to Israel ("Everybody left their front door open then . . ."), how his daughter and her fiancé were both killed at Kfar Etzion in the War of Independence. But that night his wife had called for the nurse and asked for her nails to be manicured. Soon afterward she was home.

The cemetery in Sanhedria is especially beautiful. It is protected from the road by a row of tall cypresses and divided into sections by green hedges. There, most of the great rabbis of Jerusalem are buried. To read the tombstones is to learn how they came from Poland, brought their communities with them, ransomed captives, and spread the knowledge of Torah. Among the graves, those of Reb Aryeh Levin and his wife, known as "the friends of the prisoners," are so covered with stones and petitions that one can scarcely read the wording. There too, near the path because her family are *kohanim,* is my uncle's mother. The inscription reads, "Born on Ḥanukkah, she is a source of light."

TU B'SHEVAT

The Speech of Trees

"Take with you of the song of the land," said Jacob to his children. "What is 'the song of the land'?" asked the Rebbe of Apt, "if not, 'The earth is the Lord's and the fullness thereof'?"[1]

Where would we be without the song of the land? Of course, this classic ḥasidic interpretation is in fact a creative mistranslation. What Jacob really said to his sons at the height of the famine, when they were obliged to return to Egypt to buy grain, and insisted on taking Benjamin with them, was, "Take of the pruning of the land," that is, of its produce, fruits, and spices. Yet perhaps there is a certain kind of song in the very flavor and fragrance of such a harvest. Perhaps, like Joseph, we, too, are strangers in a foreign land, and may be reminded by such things of our home.

For the trees and the whole of nature speak to us. To be denied their presence is to be subjected to a serious deprivation of the spirit, as city dwellers partly are. To reach the point where we don't care whether we see anything green or not is precisely to prove our alienation. Indeed, there may be parts of the heart which simply fail to receive their due education because of the absence of the language of trees and grasses, animals and birds. We do not experience their inspiration, we are not cleansed by their chastening presence and we live without any relationship to the rhythms they form through day and year. Part of our essential being starves; we are that much more vulnerable to the subtle desensitization of our moral and spiritual being.

Maybe this is the insight that underlies the frequent poetic references to trees throughout the Bible, but especially in the Books of the Prophets and in the Psalms. In the Bible, trees do not only speak; they sing, dance, and clap their hands for joy. Trees are among the first plantings of God in Eden and trees are mentioned as part of the first recorded sale of land, by Efron to Abraham. Abraham himself plants a tree, in Be'er Sheva, and calls on the name of the eternal God. But it is Isaiah's description which is perhaps the most beautiful: "You shall go out in joy and be led forth in peace; the mountains and the hills shall break before you into song and all the trees of the field shall clap their hands" (55:12). Surely there can be no greater blessing than that.

I simply cannot describe what I owe to the natural wonder of this world. My soul in its fullness — and its frequent emptiness — knows. Almost every day I am affected by nature's rich and gracious generosity. My mind has been sweetened, my blood has been quickened, and my spirit has sung. Whatever love my heart feels is nurtured by many things; but essential among them are the grass, the leaves, the rain, and the trees, which feel pure and profoundly sustaining.

Yet there is a paradox here. For, while in itself substantially amoral, following the rules of seasons and species, and largely indifferent to the law of compassion, nature is widely experienced by human beings as morally and spiritually renewing. Wordsworth, revisiting the hills above Tintern Abbey, reflects on the solace that thoughts of the scene have brought him in the years since he was last there:

> I have owed to them,
> In hours of weariness, sensations sweet,
> Felt in the blood, and felt along the heart,
> And passing even into my purer mind
> With tranquil restoration:[2]

At a similar point in time, but amidst other forests and from a very different culture, Rebbe Naḥman of Breslav asked God to help him make it his custom:

> to go outside each day among the trees and grasses — among all growing things — and there . . . be alone and enter into prayer, to talk to the One to whom I belong.

Maybe we are subtly selective in what we see in nature; or maybe we simply feel embraced by a greater life, and forgetting our pettiness, rediscover our capacity for awe.

Perhaps this is the meaning of the remarkable encounter described by Viktor Frankl in his account of his experiences in the concentration camps. A young woman is dying, yet she is cheerful in spite of that knowledge:

> "I am grateful fate has hit me so hard," she told me. "In my former life I was spoiled and didn't take spiritual accomplishments seriously." Pointing through the window of the hut, she said, "This tree here is the only friend I have in my loneliness." Through that window she could see just one branch

of a chestnut tree, and on the branch were two blossoms. "I often talk to this tree," she said to me. I was startled and didn't quite know how to take her words. Was she delirious? Did she have occasional hallucinations? Anxiously I asked her if the tree replied. "Yes." What did it say to her? She answered, "It said to me, 'I am here — I am here — I am life, eternal life.'"[3]

The courage and generosity of this young woman are striking: she is comforted at the ultimate moment by the presence of a tree. For sure, she is not the only person to have held such a conversation or to have heard in the speech of trees the voice of a mighty force for life. But she surrenders to it as to God, reconciled and consoled. Strangely, there is a chestnut tree in the tiny back garden behind the secret annex, below the window of Anne Frank's room. I have often looked at it during my visits there: did it too speak?

Tu B'Shevat has come to mark our special bond with trees; it has become our festival of planting, particularly in Israel. When one plants a tree, one has to pay particular attention to the roots. One must dig a hole deep enough and wide enough to spread them well out; they should never be cramped or forced to point upward. It is worth taking care when planting trees, for in tending to their roots, we nurture our own.

On the Life and Death of Trees

If the Messiah comes and you are planting a tree,
first finish planting, then go to greet the Messiah.

Avot deRabbi Natan, Recension B31

In the garden of my grandparents' house stood an immense pear tree. Each year we would gather to pick the fruit. The ritual began indoors with the collection of a mixture of ancient bowls, baskets, and shopping trolleys. It was my prerogative to climb and, with my grandmother giving incisive instructions, reach for the more recalcitrant pears high in the center of the tree. Meanwhile my brother, assisted by my grandfather and an umbrella, would hook the fruit on the far-spreading branches. Afterward, we would drag the worn and bursting shopping baskets inside and carefully store the fruit on the tops of cupboards, where we would climb each week to check the diminishing stocks of withering pears for the ripe, the rotten, and the eternally hard.

That autumn day was not the only moment of the pear tree's glory, however: for some ten days each spring, more if the weather was clement and the wind still, it wore a stunning whiteness, a beauty that still accompanies the family in flourishing memories, many years after the house has been sold.

My grandparents loved this tree and the even greater oak that spread its old branches behind it, frighteningly brittle, and the minor thicket of rose and honeysuckle by their window where the small birds that foraged in their garden would sometimes nest. I remember their distress when a neighboring cat caught both the brood and the returning parents. They would often talk of their joy in the squirrels and the sparrows, in the leaves and the evening light behind them. One day when I visited my grandfather, by then in his nineties, he was feeling too weak to get out of bed. "What have you been doing?" I asked him. "Praying a little," he said, "and thinking a little." At that moment my eyes followed his to the trees just beyond the bedroom window, and I realized that the contemplation of the life within them had long since formed an intrinsic part of his inner world.

"A tree of life is it to them that grasp it," says Proverbs (3:18) in a verse that links Torah to the vitality of bark, trunk, and sap, inviting us to see the beauty of everything natural in God's law and the workings of God's law in every tree. Many times since that day at my grandparents' house, I have wondered at that connection. Trees are for beholding, but they are to be listened to as well. There is a still, strong voice in their vibrancy, ascending and descending between root and leaf. As their leaves purify the air, removing choking gasses and making it breathable again, so the trunk and branches have power to cleanse and refine the soul. Hearing the sap's flow the spirit grows still, sufficiently attentive for a moment to be aware of its participation in the unlimited life of all that is. Thus the tree, like the Torah, is the guardian of the soul's integrity. Perhaps it was for this reason that prophet and psalmist beheld the trees dancing before the coming of the Lord. To a hidden melody day by day, and to a visible rhythm through the seasons, they surely do.

For these reasons I appreciate the protection of trees. Most of all on a winter night, when the frost has seized the ground beneath and the stars shine out among the frozen branches above, I value a tree's companionship. Sometimes in my best moments I feel I have it and listen to its purifying speech. The rest of the time I fail to be worthy. But the tree will be there when I ask for its fellowship again; it will be there with its vitality to support other lives, when my life is over.

This is what Job ironically observes when, full of grief at death's nullification of human existence, he makes the comparison: "There is hope for a tree when it is cut down . . . If its roots grow old in the earth and its trunk dies in the soil; at the very smell of water it will grow" (14:7–9). Who knows if Job would say the same if he were alive today and witness to the fate of trees? At any rate, Job is bitter — and justifiably so. The author of this poem also had much to feel aggrieved about, but he wasn't when he wrote of the nightingale:

> 'Tis not through envy of thy happy lot,
> But being too happy in thy happiness, —
> That thou, light winged Dryad of the trees,
> In some melodious plot
> Of beechen green, and shadows numberless,
> Singest of summer in full-throated ease.[4]

I think my grandfather was at one, that day when I spoke to him, with the generous attitude of Keats's poem, a spirit all the more remarkable because Keats knew he was dying when he wrote it. We are in a better state of mind if we can share his gratitude that there is life which outlives us. Let "beechen green and shadows numberless" long be the guardians of life!

> If a man kills a tree before its time,
> it's as if he had murdered a soul.
>
> Rebbe Naḥman of Breslav

Our dear family friend Hilde Bach was a wise woman. A refugee from Nazi Germany, she began to make her way in this country as a domestic servant and learned to live with little. Her final years were spent in a single room, surrounded by a few books, a few plants, and the bare necessities of life. But the sphere of people and issues she cared about was large indeed. It therefore fell with the force of a profound and considered judgment when she said one day, "Our age will be known as the Age of Waste."

Trees are among the biggest victims.

119

The Torah forbids the destruction of fruit-bearing trees. The context and reasoning are pragmatic. If one lays siege to a city and needs timber for bulwarks, battering rams, camp fires, and whatever else, fruit-bearing trees must not be used. They are not enemy soldiers to be destroyed, so why waste a valuable source of food? (Deut. 20:19). Rabbinic Judaism found in this specific, pragmatic proscription the basis for a general prohibition against needless waste of any kind, and the key words of the verse "*Lo tashḥit* — Do not destroy" were adopted as the name of the rule. Its subsequent history can be traced through the various layers of the sources. The Talmud contains a number of references to the law and its wide application is taken for granted. Maimonides (1135–1204) saw in it a broad educational principle: "One should be trained not to be destructive."[5] In our day we should apply his formulation to all trees cut down thoughtlessly, with no intention of preserving the habitat of which they formed the crucial part.

Of course, even trees don't live forever. If a tree dies naturally, it slowly turns into a custodian of forest life; ants, beetles, maggots, lice, and all the birds that eat them find their home in its generous decay. The situation is otherwise when whole stands of trees are destroyed. They are dragged away, the creatures that lived there must seek another home or perish; in the forest there is left an arid patch of waste and a path slashed by the machinery of extraction. It is one matter if there is swift and careful replanting. Hugo Gryn wrote of how his father was responsible for the felling of timber in the Carpathian forests and its transport downstream by river. He recalled how his father would insist that before the wood was taken away the forest must be replanted.[6] Such a use of natural resources is widely considered acceptable, so long as it is made with due thought for habitats, nature's rhythms, and the needs of the people who live in the area. It corresponds with God's instruction to Adam and Eve "to work and protect" the Garden of Eden (Gen. 2:15), which at once gives us permission to use, and requires us to preserve, the natural world, a balance substantially reflected in the modern term "sustainability." But it is otherwise when there is to be no replacement of the trees, when greed is the main factor, when there is only the dying.

When whole tracts of forests are obliterated, the loss is far more than that of the trees. When a fruit tree is heedlessly cut down, teaches the author of *Pirkei deRabbi Eliezer*, "its moan is heard from one end of the world to the other, yet no sound is heard."[7] What might the content of that silent cry be? What is the tree trying to tell us? It goes to the heart of our tragedy that we so often fail to be attuned to the wavelength on which nature is articulate. Only in fairy tales and poetry do trees talk like us.

There can be few places in literature where trees have something more terrifying to say than in Dante's *Divine Comedy*. Descending to the seventh circle of hell, the poet, led by Virgil his guide, enters a pathless and degenerate forest of writhen trees with discolored leaves. He hears a dismal wailing, but sees nothing that might be the source of the mournful sound. "Pluck off a twig," says his mentor, and your "thoughts will stagger at their own dumbfounding." He follows the instruction and to his horror the trunk cries out, "Why tear my limbs away?" while blood oozes from the wound. Encouraged by Virgil, who apologizes for persuading his protégé to break the branch, the sorrowful voice explains that in these trees are trapped the souls of suicides. They are condemned to this bleak imprisonment until the resurrection of the dead. At that time they will be joined by their bodies, which will be hung from their branches.[8]

Whatever the reason that led Dante to make the link between trees and self-destruction, the modern reader experiences these lines with a new kind of horror. For there is today a basic, literal connection between the fate of the forests and the fate of all creatures. Perhaps the other animals realize this more than we do as they shrink back into their contracting habitats. Perhaps it is only we human beings who are deaf. Maybe this is the message in the unheeded warning to which the *Pirkei deRabbi Eliezer* refers.

Spirituality Goes to the Dogs

I believe I'm often called behind my back "The rabbi with the dog." There are worse names, for my life, including its spiritual side, is enriched by the companionship of my canine quadruped. He arrived in our home some nine years ago after being rescued from the streets by members of my congregation. We called him Asaf, or Safi for short, because he is a scavenger and because of a Jerusalem rabbi of the same name, known for the love of his dog who followed him everywhere.

Safi loves to come to shul; furthermore, unlike many humans, he regards it as a travesty to travel there by car. Safi attends every lesson, where I'm afraid he sets a rather bad example by yawning loudly and falling asleep at the first word of Hebrew. But then, he's probably nervous lest he stand out by showing too different an attitude from so many others. He loves Shabbat and the festivals and is troubled only by Pesaḥ when, because all or almost all dog foods contain leaven, he suffers from the same dietary restrictions as everyone else.

I have learned a great deal from that dog. I think it was She'ar-Yeshuv Cohen who said when he was Chief Rabbi of Haifa that every Jewish family should have a pet, to teach the children compassion. He is right. Judaism, without being sentimental or equating animal with human life, understands that "God's mercy extends to all God's works" (Ps. 145:9), that to inflict suffering on bird or beast is wrong, and that we should value the whole of creation as God's work. In our urbanized communities, focused on cyber and screen, studying the texts of Torah, we should not forget the great text of creation itself, nor our responsibility toward it.

I have learned about fidelity and affection from that dog. Every dog owner says it, but it's true. Whenever I come home, there he is, wagging his tail. I sometimes come back in a bad mood and go straight to my study; I sometimes don't greet the family because I'm busy, bothered, or bad-tempered. But Safi is always there with a bark, a lick, and a sniff. "The great principle is equanimity," taught the Ba'al Shem Tov, founder of Ḥasidism; Safi often shows a more even state of mind than his owner, something from which the latter tries to learn.

People talk about "cupboard love," but his love is not contingent on what you bring him. He doesn't have to agree with you to like you; he sits on no committees, holds no ideological positions, conducts none of the arguments over trivia that so often prevent people from treating each other with a modicum of warmth and welcome. He is the perfect undogmatic dog, the ideal post-modern, post-denominational creature. He teaches me to try to be welcoming always and to see the person in the person, whatever his or her beliefs or state of mind. I try to follow this in my life, appreciating the wealth I gain from all my teachers, be they Reform or ḥasidic.

I have learned about trust from Safi. The trust of children, and animals, may be absolute. To be so trusted is chastening; it is an honor and a great responsibility. We are rightly outraged when trust, especially that of children, is betrayed. So, albeit this is a small matter in comparison, when I see how that dog trusts me for everything, for food, for walks, and for affection, I take it to heart. It leads me to reflect on the wider meaning of trust; on how we as human beings are entrusted with the welfare of one another, how God has entrusted us with caring for this world that is not ours.

I have learned about compassion. Safi can't abide crying. Some years ago a man came to see me and, while talking of his troubles, burst into tears. Before I knew it, the dog was sitting on his lap, licking tears away. It's not, perhaps, the ideal approach — I think it's called shock therapy — but I wish we all cared about one another's sorrows quite as much. (I admit I'm being anthropomorphic — perhaps.) Anyway, Safi's pastoral skills have improved over the years and he now just sits quietly and listens, maintaining a perfect confidentiality.

Sadly, I'm aware that I shall also learn about grief. Already I regret the speed with which the old boy is going grey. I suppose his aging marks the passage of my days, too; for the last nine years I've measured out my life in dog-food tins. On several occasions I have been consulted by Jews in and out of my congregation on what to do when. . . . Again, a pet is not a person, but it is both inevitable and appropriate to feel sorrow.

Not everything has been perfect, of course. Safi is sometimes rather better with people than with his fellows, just as some Jews manage interfaith relations better than cross-communal ones. Though actually, Safi himself hasn't always been good with other religions, as on the inauspicious day when he saw a Christmas tree for the first time and, deciding he must be in the safety of the woodlands, lifted a leg over the beautifully wrapped presents. But don't we all make mistakes?

In the end, I agree with the words of the Indian chief who reputedly wrote to the president of the United States that if it weren't for the animals, we should die from loneliness of the spirit. (With that I must pause, because Safi's waiting for his dinner and it's a mitzvah to feed him before I myself eat.)

PURIM

Evil

Remember what Amalek did unto you, by the way, when you came out of Egypt; how he . . . smote those trailing after you, when you were weak and weary . . . You shall blot out the memory of Amalek. You shall not forget.

Deut. 25:17–8

For hate is not conquered by hate: hate is conquered by love. This is law eternal.

The Dhammapada 1:5

Why remember ancient hatreds? Aren't they best forgotten? Judaism is permeated with memory. There is not a day on which, evening and morning, we do not remember the Exodus. The week is structured around the memory of the seventh day. Rosh Hashanah is Yom Hazikaron, the day of remembering. In the *Yizkor* service and on their *yahrzeit* we think of our family who have died. But Shabbat Zakhor, the Sabbath that precedes Purim, is different. Here, and only here, are we commanded to remember evil.

Although unspeakable wickedness has been perpetrated against the Jewish people since then, the attack by Amalek, from behind, against the old, the sick, and the weary has always represented the epitome of evil. In commanding us never to forget it, Judaism sets itself against the pretense that evil doesn't really exist, or doesn't really matter.

As a nation Amalek no longer survives. Haman, son of Hamdatha, descendant of Agag the Amalekite king, is among the last of his people. For the Talmud records that ever since the Assyrian emperor Sennacherib carried out his policy of mass deportations throughout the Middle East in the eighth century B.C.E., the ancient peoples as referred to in the Bible ceased to exist.[1]

There are those who have sought to identify the Nazis, and other recent enemies of the Jewish people, with Amalek. But that is not correct, and there are obvious dangers in labelling any group, however wicked their actions, in this way, so as to claim that God is on our side in an eternal war against them.

127

The way in which Amalek does live on is as a principle. What Amalek means today is quintessential evil. This includes both evil without, and evil within. *"Lekha Amalek,"* teaches the ḥasidic tradition, as so often creatively rereading the words of the Torah, "To you Amalek" — Amalek is within you, within us, also. For that, and only that, reason, is there "a war of the Lord against Amalek from generation to generation" (Ex. 17:16).

Evil is real enough. To be its victim is not only a terrifying but also a profoundly bewildering experience. I recently heard a woman talk about her childhood in an East European capital in the late 1930s. Once, when she was a little girl, her father left her on her own for a few minutes in the central courtyard of a housing block while he went to greet a friend. She recalled how children emerged slyly from various doorways, taunted her for being Jewish, and started to throw stones. She hadn't been afraid, and it hadn't hurt her physically. What she had experienced was sheer incomprehension that someone like her could possibly be the object of another person's hate.

Perhaps the same sense of incomprehensibility remains when the situation develops into a major tragedy. A local Bosnian man acted as a translator for the United Nations in Srebrenica during the Serbian onslaught. The UN force was surrounded, and the so-called safe haven abandoned, together with the entire civilian population it had been established to protect. The man pleaded with the United Nations to place his father, mother, and brother — who were standing there in front of them — under the same protection to which their own personnel were entitled. With the guns of their adversaries pointing at them, the UN refused, and the man watched as his family was taken away. He never saw them again.

The war against Amalek requires us to do all we can to prevent such savagery from being perpetrated anywhere, ever. Furthermore, Amalek does not just represent evil committed against Jews, but every form of outrage practiced against any people.

But we must be very careful not to imagine that evil is always "out there." It is also within us. From the beginning of our life until its end, we are subject to conflicting impulses and temptations and none of us is entitled to make assumptions about our future conduct. "Do not trust in yourself until your dying day," taught Hillel.[2] Remembering the — potential — evil within is, therefore, part of preventing the recurrence of evil in the world out there. None of us is immune to hatred, envy, and fear.

Few of us like to think that we are capable of hating and being hateful. However, most of us have a sore patch somewhere; rub it hard enough and the poison bursts out. Most of us have said or done things of which we are truly ashamed, things we would fear to admit to our closest friend, things we only dare think of in a secret corner of our heart.

Envy perverts judgment and twists the soul. Fear leads to prejudice and inhumanity. Imaginary fears, especially of people from different ethnic groups and religions, often cause us to label others with all the evil characteristics we like to dispose of on any ready target but ourselves. Actual terror prevents all but the most courageous among us from doing what we know to be right. If we haven't lived in a society where there is no trust, where the innocent are persecuted, and any demonstration of humanity is punishable by death, then we should consider ourselves not innocent, but lucky.

The war against Amalek means fighting evil both within ourselves and without. If we ignore the former, we too quickly become like Amalek. As we know to our cost, Purim still has the power to engender violence. We have only to remember the appalling massacre of Moslems at prayer by Baruch Goldstein in 1994 and the spate of bus bombings which killed so many Israelis in 1996. The purpose of recalling evil is not to pursue an eternal vendetta. For hate only breeds hate, and evil evil. The aim is to transform hatred. That can be the only meaning of the strange paradox in the commandment to simultaneously remember and to blot out the memory of Amalek. We remember in order to learn and blot out memory by working for a world which is different.

Amoral World?

> Be careful in your dealings with the ruling power;
> They favor a person only when it suits them.
>
> Rabban Gamliel, son of Rabbi Judah the Prince,
> M. Avot 2:3

The principal experience of Purim is of being plunged into the world of the Scroll of Esther. There is a wondrous quality to the scenes evoked by this brilliant novel in miniature and the events that it recounts. Here are richer fabrics and brighter colors than in almost all of the rest of the Bible; here are eating, drinking, and beautiful women, queens with minds distinctly of their own, spies, schemers, eavesdroppers, horses on parade, and, looming high above it all, the gallows. Here is the overt absence of those concerns that so powerfully animate virtually the entire sacred canon: God, justice, the purpose of life. If the world of the Megillah is a moral universe, it is not so in any obvious sense.

It may be argued that a single tension inhabits the Bible and draws the long fabric of its narrative taut: the difference between what is and what should be. This dialectic is expressed in countless ways. Often, but not always, it springs across the polarity between God's law and what the people actually do. Sometimes the debate is directly about God: Why isn't God fair, as God is supposed to be? Why doesn't God act in the way we think God ought to? More often it animates narratives so complex with hopes and failures as to defy our ability to know exactly who is at fault or how, leaving us with nowhere comfortable to put our feet. Yet the tension remains.

In the Megillah, this tension seems to be absent. No overt moral discourse governs the events of the story, no moral purpose unites the actions of its characters. There is no shared ideal. Even Mordekhai and Esther, who act selflessly and courageously, must devote all their energies to the survival of their own people. At best, in this world of shades and appearances, moral order is a winter shadow amidst many more prominent phenomena. Or the moral order resides in the mind of the reader who, unhappy at its absence, finds ways and means of putting it back.

What then does impel people to act? Why does Aḥasuerus give his magnificent party at the beginning? Why does he summon his queen? Why does he raise up Haman, why accept with such blithe speed Haman's offer to deal with the Jews? Why does he later seek to trip him up and pull him down? Why does he elevate Mordekhai instead and, by cue and collusion, have him deal in such a bloody way with the old Hamanite faction? The answer is always the same: self-interest. Not only is there no other motive, there is not even the thought that there ought to be.

That is not to say that the king is stupid. This issue is touched on briefly in the Talmud, which notes the difference of opinion between Rav and Samuel, one claiming that Aḥasuerus is a wise ruler, the other that he is foolish.[3] The latter view may be based on the insight that ultimately a ruler without moral vision is bound to fail, but in the story Aḥasuerus doesn't behave as a fool — far from it. He has one hundred and twenty-seven provinces to govern and no principle whatsoever under which to unite them. His goal is therefore survival, and it is toward that simple end that he directs his decisions. This is the key to understanding Haman's influence over him. How cleverly he plays on Aḥasuerus's insecurity when he tells him that there is a people who are everywhere (unlike your authority), who have a common language and tradition (which you do not), and who don't obey the king's laws. Would Aḥasuerus have thought of these things — or dealt with the consequences — himself? Perhaps not. But when someone like Haman offers to do the dirty work, why not take advantage of his convenient ambition and be rid of the Jewish threat? After all, having someone else do the job allows him to keep his own hands clean, and Haman himself can always be dealt with later should that prove necessary, especially as he too is an outsider, a mere Amalekite, another refugee, with little influence in the kingdom.

If such were his plans, what makes the king change his mind and overthrow his new protégé? His fresh course of action is determined by considerations every bit as unprincipled as the first. Haman, he is made to realize, is not such a safe bet after all. Does the king revoke his decision to cleanse his provinces of the Jews just because he fancies Esther so much? Of course not! But by inviting Haman, and only Haman, not once but twice, to a party with her royal partner, the new queen succeeds brilliantly in her plan to make him jealous, sexually jealous perhaps, politically jealous certainly. Perhaps, thinks Aḥasuerus now, there is something between the two of them? Perhaps Esther knows something about Haman which he, the king, doesn't? It is high time for a sleepless royal night; high time to search the annals and find a tool for Haman's humiliation! Note how Esther says not a word about her real request — to save her people — until the poison has worked upon the king. By the time he arrives for his second drink, Aḥasuerus's mind is made up anyway; it is precisely upon this point that the queen has been relying. When she tells him who her enemy is, she provides the pretext for a course of action on which the king has already decided. He may even have been hoping that she would say something of the kind. After all, it keeps his hands nice and clean.

For if the Jews were the threat before, Haman is the problem now. He has to go. How excellent to devise a way of letting Jew and Jew-hater deal with one another directly. Let dog eat dog! Even better if — once the tables are turned — he can persuade the Jews to kill as many of their former persecutors as possible. Let the Jews root them all out, and in so doing make themselves hateful in turn. All the sooner will someone else emerge to give them their due, while the crown and sceptre remain safely on Ahasuerus's seemingly innocent head, and in his bloodless hands.

Thus in the world of the Megillah, morality is replaced by cunning, cunning, and plenty more cunning in this competition to be the fittest and survive. The winner, of course, is Esther. She proves to be not just the fairest, but the cleverest, of them all. Who will triumph in the subsequent battle, with the next turn of the screw, one cannot say. Mercifully, the story of the Megillah stops before that happens, before Mordekhai, Esther, and the Jews reap the reward of their unsolicited ascendancy to power. For ruthlessness is all.

Yet that is still not quite the whole truth. There is an essential sequence in the story in which conscious decisions are made for motives other than self-interest. Mordekhai sends to Esther in her moments of despair before she resolves to act, "If you are silent now, rescue and respite shall arise for the Jews from somewhere else, and you and your father's house shall perish. And who knows," he goes on to admonish her, "if it was not for an occasion like this that you attained royal rank." This is an appeal to a sense of responsibility based on the consciousness of a higher destiny. Mordekhai invokes an authority in the name of which self-interest must be subjugated to self-sacrifice for the sake of a greater goal. This is the clearest glimpse of moral grounding in the story; it is no accident that the action founded on it should prove to be decisive. But in the world of the Megillah, this moment remains an anomaly. Or rather, the rest of its world must be judged in its light, judged for what it lacks.

What does it feel like to be a citizen of Persia and inhabit this story for a day? As Jews we have always made fun of the experience. This time we won; we lived, and we still live, to eat and drink for another day. It is, as the Megillah itself declares, a topsy-turvy world, so let's make the best of it while we can!

Yet there is an unpleasant aftertaste to all the food and laughter; it sticks in the throat. For which world is it that is actually upside down? One doesn't go to such elaborate lengths to laugh something off unless it is sufficiently uncomfortable to require such casual, determined, evasion. Too much is real about the court of Aḥasuerus for it to be dismissed as mere farce. Too much about our own world uncomfortably resembles the universe of the Megillah.

If that is really the world we inhabit, if in the end it is only an Aḥasuerus who sits on the throne of his one hundred and twenty-seven provinces, we will all be damned sooner or later. Killer and killed will remain forever equally expendable, rising and falling in fortune's scales as they sway on their soulless pivot. Nothing will ever unite the many domains of our planet, and those who inhabit them will have nothing, not even a word or language, in common, except the fight for survival. Even this, which could have the power to unite us, will be seen as a goal that justifies endless conflict. A deeper sense of purpose will never take hold. There will never be a reason to cease from killing; there will never be a greater objective than "live and let die."

If there is a God who sits on that throne, or if humanity can find a shared moral vision, then it may be possible to establish a common purpose so that we can all work to protect the vulnerability from which every one of us suffers. Then we may find that there are things for which it is even worthy to "die and let live," as Esther was ready to do. Then, and only then, will we all be able to hope for safety, prosperity, and peace. That is what we glimpse in the Megillah's most extraordinary moment, when Mordekhai persuades Esther to risk her life, "If you are silent now. . . ."

Into Confusion

You are not permitted to hide yourself away . . .

Deut. 22:3

A puzzling rabbinic saying maintains that in the time to come only two festivals will remain out of the entire cycle of yearly celebrations: Purim and Yom Kippur. Beyond the play on the names (*Pur*im / Kip*pur*), and the fact that they have in common the drawing of lots, the two days are profoundly antithetical. The relationship between them poses a difficult question:

Which is more difficult — to find the way back from a world of confusion to self-knowledge or to travel out from home into a world of confusion? Every Yom Kippur we try to make the first journey. Every Purim we are reminded uncomfortably of the reality of the latter.

On Purim we are transported to a universe we are encouraged to imagine as irredeemably foreign and utterly unfathomable. We spend most of our time in the capital, Shushan, where there is painted before our eyes a palace furbished with virtually every precious material under the sun and in every color we can imagine. On Yom Kippur, however, there is only one significant province, God's world. We are repeatedly reminded that for all the differences we perceive in it, and magnify or even manufacture between peoples, that world is one dominion, God's. The palace at its center is God's Temple. In the heart of it is the Holy of Holies, and, far from richly furnished, it is empty save for the Ark of the Covenant and God's invisible presence.

On Purim we read of clothes made of all kinds of fabric from sackcloth to silk. The characters in the story don robes and roles and are invested in them or divested of them by the fickle hands of tyranny and fate. Vashti is stripped of rank for refusing to strip at the king's command; Esther puts on royal apparel and is garbed in radiant grace. Even today we are encouraged to let ourselves go in imitation. What would Purim be without its fancy dress? But on Yom Kippur we are taught to dress down, so as not, in Isaiah's words, to "hide from [our] own flesh." Though outwardly we may wear our best clothes, for the day is still a festival, inwardly we try hard to remove the fabricated layers that may conceal from us who we are.

In the Megillah, speech and the written word are frequently instruments of confusion. One hundred and twenty-seven provinces, as we are repeatedly reminded, each rejoice in a different language. It was clearly a bonanza season for translators. Who else could supply the runners with the missives sent in such haste at each turn of the story to inform every province according to its own script and language? Yet, for all that, the plot depends on contrived misinterpretation, and distrust and disinformation rule.

On Yom Kippur there is only the striving to tell ourselves the truth before God. In the silence of self-knowledge God knows, and we know too. On Yom Kippur we try to avoid playing roles and see ourselves as we really are. Yom Kippur is a day for stripping away inessentials: the challenge is to divest ourselves of the physical activities that make us unconscious of, and the delusions which divide us from, our true nature. We try to acknowl-edge who we really are. Nothing extrinsic matters as we stand before God and people in truth, as moral beings, as mortal beings, as flesh before dust and spirit before spirit. The day is the touchstone of our being. But Purim is a day of borrowed robes and undeserved titles, of excessive food and drink. It marks not our triumph before our deeper destiny but a temporary victory in the face of fickle fortune.

It would be easy to say that the world of Yom Kippur is the true world and that of the Megillah purely artificial, but it is not so simple. Purim also presents us with a moral challenge. Its question is: How far out into the world can we go without losing our integrity?

For Yom Kippur is just a day, an essential, but only a single, day. Few of us live in a state of prolonged inner concentration. The world we actually inhabit is a place of constant action and confusion. We take on roles, wear various robes, learn to speak, if not in different languages, in different ways in numerous situations. Most of us travel a long way out from the center of ourselves. Sometimes we manage to take with us the person we really are, or hope to be, but often we get lost in a world of countless provinces and innumerable disguises.

Yet travel out we must. Just as Esther could not hide at the crucial moment in the story of the Megillah, so we too have no permission to be silent. We must, we are in fact commanded, to live on earth engaged, com-mitted — to other people, to complex situations, to pains and pleasures, even to things. We are required while here to be here.

For a long time I had an unconscious attitude of avoidance. It wasn't a deliberate policy; I didn't understand at the time that this was what I was doing. I worked at many different things; I kept busy but avoided any sin-gle employment that would occupy more than a small part of my time. I wanted space, plenty of aloneness, time to reflect. I thought that what I was in pursuit of was integrity, soul. That was no doubt partially true; it was a time of growth and preparation. But now I also realize that part of what I wanted was life chiefly for myself, my spirit and myself. Taken to its extreme, such an attitude is selfish.

This is a long way behind me now, and today I am conscious of a differ-ent danger. I have become involved. Involvement leads me into complex situations; inevitably there are also conflicts. I end up arguing a point of view, taking sides, assuming a role, adopting a position. I make mistakes, misunderstand, feel misunderstood. Sometimes I even feel the victim of my role. I wonder, Who am I really? Who is this person, rabbi, teacher or whatever, whom people imagine to be so-and-so and respond to in such-and-such a way? In my personal life I think, I'm a husband now, a father. Is it really me who is that person with those responsibilities, or am I only playing this role? There turn out to be so many languages, so many disguises, so much possibility for misunderstanding between ourselves and who we are perceived to be, ourselves and who we think we are.

Thank God, then, for Yom Kippur, which brings us home to ourselves.

But Purim is also the real world; mad, perhaps, but most definitely, real — only in a different dimension of "real." We have to be out there in the social and political world, yet still know who we are. That is the challenge. Can we, as the Talmud puts it, drink from life until we don't know the difference between "cursed be Haman and blessed be Mordekhai," yet still know very well the difference between the two?[4] It's fine to have our integrity when and where it isn't challenged. But do we dare to put it to the test?

PESAḤ

Whose Story?

> The people need poetry that will be their own secret
> to keep them awake forever.
>
> Osip Mandelstam[1]

All people seek the secret of their own continuity. This is the power of the seder night; it lights up the past as the full moon illumines the path through the forest. The light of where we come from shines into the uncertainty of who we are. For where we come from is always at the heart of who we are, and until we understand the greater journey of our family and people we cannot recognize the direction of our own life.

The past enters the present through the telling of stories. From camp fires to formal liturgies, all peoples have rituals for the telling of their story. The story of the Exodus from Egypt is the most important Jewish story and the essence of the seder night. That, after all, is what *haggadah* means — telling: "*Vehiggadetah le'vinkha* — and you shall tell your child," teaches the Torah, furnishing the basis for the seder.

Everyone loves to be told a story. My wife was on a train with our children and read them a book. When she finished she looked up and noticed that half the carriage was listening. Some of the passengers even thanked her. Any story well told becomes, at least to a degree, our own story. Its heroes and heroines express some facet of our own humanity, and we travel with them on their adventures. But the story of the Exodus grips us with exceptional power. For, in outer fact or inner truth, we have all fled oppression and travelled through the desert in search of liberation and the promised land.

The Exodus is our family story. If it did not happen to us, then it happened to our parents; if not to them, then to our grandparents. But again and again through Jewish history it happened; we fled Pharaohs, crossed borders, sought deliverance by night. Many of us, once we become aware that this is our story, experience an unquenchable thirst to hear it. Often it is the child who wants to know, even more than the parent desires to tell.

"Tell me a story about when you were a child," I used to pester my parents. "Tell me how you came to this country and what it was like."

"I left it until it was too late!" say so many people when the last member of the older generation passes away. "Why didn't I make a tape or persuade her to write it all down? Who will identify the faces on the photographs now?" An era and all its stories have gone down into the silence. What joy, then, to discover a relative still living in Israel or New York, who remembers and, yes, who would be delighted to see you when you visit in the summer. The same desire to know underlies the pilgrimage so many people make to Eastern Europe. How exciting to discover the house where one's grandmother was born down a small lane at the back of some village in Lithuania. How sad, but how stirring, to pull away the ivy from a tombstone in an unkempt cemetery and read the family name.

The seder night transforms all these journeys into the ancient, ancestral journey out of Egypt. They become another chapter in the same long wandering in the wilderness, part of the same unending pursuit of God's revelation and the borders of the promised land. The deeds of the ancestors are a sign for the children, teach the Rabbis. Every facet of their journey, the plagues, the crossing of the sea, the oases, the thirst, the hunger, and the loss and rediscovery of faith become potential symbols for our own.

The journey we recall on seder night thus becomes an inner voyage as well. There are formative moments in the spiritual life of every person. In the desire to keep inwardly alive, we revisit these moments with yearning. In particular at times of crisis or change, at the birth of a child, on the Day of Atonement, perhaps most seriously when we face illness and death, our souls return to the places where they found their deepest inspiration and the greatest wealth of life was revealed. One person longs for the sea, another to stand on the same balcony and relive a moment shared with a partner thirty years ago and sacred ever since. Someone else remembers a line of poetry, or the sound of a voice — anything that made a hole in life's darkness and penetrated the heart.

It is the same with the collective spirit of a people. We return together to our great and decisive experiences. We put on our sandals, take up our staff, and wait with anxious hope for God's deliverance. We rejoice in our freedom, we eat the bread of liberation for the first time. We stand at God's sacred mountain. We become frustrated; we tell ourselves that we will never see the borders of the promised land. Egypt, Exodus, Sinai — these are the defining moments in the life of the Jewish spirit. They happened long ago, but they never become irrelevant because our own journey continues and, year by year, they illumine our wanderings with a different light.

The story of the seder is an invocation, a call of awakening to the soul. On seder night we see ourselves as travelers again, choosers of routes, seekers of revelations. An old freedom reasserts itself, and we attach ourselves with joy and hope of restoration to the ancient journey. The spirit travels forth. It seeks, along the beaten path of its people's past, the poetry of its future.

Too Young to Ask?

> The Torah speaks of four children: one wise, one wicked, one simple and one who knows not how to ask.
>
> from the haggadah

Like most others, I imagine, I have been beguiled by a mental picture of the youngest child, the one who "knows not how to ask," as too little and too sweet to formulate a question. That is why I have never even thought about the words our Rabbis so carefully chose to describe the due response to him — or her: "*At petaḥ lo* — You open for him — or for her.*"

"You must make an opening!" This simple phrase, the haggadah's instruction to the parent of the fourth child, is the hardest task of all. How does one make an opening for someone, a place and welcome around the table? How does one fashion an atmosphere where questions are comfortable and where not to know is acceptable? How does one make a passageway, an opening, in one's own self and give freedom to one's spirit? These challenges begin with the seder but quickly spread out into the whole of our Judaism, and, indeed, the rest of our life.

Before considering how to respond to the fourth child, I must admit that I've never reflected on what might in fact be preventing him or her from asking a question in the first place. I had simply assumed that this *child* could not yet muster the necessary vocabulary and was incapable of asking. Yet that is not what the Hebrew says. The text doesn't read "*she'eno yakhol lishe'ol* — who can't ask," but *"she'eno yode'a lishe'ol* — who isn't skilled at asking," or perhaps, "who isn't confident at asking." Compare, for example, Jeremiah's attempt at evading his calling, when he tells God that he is no good at speaking. His excuse — *lo yad'ati dabber* — doesn't mean, "I can't speak," for he obviously can. What he's really saying is, "I'm not confident at speaking and the thought of having to do so in public utterly terrifies me." So it's not that the child can't ask. Have you ever seen a child incapable of asking or, indeed, demanding? It's that he or she is nervous or afraid.

These considerations help us to enter the mind of the fourth child and to appreciate the part of ourselves, and others, which is like that. How painful to feel that one's ignorance is going to be exposed. How humiliating to think that everyone else knows, except me. How nerve racking to be tortured by the conviction that if one should so much as dare to open one's mouth, the words would be bound to come out all wrong! Or perhaps one feels so overwhelmed that one simply doesn't know where to begin. Judaism can feel extremely intimidating. So can the rest of life; but in the context of religion, with its judgmental image, one is even more likely to feel that one is going to be found wanting.

To reply to any of the four children is a big responsibility; to respond to the child who doesn't know how to ask is probably the greatest of all. Yet every one of us harbors this child within us and is familiar with its fears. How then should we answer?

First of all we need the sensitivity to listen to the questions that aren't asked. It is perfectly possible to spend a lifetime without hearing them. Most people have a shrewd instinct for what those around them are incapable of hearing and unconsciously edit their words and manner accordingly. Sometimes we can't hear because the part of ourselves that might be capable of doing so has not yet been opened and plumbed by our own experience. Sometimes we fail to perceive the pain, or need, or even the quiet joy of another because we are so busy with our own noise. If one has to make space for another person's words, how much more so then for another person's silence.

Once we have become aware of the presence of what is unsaid, we need to find the warmth and gentleness of tone that might, with a soft inquiry, draw it forth. This is not just a matter of "knowing what to say," as if there were some such clinical skill. We don't have to know the right answer, even if there were such a thing. Indeed, the very word "right" is wrong; there is no correctness except what is genuine. This will express itself in our attitude, whatever our words, so long as they are not careless. Let that attitude therefore be one in which we acknowledge our listening to life, to ourselves, to the sound of the birds and the trees. For the child who does not ask is both everywhere and within us.

It is for this reason that the fourth child probably has the most to teach us. If we believe we already know everything, we cannot possibly hear him or her; to listen we must become attentive to our own ignorance. The unasked question is therefore always, at some level, also our own, but it is good to be brought to the threshold of our not knowing. Perhaps this is why the answer to that child is so personal: "Because of what God did to me, when I went out of Egypt." We can blind the wise child — and ourselves — with science, beguile the naïve child — and ourselves — with a story, but here we have no other answer to draw on except our own most personal response. We have no choice but to struggle with what it all means to us: God, Exodus, freedom, long journeys through the desert of our own life. If it is genuine, our answer will itself remain an exploration, a departure with words into new desert spaces, an Exodus in miniature. But should our answers turn into old lectures, should our "answers" lose their questions, the child who knows not how to ask will do as we do and not listen any longer.

The moment that child leaves our table, we will be back with last year's words, sitting at last year's seder; this year's journey to this year's freedom will have ceased. It is the very beauty of the seder that it forces us out of Egypt, year after year. Back in the desert, unknowing but attentive, we have at least a chance of meeting God.

Weaving

A thing I love is the action of spinning:
the shuttle fluttering back and forth, the hum of the spindle . . .
Everything's happened before and will happen again,
but still the moment of each meeting is sweet.

Osip Mandelstam, "Tristia"[2]

Rabbinic literature reserves the word *massekhet,* translated by Jastrow in his classic dictionary as "web on the loom," for its most important text, the Talmud. Indeed the volumes of the Talmud deserve their names, *Massekhet Berakhot, Massekhet Shabbat,* and so forth, because they are composed of the weaving of threads from the teaching of seemingly countless rabbis. These threads carry the colors of different times and places, and vary in texture from the strong fibers of legal definition to the lithe strands of poetic interpretation. So many voices, so many disagreements, so many stories, and so many apparent non sequiturs — all these help to make the great text of the Talmud everyone's companion.

The most famous and familiar *massekhet* of them all is surely the haggadah — although it is never called by that name. The weaving begins in the text of the haggadah itself and continues by means of commentaries, be it by word or illustration, before the threads are taken up by everyone around the table and woven in different patterns at each seder and in every generation.

The way the story of the Exodus is told in the haggadah provides a classic example of the rabbinic method of weaving. The core narrative, which begins after the four questions and the description of the four children, is simple. It is taken straight from the Torah: "A wandering Aramean was my father, and he went down to Egypt and sojourned there few in number; and he became there a great nation. . . ." (Deut. 26:5–8). These words are like the weft and woof of the loom; it is into them that everything else is woven.

How did the Rabbis know which threads to choose? To them each word of the Bible had a distinctive color, which they recognized whenever it occurred elsewhere in the sacred canon. Thus when Deuteronomy tells us that the Children of Israel "sojourned there" (26:5) in Egypt — *vayagor sham* — the Rabbis connect this with the words of Joseph's brothers when they were first presented to Pharaoh and said, "We have come to sojourn in the land — *lagur ba'aretz banu*" (Gen. 47:4). What the brothers were trying to say was that they didn't intend to stay in Egypt for long. The connection with them teaches that the Jewish people had no wish to stay there for any length of time either. We meant only to stop in Egypt for a while, like countless other fugitives who hoped to return to their homes, or to travel on, like the Spanish Jews who took their keys with them when forced to flee in 1492, or like my mother's family who came to England in 1939 on transit visas to America and are still here now.

Such interweaving of core and intersecting verses forms the basic structure of the narrative of the seder. Next come the commentaries. They should be as rich and varied as possible, using every medium, from words to puppet shows or art, and should be suitable for every age. (Last year we had two crocodiles in the river Nile discussing how God had told them not to eat the baby in the bullrushes.) It is a sign of a convivial seder when there is an enthusiastic comparison of haggadah editions. "Listen to what my haggadah says. . . ." "Mine is totally different!" Thus the engagement with the text, which the compilers of each edition sought to convey in their particular manner, is transferred to the table. What, to refer to the example already given, does "sojourn" mean? For how long does the sojourner remain a *ger* (from the same root as *vayagor*), an outsider, a stranger? At what point do you cease to be a refugee and become a settled citizen? Is it when you buy a house, when you dream in the new language, when you give your children English names, or when they speak without a foreign accent? Or does their sensitivity to their parents' pronunciation or the fact that their home is different make them and every single Jew a stranger and a sojourner forever? As the psalmist puts it (119:19), "*Ger 'anoḥi ba'aretz* — I am a stranger on the earth." Or is everyone always a stranger? Is that the human condition?

Thus the words and commentaries leave the book, and all around the table the threads are woven into our own stories. Let it happen! As Rabban Gamliel taught nineteen hundred years ago: "Everyone must see themselves as if they had personally gone out of Egypt" — "We came here with ten shillings in our pockets; can you imagine, ten shillings?!" — "When I came, like so many other girls, as a domestic, I found more friendship in a small village in Wales than in a whole English city."

That's what makes a seder.

Where does it all finish? A seder has, of course, to have an ending — or at least a middle, when it's time to eat. Otherwise there will soon be complaints! But the Exodus itself is unending. We go on weaving threads all our life. We are forbidden to tie a knot and put them down. That is why the seder so pointedly includes the children. We can guess at the questions they may ask, but we cannot know what answers they in turn will give their children. Our duty is to hand them the threads with confidence and love. The story will surely, inevitably, be meaningful for them too:

Everything's happened before and will happen again.

The Challenge of Freedom

Every person is a world in miniature, containing Moses, Aaron, and Egypt.
Rabbi Ya'akov Yosef of Polnoye, *Toldot Ya'akov Yosef* [3]

All our life we have to struggle for whatever freedom we can attain.

Limitations are with us from the start. Over the last eight years I have had the privilege of watching the birth of my three children. When my son was born I had a powerful feeling that at this moment, or perhaps at the time of conception, a clock had started and the sand in the hourglass of his mortal time had begun to flow. I had been present at a border between worlds and watched a new life cross it and commence. I have since likened this to what I have sometimes experienced in the presence of a person who is dying. Clearly the situations are antithetical, yet, in both, two worlds meet; the known and the unknowable, infinity and the finite, the timeless and time.

According to a famous midrash, the soul protests when the Almighty summons it to birth and commands it to enter the womb, saying: "You expect me to enter this fetid drop!" But it is not free to decline. During the months of pregnancy the unborn child is shown the whole world and taught the entire Torah. At birth the mind and soul enter the confines of the flesh, and the portals of eternity are all but shut: an angel smites the new-born baby on the lip and the child forgets everything it has ever known.[4] Whatever the child now learns, it must do so by struggle.

Thus the paradoxes of freedom are innate to our condition, they are literally born with us. We enter a world of limitations, bound by time, constricted by our bodies, contracted in consciousness, and little in knowledge. Yet it is precisely here, within these bonds, that we live, act, and make our choices. Other worlds may offer wider expanses, we may dwell with God unconfined. But there we have no options, hence no freedom in any meaningful sense. For freedom is born out of choices, it is gained by struggling with limitations.

Perhaps that is why Judaism always speaks of freedom in the context of slavery. We were slaves in Egypt; God brought us out from there with a mighty hand and an outstretched arm. This is our story and we remember it not only on the seder night, but every single day. It is more than a history; it is the configuration, the meta-history within which we comprehend our existence now as then, within which the drama of all life and every life is framed. Here is the recurring pattern of servitude, oppression, liberation, journey, responsibility, promised land, and we are always somewhere in the middle of this process. From it, we derive the key lessons of our morality in that our nationhood commences not with the memory of a victory, but in the recollection of being downtrodden: *Remember God who freed you. In all other strangers, perceive the stranger you were, love your neighbor, follow justice.*

The individual life falls within the same framework and may be viewed according to the same pattern. Egypt (symbolic, of course) is my birth, and all my ensuing limitations. Indeed, the collective *mitzraim*, Egypt, is understood by dint of a word play to be each individual's *metzarim,* or narrow places. Thus in my personal slavery, I am the Pharaoh of my life and my Moses and my Aaron as well (though others may enslave me, too, or assist in my liberation). I seek my burning bush, I listen for the voice that declares, "I am the Lord your God who brought you out," I endeavor to bear my responsibilities, I travel toward my promised land, I search for my redemption.

Am I actually liberated, or at least changed, by going on this journey? The Children of Israel are notoriously complaining and unbending in the Bible. Are we any different as we traverse the wilderness of our own life? I have moments when I look at my own inner pharaohs and feel that they are sitting on their thrones exactly as they did when I was a boy, and that all my life's attempts have taken me no further than the place where I began. Yet perhaps just this is why we are required to repeat the cycle of slavery and departure every year. But do we in the end get anywhere? If the journey neither changes me nor leads me to greater freedom, is it worth it? Am I using my life properly? Will I return any different when I die from how I was when I first came?

The belief in free will is virtually a tenet of the Jewish faith. We, not God, make our decisions. Maimonides appears to speak for Judaism when he declares:

> Every human being may become righteous like Moses our Teacher, or wicked like Jeroboam; wise or foolish, merciful or cruel, niggardly or generous, and so with all other qualities. There is no one who coerces them or decrees what they are to do, or draws them to either of the two ways; but every person turns to the way which they desire, spontaneously and of their own volition.[5]

We are, then, precisely as free as we choose to be.

I often hear people wax lyrical in praise of Maimonides' defense of freedom. But is Maimonides right? Not all his readers have been convinced. Thus we find the following small note in the commentary *Haggadot Maimoniot* by Rabbi Meir HaCohen. Its author expresses puzzlement, observing that, in apparent contradiction to what the great sage has written, the Talmud teaches that:

> An angel appointed over pregnancy, and named Laylah (night), takes the drop [of seed to be impregnated and determines the details of the life that will develop from it] down to [such questions as] whether the person will be strong or weak or foolish or wise. This clearly implies that even these things are in the hands of Heaven.[6]

It is not difficult to appreciate what the *Haggadot Maimoniot* is saying. Surely experience tells us that there are a whole host of areas, including matters as intrinsic to our identity as physical ability, intellectual capacity, and traits of character, concerning which we have no freedom of choice at all. We would probably not ascribe them to the influence of an angel but rather to our genetic inheritance or the effect of our upbringing. But the implications are the same. How can we pretend that all these factors make no impact at all upon our supposedly absolute freedom of choice?

However, the *Haggadot Maimoniot* does not let the matter rest there. Following the beaten path of Jewish commentary, he seeks a harmonizing opinion. He refers us to his "teacher in Ensisheim," who finds a way of reconciling Maimonides' comments with the Talmud by saying that the latter speaks only of the difference in natural endowment between person and person, something indeed determined by birth, whereas Maimonides addresses the issue of what we do with the capacities we have. Here, the teacher maintains, we are indeed free and may make of them what we can and will. The significance of this distinction is brought home to us when we learn that the "teacher from Ensisheim" is none other than Rabbi Meir of Rothenburg, who was captured and held prisoner in the fortress of that name for some nineteen years until his death.[7] Nobody could be better placed to appreciate that one's opportunities may be limited, but that the challenge remains of making the most of the circumstances with which one has to contend. It is in this arena that the real battles of freedom are fought.

There are moments of glory. When a man like Natan Sharansky defies the entire repressive apparatus of a vast state, disciplines himself not to be swayed from total integrity of action by any emotional tie, however powerful, and discovers the fear of God in a prison cell, this surely proves that the capacity to exercise freedom in the name of right is ultimately inalienable. Even the mightiest tyrants know this; perhaps it is this very recognition that feeds the mania of their cruelty. In the secrecy of their heart they realize that the human spirit will always be stronger than they are, that, however many people they kill, there will always be a voice that speaks out in the name of a freedom which is infinitely stronger than they are. It is to this that Osip Mandelstam testified when he wrote, in exile under Stalin:

> You took away all the oceans and all the rooms.
> You gave me my shoe-size in earth with bars around it.
> Where did it get you? Nowhere.
> You left me my lips, and they shape words, even in silence.[8]

Yet the freedoms that matter to us are always hard won. Often we fight all our lives for victories that seem temporary and small, but it is the effort itself, as much as the change we do effect, both in the world and in ourselves, that testifies to the value of the struggle. For it is through that effort that our moral and spiritual personality matures and that, working with the raw materials of our birth, we become the person we are capable of being.

Journey Round the Seder Plate

KARPAS

Pesaḥ is *Ḥag Ha-aviv*, the Festival of Spring. Spring is present on our table in the greens that make up the *karpas* — in the parsley, watercress, or radish. Spring should be on our table with buds and flowers and songs from the Song of Songs — which speaks of the tiny grapes emerging on the vine and the small fruit on the nut tree.

Pesaḥ is the springtime of the mind. If lethargy is mental winter, then curiosity is spring. Everything is exciting, everything provokes a question. That is how we should be at the seder, like the child who asks why so often that its parents tear out their hair: Why is this night different? Why is there still slavery today? What is the purpose of freedom? How do we reach the Promised Land?

Let the spirit rejoice in the spring; let it go forth from captivity as the herd over-wintered in a musty barn goes out into the meadow and delights in the clean air. Let it rejoice in beauty.

And (crazily enough) I feel the same excitement when I think of emptying the kitchen cupboards and turning all their stuffy contents out. Most people hate Pesaḥ cleaning, but it has always seemed to me as much an adventure as a chore (though there are hours when it drives me mad). I want to see the shelves clear and the surfaces bare, to turn the cobwebs over to the winds and the pots and pans to the air, to let the freshness of the spring sweep the floors and repossess the cupboards and the drawers. It should be as if the wind that blows the blossom off the branches were to whisk away the dust and dirt and all the remnants of the leaven, filling every corner with an elemental brightness, so that when the seder is set, the season's fragrance floods the house.

Perhaps even that very worst part of Pesaḥ, the cleaning, should be understood as the springtime's service to God. *Karpas* is the offering of the spring.

MAROR

Maror is the herb of sorrow. As the Torah says, it represents bitterness, "because [the Egyptians] embittered [our ancestors'] lives with clay and bricks and all kinds of hard labor." Yet plants are growing things, and herbs are for healing: How can bitterness lead to growth and healing?

The message of the *maror* is as simple as its taste. Slavery is intolerable. It is forbidden to enslave another human being. It is forbidden to support any institution or government that does so. It is forbidden to be indifferent, as if such matters are not our concern. Just as we are not allowed to swallow the *maror* without chewing it, so we are not allowed to witness human misery and ignore it. We would use our time differently, care for others differently, and shop differently to avoid exploitation if we took that message to heart.

The *maror* has not only to be bitter; it must also be a herb, something that grows. Jewish law prohibits the use of artificial compounds and forbids eating the *maror* pickled or boiled to diminish its taste. It has to be as close to its natural state as possible. Something has to grow out of our misery; it is not enough to eat the *maror* and forget.

Many things may emerge from the experience of bitterness: the courage of a midwife in defying the edict that condemns a baby to death, the anger and compassion that mark the birth of leadership, the strength of spirit that ultimately overpowers tyrants. These are all responses to misery, all forms of moral and spiritual growth. That is why the *maror* on the seder plate must be a growing thing.

That, too, is why remembering the slavery in Egypt is so central to the Jewish experience. It is the touchstone of our values, the place where our moral vision begins. Through remembering what slavery is like, by recalling what it means to have our history impugned and our nationhood despised, we reaffirm the basic rights that are the due of every human being.

There is, however, a further, and more painful, aspect to the taste of the *maror*. This is its most intimate challenge to us — to grow within and through suffering. Few of us will be fortunate enough to live our whole lives free from any pretext for feeling bitter. We may, in fact, have much cause for bitterness, we may feel betrayed by life and robbed by death. Yet, fair or unfair, bitterness destroys; slowly but surely it devours the person who harbors it. It is one of life's greatest challenges to grow in spite of our anger, or grievance, or pain, however justified it may be. That is why the *maror* must be a herb of healing.

A man once came to see Rebbe Menaḥem Mendel of Kotzk. "I'm depressed and miserable and I want to put an end to my life," he said. The Rebbe reflected for a moment before replying, "The Talmud teaches that on seder night we must chew the *maror.* We have to taste it. We are forbidden to swallow it whole. This too you have to chew."[9]

The taste of bitterness may become the beginning of growth.

ḤAROSET

Like every other item on the seder plate, the *ḥaroset* expresses both something and its opposite. It is made of ingredients that represent the degradation of slavery and mixed out of fruits that remind us of the power of love. Consider this recipe, for example, from seventeenth-century Italy:

> Take apples or pears, cooked in water; hazelnuts or almonds; shelled chestnuts or walnuts; figs or raisins; and after cooking, grind them thoroughly and dissolve them in the strongest wine vinegar that can be found. Then mix in a bit of brick dust, in memory of the bricks which our fathers made in Egypt.[10]

Like the *maror,* but more subtly, the *ḥaroset* reminds us of the wretchedness of slavery. Hence the brick dust and the wine vinegar, in memory of the blood, toil, tears, and sweat of our ancestors. Some also say that the wine represents the blood of young children crushed to death between the heavy bricks. Perhaps the Jewish soldiers of the Union who could find nothing else to serve as *ḥaroset* during the American Civil War were right when they simply put a brick on the seder plate instead.[11]

There is another side to the *ḥaroset,* based on a seemingly strange rabbinic legend about the family life of the Children of Israel when they were slaves. To prevent them from having children, Pharaoh forbade the men to sleep at home. After the decree that all male babies were to be drowned, no one wanted to make his wife pregnant anyway. But the women thought differently. They made themselves attractive, went out into the fields where their husbands were working, and seduced them. These acts, at once of love and defiance, are remembered in the *haroset*, which according to some traditions must be made entirely of fruits and spices mentioned in the Song of Songs, that beautiful and enigmatic scroll in which woman's love for man and God's love for Israel form part of the same continuum.

The *haroset* therefore represents a double bond of slavery and love. It is at once both anguish and balm. No wonder we are instructed to dip our bitter herbs in it. Love makes it possible to survive even slavery. Love is the ultimate protector of faith and hope. Perhaps even God remembered the people in Egypt, not just because of their suffering, but out of love. For the Torah says of that moment that "God knew" (Ex. 3:7), using the very word with which it describes man's intimate knowledge of woman.

Countless testaments bear out the truth that love can make even the most appalling suffering more bearable. This is how Marie de Hennezel describes her work with those who are about to experience the ultimate human subservience, to death:

> I've been witness to limitless solitude; I've felt the pain of being unable to share certain times of distress, because there are levels of despair so deep that they cannot be shared. But alongside this suffering, I feel I have been enriched, that I've known moments of incomparable humanity and depth that I would not exchange for anything in the world, moments of sweetness and joy . . .[12]

THE EGG

When the seder is over and the guests have all gone, when the dirty dishes have been cleaned and the rests all removed, there remain on the table two items untouched, the egg and the bone. Everything else has been eaten, drunk or dipped in, but the egg and the bone, the beginning and the end, are intact.

They are part, of course, of a well-established symbolism. As the *Shulhan Arukh* puts it:

> On the seder plate are two cooked dishes, one in memory of the Paschal and one in memory of the Festival offering. The custom is to use meat and an egg. For the meat a shank bone is generally used, the custom being to roast it over the embers. The egg should be boiled (or roasted), and this is the custom in our city.[13]

To the vast majority of Jewish people today, however, the sacrifices they commemorate are neither evocative nor compelling. Yet the presence of the egg and the bone on the table is, strangely and powerfully, both. For they symbolize the future and the past and the close relationship between them, the story that has been told and the story that shall be told in its image. Their very neighborliness on the plate indicates the constant presence of the one within the other, just as the seder as a whole places the bones of ancient memories upon the shoulders of the children.

The egg is future, half encoded and half mystery. It is life's potential in the moment beyond. I have never forgotten the teacher who told our class how wonderful he found the knowledge that, when his daughter was born, she, like all baby girls, already carried inside her the eggs of the next generation. On the seder table, the egg is life cracking open and unfurling, dividing and growing. It heralds a joy which is sensuous and spiritual at once. On this spring festival it contains all the excitement of the fresh season, the odor of warm earth in the morning and the fragrant fertility that follows the rains. It is the lung's delight in the scent of spice and the heart's dance with the leaf, the buds, and the wind. It is the soul's setting forth, the defiant affirmation of a lifelong desire, a quickening once again at the thought of the quest: "Arise, my beloved, my fair one, and come away" (Song. 2:13).

Yet Judaism also sees in the egg a symbol of mourning. Is this just another example of the heavy hand of kill-joy religion? Surely not! Rather it expresses a shrewd insight into the interrelationships of time. It reminds us that our journeys invariably lead us not simply into the future, but into the future by way of the past. The bone is not just next to the egg; its cultural and spiritual DNA are within it. All our travels out are also travels back. Even if it is the very farthest point on the map that calls to us, it does so because we intuitively hope that it will also prove to be home. It is always the secret of our own consciousness for which we search, and it leads us back, even in our setting out, to our ancestors, to their journeys and their God. For they are within us, birthright and burden. The very shape of the egg hints at this, defying us to tell the difference between end and beginning. In our going out is our coming home, and home itself is a beginning. We go back to Egypt, we rejoin our elders, in order to set out with them once again. And wherever we go, we will travel no farther than they; time and again we go back to begin with them anew. No one fails to set out, but no one arrives. The Promised Land will always be beyond the mountain where we die.

THE BONE

> And [the Lord] said unto me: "Son of man,
> shall these bones live?" And I answered:
> "O Lord God, thou knowest."
>
> Ezek. 37:3

The egg's companion is the bone. Carrying the bones of the past may frequently feel onerous, but there is also a mystery in their presence beside us. Like, I imagine, everyone who mourns relatives and who wishes they had known them better before they died, I love to learn about the members of my family who are no more. Someone unexpectedly says, "Of course I knew him." I ask how and when, and what it is that they remember, and am glad that flesh has been put on bone, a pen in a hand, a look of surprise on a face. The feelings evoked are similar, if vaguer, with more distant generations; people are drawn to the graveyards where their ancestors lie, they treasure a book or an ornament that once belonged to a great-grandmother, to an unspecified relation. Perhaps our sense of kinship expands as it recedes in time; the very fact that the bones are those of our people becomes sufficient to make them in some way ours. Inevitably they haunt us, but not with an evil haunting. There is nothing morbid about their presence among us, their voices inside us; one way of putting it might be to say that their poetry is ours. This is what Ezekiel conveyed in his great vision, which the Talmud described as both parable and truth at once:

> The hand of the Lord was upon me, and the Lord carried me out in a spirit, and set me down in the midst of the valley, and it was full of bones . . . And he said unto me: "Son of man, shall these bones live?" And I answered: "O Lord God, thou knowest" (37:1–3).

Whether, and how deeply, they live depends on how thoughtfully we care for them. In talmudic times burial practices were different from how they are now. Initially, the body was placed in the family vault; later, the bones were gathered by the closest relatives and placed in an ossuary.

Macabre as this custom may seem to us today, there may well have been a loving honesty in the performance of the task. It would certainly have been honest, because there can be no closer confrontation with the actuality of death. It may also have been loving by virtue of the careful devotion required in gathering the bones, and the memories, together: *This was the knee on which I sat, this was the hand which seemed so big when I held mine against it.*

We may be at a greater distance from their actual bones, but the challenge to us is the same: How lovingly can we gather up our ancestors' experiences? How can we enable them to speak to us? Will they still sing? Will they travel with us as we set out on their journey? Will these bones live?

It is sometimes thought that the bone must be an impediment to the egg, that it is both an opposite and a hindrance, but this is not the case. New life is all the more vigorous when old life walks in its footfalls.

MATZAH

Matzah is the bread of paradox. At the start of the seder we hold up the matzah and say, "This is the bread of affliction which our ancestors ate in Egypt; let all who are hungry come and eat." It makes sense that this hard biscuit, made only of flour and water, should be the food of slaves. "Because poor people, in the severity of their destitution, will take some flour, knead it, and bake it into unleavened cakes which they eat immediately," wrote Shmuel HaNagid, who probably knew first hand the harshness of servitude and exile.[14] Yet later on we remind ourselves of how "our ancestors' dough did not have time to rise before the King of the king of kings, the Holy Blessed One, was revealed to them and redeemed them."[15] Thus we learn that matzah is the bread of redemption and that its simple taste is in fact the flavor of freedom. Which is it? And what does it tell us about freedom?

For there is, perhaps, a paradox at the heart of freedom. We squander it, we fail to recognize it at all, if we have never experienced anything else. Ask someone who has been ill what it feels like to get up and walk around after many weeks in bed. This is how Milton Steinberg describes looking up at the sky on his first trip outdoors after a severe illness:

> In that instant I looked about me to see whether anyone else showed on his face the joy, almost the beatitude, I felt. But no, there they walked — men

and women and children, in the glory of the golden flood, and so far as I could detect, there was none to give it heed.[16]

We only experience the real taste of freedom if we have first eaten the bread of slavery. That is why at the beginning of the seder we call the matzah the bread of poverty, and at the end, the bread of redemption.

There is another paradox to the matzah. Matzah is unleavened bread made from specified kinds of flour. Strangely enough, it has to be made from the very same ingredients that constitute leaven; both of them are flour and water mixed. The difference between them lies not, therefore, in the ingredients, but in the way those ingredients are mixed. To make leaven they are left to rise; to make matzah the slightest rising is stringently avoided.

At one level, slavery and freedom are outer states, and we all know the difference between them. But at another, the extent to which we experience freedom, or slavery, depends on us. The issue is not the raw ingredients of our life but how we mix them in our mind. After all, we talk about being the slave of pleasure, or of our appetites or vices, where the tyranny comes not from outside us but from within. How much outer freedom we have may well depend on others, but how much inner freedom we can find is up to us. The challenge may be enormous, but it is here in the struggle between fate and character that our true degree of freedom is defined. As Viktor Frankl wrote:

> We who lived in concentration camps can remember the men who walked through the huts comforting others, giving away their last piece of bread. They may have been few in number but they offer sufficient proof that everything can be taken from a man but one thing: the last of the human freedoms — to choose one's attitude in a given set of circumstances, to choose one's own way. . . .[17]

The Song at the Sea

Moses and the Children of Israel answered you in song . . .

Ex. 15:1

Each year the sound of the Shirah, the Song at the Sea, brings back memories of my grandfather. My grandfather gave his first sermon when he was only three. Family legend has it that he climbed on to the table, donned a handkerchief as *tallis,* and addressed a sole and somewhat reluctant listener, his brother, who presently left the room, revealing his equally early preference for the forests and all things green. My grandfather's last sermon was, I believe, delivered at the *Ne'ilah* service in the Fasanenstrasse Synagogue in Berlin when he was approaching ninety years of age. Of all the themes about which he spoke in his long life it is that of song which most appealed to his spirit. We are, he would say, *ein singendes Volk,* a people of song. "Sing to the eternal a new song," he would quote (Ps. 96:1); this was the theme of his life.

Twice in the year, on Shabbat Shirah, the Sabbath of Song, and on the seventh day of Pesaḥ, we read from the Torah the Song at the Sea. But we refer to the song morning and evening every single day in our prayers. "Moses and the children of Israel answered you in song," we say. I often used to wonder why the liturgy uses the word "answered," rather than simply "sang." Maybe the reason is because song has been *the* answer, *the* response par excellence of the Jewish people, not just once long ago at the Red Sea, but again and again throughout a harsh and challenging history.

The song begins in the most unlikely of places. The Children of Israel have left Egypt. They have traveled three days' journey and the desert is all about them; as Pharaoh cruelly observes, it has closed them in. That is why he decides to pursue them with chariots manned by the best officers and drawn by the strongest horses. As the Children of Israel hear the sound of beating hooves and begin to discern the distant chariots swiftly racing nearer, they realize that they are cut off from behind by the Egyptians and from in front by the sea. They must have felt utter terror.

Two and a half-thousand years later when the Jews were expelled from England, a sea captain promised a number of them safe passage across the

Channel. Having tricked them on board, he deposited them at low tide on a sandbank far out from the shore, abandoning them with the taunt that God who divided the waters for Moses could surely do so again. They all, of course, perished.

Jewish history is filled with the experience of being trapped. However, it is not only in our collective past, but also as individuals in our internal life, that we feel surrounded by troubles and cut off from all help. When life seems unbearable and everything looks hopeless we say, "I simply can't go on," or, "I don't know where to turn." It may be a particular painful event that makes us feel that way, or a general mood of hopelessness. We feel trapped between our private desert and the impassable sea, while all around, our troubles close in about us. In Pasternak's novel, *Doctor Zhivago*, bereft of his beloved Lara and looking out on the bleak winter of the Russian revolution, writes:

> When the great white world
> Is hidden by the frost on the window,
> The hopelessness of sorrow
> Is even more like the desert of the sea.[18]

Here we are then, between the desert and the sea. What do we do? Our thoughts spin round and lead us nowhere. We may cry out in complaint, "Why did you do this to me; what's the point of it all?" We may give way to despair or turn to anger and blame. The Children of Israel round upon Moses, "If only you had left us alone! If only we'd never left Egypt!" (Ex. 14:11–12).

Yet in our hopelessness there may come a moment, occasioned perhaps by sheer exhaustion, or engendered by some inner movement toward stillness and submission, when we fall silent. In this very silence something may happen that enables us to go on. I once overheard a conversation between a professor of music and one of his students: "The songs have all dried up inside me," the student complained. "It's like getting blood out of a stone; there isn't any music left." "Just be still for a while and listen; just be silent and wait," the teacher responded. "The songs will take strength and return." So it was with the Children of Israel at the sea. Moses said to them: "God will fight on your behalf; as for you, be silent" (Ex. 14:14). It was in that silence that it became possible for them to go forward. That was when the song began, in the silence before it started.

Where there is song even the waters of the heaviest seas can divide, forming a protective wall on either side. A number of years ago, the BBC screened an amateur film made to mark the passing of twenty-five years since the Aberfan disaster. A huge heap of slag had slid down the mountainside, submerging the local school and killing over a hundred and fifty children. The village was left bereft of almost all its little ones; even the street sweeper had been seen to weep and say that he missed them messing up his leaves. The film was not a professional production; it was made by the people of the village and was simple and moving. It included an interview with a mother of a child who had died in the disaster. She was asked, "What helped you find the strength to carry on?" The film showed her walking beside the mountain stream that flowed through this lovely Welsh valley. "It was the waters of this river that gave me the strength," she replied. The waters had spoken to her; they had sung to her as they ran between the small stones and tumbled over the rocks. For her, as for the Children of Israel long before, "The waters were . . . a wall, on their right hand and on their left" (Ex. 14:22).

It is the songs that begin in the silence of helplessness, in moments of surrender, when inspiration nevertheless overtakes us and courage comes upon us, that have carried us across the many seas we have traversed since then. That was the song that bore up my grandparents and all the family when they fled Germany and began life anew in a strange country. That was the song that never left him: "Sing to the Eternal a new song."

On my grandfather's grave are the words from the Psalms, "I shall sing to the Lord in my life; I shall make music to my God as long as I live" (104:33). This he surely did. But the Hebrew also bears a slightly different translation, because the prefix *be* can either mean "in" or indicate agency and signify "with." Perhaps the song that really bears us up, the song that carries us through the seas of fear and hopelessness, is the song we sing not only *in,* but *with* our life, *with* all our being. Such songs are truly a wall against the rushing waters.

The Song of Songs

Tell me, you whom my soul loves,
where do you pasture your flocks,
where do you make them lie down in the afternoon?

Song. 1:7

The Song of Songs, traditionally read on the Sabbath in the middle of Pesaḥ, describes a joyful and wondrous encounter with the world around us that takes place on every level of our being.

The book is permeated with a sensuous delight in the land itself, its plants and animals, their form and color, their motion and scent. The fig tree, the apple tree, and the vine, the nut tree and the lilies — they are not merely seen but experienced. They give forth their fragrance and are breathed into the very being. The doves, the foxes, and the deer are observed, but not with a dispassionate eye. Their appearance and comportment herald the change of seasons and create our sense of time, the passing of winter, the time to draw close, the time to flee away. Thus nature fashions the breadth and depth of our belonging in the world.

Thus, too, the natural world becomes the context for the mysterious and compelling love relationship that the book describes. "Trace the tracks of the flock," the girl is told by her lover (1:8). "He feeds among the lilies," says she of her beloved (6:3). "Beneath the apple tree I aroused you," says the girl (8:5). But the pastures and orchards and gardens are more than the setting for love. They provide more too than the imagery, intimate as it is, through which the lovers describe one another, eyes, hair, and all the body. Their love is simply bound up in the bond of these places, these shapes and sights that describe it, the heap of wheat that is her belly, the fawns her breasts resemble. In the same way those places, those hills and trees and flowers where we met . . . are haunted by our love.

Nor is nature part of our personal story only; it is the landscape out of which our people's story grows. The passionate belonging that a beloved landscape evokes becomes part of the national memory whose images and legends are defined by its pools and fountains, beasts and birds. Like a horse among the chariots of Pharaoh, like the palanquin Solomon made of the trees of Lebanon, so the national story and the natural image interpenetrate the web of association and response. In this manner, where we are becomes part of who we are in the consciousness of the group.

Most profoundly, nature is the setting for our spiritual life. The Song of Songs is a work haunted by mystery and wonder. Just as its pathways lead us to the human beloved, so they impel us toward the elusive presence of God. Where precisely God is remains as inexplicit as the intimate encounter of love; both are ultimately "a locked garden, a fountain sealed." The garden and the fountain are not only the haunt of desire but the habitation of the spirit.

All of these bonds are expressed in the Song of Songs through the beauty of the Land of Israel. But every land has its beauty, every people has its poets, and the relationships evoked are at least similar if not the same. For all of us, therefore, whoever we are, the loss if we destroy, neglect, or simply allow ourselves to become ignorant of our environment is devastating. It is not just a matter of having no more pretty flowers. We forfeit at once our most intimate and our most profound identity, our physical, emotional, and spiritual connection with life.

Love and Hate

All love seeks union, all hatred severance. The Song of Songs portrays a world in which all things are related to a single fluent desire, from the small fruits on the trees to the souls of man and woman, entangled in the tresses of love.

Love has eyes to discover the beauty in all things — in plant and animal, man and woman. The Song of Songs is full of herbs, spices, and fragrant plants. Some are native to Israel, such as the lily of the valley and the lilies that grow among the thorns. Others have been brought from afar amongst the "powders of the merchant" to perfume love's bower. There are the gardens too, the orchards and vineyards where the vines are fragrant with their tiny grapes. All of these places are known to the author with the intimacy that comes of deep familiarity and appreciation.

"I adjure you by the gazelles and by the hinds of the field . . ." (2:7). As the maiden knows the plants, so she understands the rhythm of the life of the animals. The movements of the gazelle conform to the seasons. Habitually secretive, it grows bold in the time of desire, appearing "behind our wall, looking in at the windows, glancing through the lattice." But if the hour is not yet ripe it is adjured to flee to the safety of the hills and blend with the night. The sudden appearance of the deer brings to those who love them not only a moment of mystery and grace, but also, with the swiftness and the beauty of their passage, an image of the soul's yearning for the invisible blessings of life itself, and God.

Amidst these wonders, a girl dreams of, seeks for, speaks with her beloved. We do not know exactly what happens; it is impossible to differentiate between actuality and desire, absence and presence. Moments of meeting seem equally to be moments of parting. But at the heart of the Song of Songs is the yearning for a coming together, a union which transcends what life permits, as the sealed fountain in the midst of the garden draws love toward itself but can never be reached. Like those who pursue the fleeing deer, the feet of the girl, roused from her bed, follow the lover she cannot find.

The Song of Songs celebrates more than the joining of one man and one woman; the act of generation is itself a meeting of generations: "I seized him and I did not release him until I had brought him to my mother's house, to the room where I was conceived" (3:4). The present will create the future in the image of the past, in a continuity that is as reassuring as it is exhilarating. This will happen amidst the scents and sights, roots and blossoms, birds and beasts of a land that has been known to parent and child like the beating of their heart.

But hatred divides, dissevers, and destroys. Nowhere is this revealed more bitterly than in the dismemberment of war.

It may seem trivial to speak of the destruction of plants and animals while human beings are torn to shreds, but this, too, is part of the great devastation. During the war in Bosnia, a correspondent from Belgrade mourned the death of her potted plants; she had been unable to give them water. A young girl, Zlata, from Sarajevo, wrote in her diary of how she wept for the death of her pet bird. These things are small indications of a much greater dying. Strangely, it is often just such "small" tragedies that enable us to begin to weep; the greater deaths are too shocking, a horror too awful to credit.

We know that there are parts of the world where weapons have been tested or used and nothing grows properly any more; in the case of nuclear weapons this will continue for millennia. War strips the valley of its lilies; its animals grow deformed and die. A recent film about the history of Serbia showed a foal caught in crossfire, dancing in terrified panic, certain to perish.

Hatred tears people apart. It divides them, then destroys them. So-called "ethnic cleansing" routinely involves the separation of men and women, these to one fate and those to another, these destined to a life of misery and those to immediate death. Perhaps the worst anguish is that of those who have been parted from their families but don't know where they have been taken, whose sons and daughters died or vanished on the march, whose husbands were removed at gun point. All too often the agony of not knowing what happened to them is followed by the misery of not even being told their place of execution.

Hatred separates, kills, and then dismembers. In the Song of Songs the parts of the body are praised for their beauty; eyes are like doves, lips like threads of scarlet, breasts like twin deer. Bombs and grenades blast limb from limb. Later, when slowly the survivors begin to return to rebuild the remains of their homes and plant their abandoned fields, buried land mines tear off their hands and feet.

It is the sign of great peace when people are able to marry in the village where their parents were married too, when a girl can bring her lover to the room where she herself was conceived. Wars and persecution sweep whole peoples from their ancestral homes. Who knows if they will ever return? If they do, who knows if it will be possible for love to be there, amidst the graves and ghosts? War sets death in the middle of the bond between heart and home.

Does God have any place in such a landscape? Love brings God near; hatred drives God away. God can make a home in the chambers of the heart, but the heart can also close its doors and leave the spirit homeless in an alien world.

We can either contribute toward the unity of all things, appreciating their togetherness in the single flow of life that animates all creation. Or we can blow everything apart and sever ourselves and all life from its source.

Welcoming Elijah

> Old message-bearer, Elijah,
> I have lost all the addresses,
> So now I write a letter to you.
> Surely you have not forgotten an old friendship,
> When, as a child, I would open the door for you.
>
> Kadya Molodowsky[19]

The opening of the door connects the beginning of Pesah with its end. At the beginning of the festival we open the door to Elijah, and at the end we speak of the coming of the Messiah.

How seriously should we take the moment when the door is opened at the seder? Every year, so I'm told, my father-in-law downs the wine in Elijah's cup without anyone ever noticing, and the children are amazed at the sight of the empty glass. My son was convinced last year that the invisible prophet had taken a sizable sip and that the level in the goblet on our table had sunk by at least a centimeter. But what happens if someone actually does come in? Once during a seder in Botchki, the local urchins succeeded in pushing a smelly he-goat through the open door into the house of the pious Reb Shnyer. Reb Shnyer proved equal to the event and, in the joyous and accepting manner of a true *hasid*, declared that the animal must surely possess a portion of the sacred soul of the redeemer and therefore be a true harbinger of the great coming.[20]

The redemptive theme of Pesah culminates on the eighth day in the reading of Isaiah's vision of the coming of the Messiah. We thus affirm the core principle of the haggadah, and of the Jewish view of history in general, that we progress *mishibud lige'ulah,* from slavery to redemption, and that time does not simply take us round in circles but onward to a higher goal. Indeed, many of the early illustrated haggadot include portraits of the Messiah, shown as a rather sweet old gentleman arriving at the gates of Jerusalem on his proverbial donkey. The pictures suggest that though the venerable man may indeed possess the secret of redeeming humankind, he certainly hasn't mastered the art of riding his recalcitrant mount.

How should we understand the messianic aspect of our Judaism? Like, I expect, most Jews today, I do not believe in a personal Messiah. The doctrine has caused the Jewish people considerable harm. Perhaps it is for this reason that the Talmud warns us not to try to calculate the coming of the end. But even the latest among the talmudic rabbis cannot have foreseen the constant harassment to which the Jewish people have been subject over why we "have not accepted Jesus." Even today, I am still sometimes asked about it in a tone of disappointed disbelief. Then there have been the many "false" Messiahs, deluded and deluding by their claims, culminating in the mass disruption to Jewish life occasioned by the fervor, and disappointment, that followed Sabbetai Sevi.

Yet the messianic idea is an essential element in the Jewish view of life. For it is this that gives us the vision of a different and a better world. This vision, of a time of justice and peace, of a time when none shall hurt or destroy, a time in which the vindication of truth will be manifest not in triumph but in harmony, for, ". . . the earth shall be full of the knowledge of the Lord as the waters cover the sea" (Isa. 11:9). This vision gives us our sense of purpose. That sense of purpose — the conviction that history is not just a succession of evils or a pointless meandering in time until the earth is eventually destroyed, but that we have a goal to work toward — makes our every action meaningful. That knowledge that what we do matters, that we either bring the age of justice and peace nearer or drive it further away, gives us our sense of commitment. And the vision, the purpose, and the commitment together mark the Jewish view of life, with its characteristic tone of hope. For even though it tarry, we still believe that the Messianic Age will come. Even though the world shows no sign of imminent perfection, even though it is full of cruelty and violence, we still maintain our vision. For Judaism perceives another world, not just in the realms beyond, but incipient in this world; and our prophets, though torn by the dissonance between what they see and what they dream, have always remained the harbingers of its ultimate reality.

We all know how easy it is to lose our hope and sense of purpose. The teachers and poets whose words are recorded in the haggadah knew what times of darkness meant. Ben Zoma lived and died between the Roman war in which Jerusalem was sacked and the Roman war in which much of the remnant population perished. Surely this is why he emphasized the word *all* in the injunction to speak about the Exodus "*all* the days of your life," insisting that it must include the nights as well. The poet Yannai lived in Israel during the withering impoverishment which followed the collapse of the *Pax Romana*. Surely this is why he concluded his poem "And it came to pass at midnight" (which is included among the songs in the Ashkenazi haggadah) with the prayer that God should make the darkness of the night bright as the light of day. We are a people who has frequently known the meaning of night. It is because of the messianic vision of the prophets that we have remained a people of hope and purpose nonetheless.

The art of Judaism, however, is not simply to have visions. It insists that all of us, in every generation, have a responsibility toward their fulfillment. This is the meaning of so many of the stories about Elijah, that venerable hero of two thousand years of folklore, to whom we open the door at our seder. I like to think that Elijah comes to every home at the seder, as he comes to the naming of every child. Perhaps Elijah comes not, as the tradition has it, to see whether this is the child who will be the Messiah, but to see the part of the Messiah that is in every child, and to look for the fragment of redemption which is to be found in every home. For there is not one of us who doesn't have something to contribute. At my seder last year we passed around a plate and each of us put on it a slip of paper on which we had previously written something we wanted to do to make the world better. One person said, "I don't want to part from anyone without their knowing that I value and appreciate them." Everyone matters; all of us are children of the same vision, and all of us are responsible for its fulfillment.

Every action matters. The Talmud tells how Elijah and Rabbi Broka the Visionary meet in the marketplace of Beit Lefet. "Is anyone here destined for the world to come?" asks the rabbi. "No," says Elijah, but just then a man appears in the square, and he changes his answer. Rabbi Broka runs after him and discovers that he's a jailer. He takes personal care of the prisoners in his charge. Every night he ensures that they are protected from assault, an abuse to which prisoners have always been vulnerable. Elijah then tells Rabbi Broka that two other men have now entered the marketplace who are also destined for the world to come. "Who are they?" he asks. They turn out to be jesters who cheer people up by making them laugh and settling the quarrels between them.[21] The message is that there is no person to whom it doesn't matter what we say and no situation in which it doesn't matter what we do.

We must never give up. If we are tempted to do so we should remember the story of Elijah and the thief. Elijah sits down wearily on a bench, tired of his harbinger's task. Next to him sits a sprightly fellow whose mind is clearly busy concocting plans. "What's your profession?" asks the prophet. "I'm a thief and I'm planning my next job," replies the man. "If this fellow doesn't give up," thinks Elijah, "how can I, entrusted with God's business, possibly think of doing so?"[22] Yet we often do want to give up, and have to learn to keep going until our dying day, until we literally lack the strength to do otherwise.

For everyone matters, everything matters, and every moment is an opportunity. This commitment to life and its value is the immediate expression of the sense of purpose that derives from the messianic vision when the world will be ruled in harmony and no one shall hurt or destroy.

Kadya Molodowsky wrote her letter to Elijah in 1942. It continues:

> Reckless, I tore up all traces of you
> And also the reach of my sky,
> And also the warmth of belief,
> And now my poems stand naked . . .[23]

We must not tear up the paper on which as a child we wrote down Elijah's address. Without the reaches of our sky, how can we manage to live?

THE COUNTING OF THE OMER

Beneath the Husk

My heart saw you and believed in you
   as if it had been standing at Sinai;
I sought you in my visions and descending
     in my clouds your glory passed me by . . .

Yehudah Halevi[1]

I have visited the Jewish Museum in Amsterdam at least ten times and am always moved. The very building resonates with memory. Housed in a number of small synagogues joined together, the illuminated books, ḥanukiyot, shofarot, and other Judaica inhabit the rooms where once their owners gathered to pray, before they fled, or perished, or went into hiding. Perhaps that is why everything feels so immediate; all these objects were made, acquired, and used with love. Among my favorite items — I transgress the commandment "Thou shalt not covet" every time I go there — are two beautiful *omer* counters. One is a delicately illustrated book, with a page for every date; the other contains a small scroll with a handle to turn until the correct number of days and weeks is displayed in the window. Both refer just beneath the enumeration of each day to the spiritual quality which it represents.

There is nothing ostensibly spiritual about the *omer*. The very name *omer*, in fact, denotes a quantity, a dry measure used chiefly for grains. The seven weeks of the *omer* are the seven weeks of the barley harvest. According to the Mishnah, the first swath of new grain was cut amidst solemn festivities at sunset after the first day of Passover, and an *omer*'s amount of it was offered on the altar the next morning. Until this offering was brought, no one was allowed to eat grain from the new crop. The Torah refers to the counting of seven weeks from the bringing of the *omer* until the festival of Shavuot. Thus what was originally a way of marking the harvest season became a manner of connecting the liberation from Egypt with the receiving of the Torah.

The kabbalists transformed this historical journey into a personal struggle to free ourselves from our inner slavery. They devoted each of the seven weeks of the counting of the *omer* to the respective purification of one of the seven *sefirot*, or spiritual centers, through which the divine energy operates in all of us and in the world. They dedicated each day of each week to one attribute within each of these *sefirot*, which contain in themselves aspects of all of the others. They counted the *sefirot* in descending order beginning with *hesed*, loving-kindness, and ending with *malkhut*, sovereignty, reflecting the passage of energy from above to below. In this way the enumeration of the days became a process of inner cleansing to ready ourselves for God's presence, as expressed in the solemn prayer *Ribbono shel Olam:*

> You commanded us through Moses your servant to enumerate the counting of the *omer* to cleanse us from our husks and from our impurities . . . May it therefore be your will, O Lord our God and God of our ancestors, that by the merit of the counting of the *omer*, which I count this day, there be perfected all that I have blemished in the *sefirah* of loving-kindness within loving-kindness, and that I may be purified and sanctified by the holiness on high . . .[2]

Thus the forty-nine days that separate the liberation from Egypt and the giving of the Torah at Sinai came to represent not only an outer but also an inner journey. We travel them both — the historical and the personal — together.

We all have "husks," we all spend much of our lives out of touch with the inner kernel of our better selves. How often do we really live from the heart? How frequently do we feel that our mind is working at full power? How much of the time are we spiritually alert? Most of us struggle for just a few minutes of such inspiration in a day, a week, or a month. The pathways to our heart and soul easily get blocked and clearing them is hard. We all need a way of cleansing ourselves, of washing out our heart and mind, both for our own sake and for the sake of those who have to live with us. The counting of the *omer* offers an opportunity to do just this. We don't have to follow all the intricacies of the kabbalistic system; we can choose our task for the day or the week, taking a few minutes to consider one quality that matters to us. Why am I so short-tempered at the moment? Why am I finding it hard to listen properly? Why have I lost my sense of beauty?

Sometimes we have to make a conscious effort to understand ourselves in order to regain our inner balance. We need to think through why we are letting a certain train of thought so dominate our mental activity. But sometimes we simply have to let go and be. I remember a holiday where I

172

took five minutes each night just to stand outside and listen. It was a beautiful place; an owl called in the darkness, a sea bird cried as it flew over the nearby water, waves splashed across the pebbles, the grass around me was alive with a constant rushing and rustling. The poison in my system was washed away. I was no longer beset by the same irritations; for a while the pressure didn't matter. I felt I had the ability to let go, understand, be generous. Something clean had entered me and blessed me with a fresh perspective. Something had been put right in my capacity for love. Admittedly, most of us can only rarely visit a place like that, but five minutes of special time can be worthwhile anywhere, in silence, in meditation, with music, to liberate the mind.

Rebbe Menaḥem Mendel of Kotsk once asked his followers where God was. "Everywhere, of course," they retorted, shocked that their teacher should even pose so elementary a question. "No," he replied, "God is where we let God in." As we create space inside ourselves, God is able to descend to meet us there. If we are full up with ourselves, how can God get in? Of course, we shouldn't expect a great revelation, but every life has its moments. God is there behind our clouds, descends into our heart, meets us in a word, in a fine morning, in some inconspicuous act of kindness. It could be anything, anywhere.

Teach Us to Number Our Days

I wasted time, and now doth Time waste me.

Shakespeare, *Richard II*[3]

What does it take to make us really value life?

Some years ago I spent a few days in Aberdeen Royal Infirmary recovering from severe food poisoning. I was considered infectious and put in a room on my own. Family and friends were far away, and I rejected the offer of a visit from the hospital chaplain with an alacrity of which I now feel ashamed. I've foregotten the discomfort, but I recall the time as a period of sanctuary. I was able to consider my life in a way which the sheer busyness of being in good health, having a young family, and holding communal responsibilities doesn't allow. I thought all the usual thoughts — about how swiftly the years pass, about how I'd come to be and do the things I'd ended up being and doing. I felt mellow, grateful. But one question beset me: How much of my life was I wasting? How many people and how many things was I taking for granted? The night before I was discharged I made a list of everything I'd learned from being in hospital. At the top was the need to value life more.

I often visit cemeteries, but I have never once returned home from a funeral feeling cynical. Every time, after talking to the mourners, after speaking about the person who has died, the love given, and the memories left, I go home thinking, "Use life! Make the most of it while you have it!" I hear the same thing from people who work in hospices. Companionship with the dying may be painful, but it is also humbling and life-enhancing. It forces us to focus on what really matters. It makes us reconsider our priorities. It teaches us to live.

One of the reasons we count the days of the *omer* is to remind ourselves that every day counts.

Sometimes we do indeed count the hours. This is true in times of special excitement. As the weeks turn to days before a baby is due, we wonder anxiously how much longer it will be. A small child cannot wait for a birthday and asks every few minutes, "Is it Monday yet?" It is also true in times of anguish. Tomorrow her husband goes off to the war; wherever she goes she hears the ticking of her watch. Tomorrow brings the critical operation; what kind of future will there be after that?

Counting the hours is not the same as making the hours count. Nor is longing for tomorrow, or mourning for yesterday, the same as living this day well. A good friend of our family used to say, "Never wish people a long life; wish them a good life." He was a doctor and had seen too much suffering to think that a long life was always a desirable thing. To linger for years in a state of increasing loneliness and ill health may be far from a blessing. It is not necessarily the quantity of our life that is important, but the quality of it. Of course, Judaism, with its cheerful toast of, "*L'hayim!* — To Life!" and its greeting for major later-in-life birthdays of, "*Bis hundertzwanzig* — May you live to be a hundred and twenty*" (like Moses), does encourage us to wish for a long life. But, more importantly, Judaism teaches us to use what time we have well. The length of our life is a mystery and belongs to the secret things of God, but the fullness of our life depends largely on what we make of it. This is the meaning of the words in the evening prayer: the Torah is "our life and the length of our days." In one way they make no sense; our days all have the same length. But in another, they make every sense; the way we live our days shortens them or lengthens them, empties them of purpose or fills them with value. Live them positively, in a spirit of generosity and responsibility, and they become warm and creative. Drag ourselves through them, and we squander them for ourselves and waste them for those around us. The message is very simple: "Look after the quality of your days, and the quality of your years will look after itself." Beyond that there are no guarantees.

Clearly, it is not always so easy. Sometimes we just can't will ourselves to be positive. There are times when we feel low and depressed, when we see the worst in ourselves and others. Hamlet speaks for most of us when he says, "O God, I could be bounded in a nutshell, and count myself a king of infinite space, were it not that I have bad dreams."[4] We all have bad dreams and sink into low spirits; in that kind of mood even the most exciting spaces soon shrink down to the dimensions of a nutshell. This is inevitable, it is only human. It is also why we need to be reminded so often of our values.

When I lose my sense of purpose, I sometimes think of a conversation I had with a friend some years ago. I bumped into her quite by chance and, on asking how things were, learned that she was on her way back home after giving blood. She said, "I did it because I felt completely useless today. Then I thought to myself, I can always give blood. At least I'll know I've done something worthwhile." Giving blood gave her back her sense of value. Since then, when I feel low, I try to do something simple for someone else. The motivation may be selfish, but it stops me feeling worthless and my spirits soon begin to rise.

The laws regarding the counting of the *omer* are very strict: every day matters and not one may be missed. Not to waste a single day should be our ideal in life. Times of mourning are surely different. But in general we could perhaps say that a day is wasted when we've done nothing that brings happiness or good to others and nothing that brings a sense of purpose to ourselves.

The end of the *omer* takes us to Mount Sinai, the site of the great Revelation. Of course, the destination is important. But, as Rashi reminds us when he points out that the text says the Children of Israel came to Mount

Sinai on *this* day, not on *that* day, the giving of the Torah is never only *then*, but always *now*. Our life is *this* day, not *the other day*, nor *one day* in the future. If we always want to be somewhere else, we end up an absentee from our own existence.

Counting the *omer* means counting today, for it is always today we have to make count.

Purity

> Your worldly deeds should shine;
> They should be as luminous as sapphires.
>
> Rebbe Meshullam Ziche of Zhinkhov[5]

The ḥasidic teachers never regard puns as beneath them; if the words of the Torah are sacred, then their sounds are significant too. "U*sefar*tem," says the Torah simply, "You shall count [the *omer*] (Lev. 23:15)." But they saw the hidden *sapphire* in the instruction and taught that the purpose of the counting of the *omer* was to make our deeds so pure they shone like precious stones.

Purity is not a popular word. It is associated with abstruse rituals on the one hand and puritanical attitudes on the other. It is the sort of concept that gives religion a bad name. But it means a lot to me, if only because I know what it can be like to feel just the opposite — impure, ugly, insensitive, obtuse. Those are the times when I hate myself, when all the best parts of me seem dead, when I wish I could either hide myself away or wash myself out. Purity, on the other hand, has to do with feeling aware, in touch, and inwardly clean.

To be pure is an unattainable ideal. At best it is a state we gain for a moment only to lose for a week, or a month, or sometimes even more. But occasionally I do have an intimation of how it might feel to be pure. It is like the song of the birds after a sleepless night, like the relief of dawn after restless, haunted hours. The birds pierce the cold air with clean, clear cries. They call out to the world with a simplicity people cannot emulate. Their songs seem at one with the timbre of the light, sharper in the first dark, soft-

ening in the brightening dawn. It is the same at dusk, when the wide rever-
berations of the many birds yield to the piercing calls and sweeping flights
of the few, as night settles over them and their perches. The simple being of
dawn and dusk and its fine articulation by the birds makes the whole confusion of human life, the very turmoil of conscience itself, seem like a sin.

At such times a prayer goes through me: Clean me with healing shame;
purify me with your awe. Let it scour my mind, wash my heart and leave
me with the simple blessing of readiness. Then fill my spirit with the reflection of your beauty, shining back from all that you have made. Let me
never damage your creation, let me not afflict what's yours. Be near me
with your presence; keep me from doing harm.

We do hurt people. How our life has really affected others is something
we simply don't know. At times I think we do far more damage than we
imagine and that there are all sorts of people who could point at us and
say, "You never even noticed, but what you did really wounded me." The
hurts we inflict make a mark on our own soul, and we carry it with us as
part of our essential identity. Perhaps a really wise person is one who
knows how to read those marks and see the conscience beneath the skin.
It is because we cause each other hurt that we can never be completely
pure. That is why I was so moved when a famous actor, asked shortly
before his death what he felt he had achieved in his life, answered that he
hoped he had never hurt anybody.

What would it be like never to have upset anybody, and how would we
know? Imagine all creation were summoned before the divine presence
and every one of us in turn were made to pass in front of each and every
living being. As we did so, God would ask, "Did this person hurt you? Did
this person help you?" And we would have to wait while the trees, the
birds, the animals, and finally our fellow human beings gave their answer.
If every single creature were to say, "This person never hurt me," that
would constitute purity before God.

It is impossible! But we are sometimes rewarded, however fleetingly,
with a sense of purity, as when the feeling in our heart ascends from nothingness to sudden awe, when we are struck by the generosity of some
action and recognize our potential to do likewise, when we acknowledge
the grace and noble conduct of another person and feel humble. For a
moment we are in touch with what it really means to be human and challenged to be faithful to what we now know.

YOM HA-SHOAH

At Birkenau

It is the voices that will compel me to return. I had not been to Auschwitz-Birkenau before, and might not have gone, had the community not asked me to lead a group on a journey there. I had seen other camps — Dachau, Terezin, but none in Poland — none of the death camps themselves. Now, however, I feel I should go back.

The books about Auschwitz say that nothing much remains of the gas chambers and the crematoria. The Nazis blew them all up when they left, except for the one destroyed in the remarkable uprising by the Sonderkommando in 1944. Only shallow pits and ruins lie where they once stood. But this is not true; there is a great deal to see and, so it felt to me, a great deal to listen for amidst the collapsed concrete, the mud, the water, and the ash.

We did not have much time that day — some two hours to climb the guard tower and view the immensity of the camp, row upon row of barracks, a universe apart; to walk along the railway spur, to stop on the platform where the doors of the cattle trucks were thrown open and the full madness of the place first hit the victims; to light our candles, remember the names of family or friends of family, and say our memorials. We did not have enough time just to be there, nor would several days have been sufficient.

Crematoria two and three are close to the end of the railway; crematoria four and five are some distance away to the right, near the area known as Canada where the plundered spoil was sorted. Beyond them are fields of ashes. We didn't go that far; we gathered around a small memorial next to crematorium two. I can't remember exactly what its "capacity" was, how many triple ovens, how many they burned each day, or how many could be gassed at one time in the chamber at the remnants of which we looked. But I thought I could feel the presence of the people; others said they sensed it too.

I've seen exhibitions of the last gifts that parents gave their children when they sent them to England on the *Kindertransport*, knowing they would probably never see them again: a siddur with a short inscription, a book with a few words from mummy and daddy, the love of generations poured out in three lines. Do the dead speak like that? Or were they taken so quickly, separated, here on this platform, amidst such bewilderment that there was no time even to be cognizant that this was it, the final parting?

That is why we have to listen; it is all we can do. Those who perished were so many, and in their living and dying said so many things that there is an infinity of listening here. There is nothing macabre about this; it is a kind of homage, a recognition of the personhood of these people, murdered in the midst of their love and terror, their abandonment, their despair, their final act of tenderness toward a child. We have to listen to what they said when they died, to the little boy who encompassed the whole outrage in five simple words, "But, mummy, I've been good." We have to listen to what they said when they lived, to the voices of the many lands and countless communities of which they were part.

If we don't listen, who will? Listening is our responsibility.

God and the Shoah

> Consider that this has been:
> I commend these words to you.
> Engrave them on your hearts
> When you are in your house, when you walk on your way . . .
> > Or may your house crumble,
> > Disease render you powerless,
> > Your offspring avert their faces from you.
>
> Primo Levi[1]

Like many children of refugee or survivor families, who grew up in a house full of memories and often with as much German spoken as English, there are times when I read compulsively about the Holocaust. I read about people. I read countless books of how people died and how people survived, of love and tenderness, final messages, courage, tenacity, and horror. My heart aches, and sometimes I wonder if this is not in some sense my very own life, as if I had inherited the soul of someone who had suffered thus. And yet I know that all these things are beyond the bounds of my imagination. I cannot know what it was really like.

I read about people, not about God. I spend my time thinking about those who suffered in the Shoah. But in the end the question can't be avoided: what about God?

I do not believe that we can explain the ways of God. On the contrary, the brief words from the Talmud come to mind: '*Agra devei tamia shetikuta* — The reward of the house of bones is silence.² And though there have been several theological answers to the question — "Why did God let it happen?" — I am satisfied by none of them. In the end, I believe that certain questions can never be answered.

Some say, "The Holocaust happened because of our sins." There is a place and a purpose to a theology which puts the responsibility for disaster not on God, but on us. It is intended, paradoxically, as a comfort: God has not abandoned us, but rather punished us for our sins and will reward us when we mend our ways. But this theology cannot be applied here. What sin could be so monstrous as to account for the Holocaust? To suggest it is the failure to practice our religion, or the emergence of Reform Judaism, or the rise of secular Zionism or anything else like it, is, in the word attributed to Claude Lanzmann in response to a questioner who dared to suggest such a theory following a showing of his film *Shoah,* "obscene." Neither the gas chambers, nor the shootings, burnings, and tortures, were anyone's just dessert.

Some say, "The Holocaust happened because of the sins of the world, which were visited upon the body of the Jewish people." I do not believe God creates scapegoats. Certainly it is not a Jewish idea that one person, or one nation, should suffer and perish by the will of God to redeem the sins of others — neither the Jews, nor the Armenians, nor the Cambodians, nor the people of Rwanda. That horrors are brought about because of the sins of the world is doubtless true, but it cannot be right to impute this to the intentions of the divine will. Those who suffer because of the sins of the world suffer because of the way human beings behave, because of the way *we* behave. We visit our depravity upon one another, and there is no atonement in such degradation.

Some even say that the Holocaust happened so that the State of Israel could be established, but the smoke clouds of this tragedy are too immense to be justified by the notion of any kind of silver lining. Nor should European anti-Semitism be retroactively rehabilitated as a justification for a homeland for the Jewish people. To impute such an argument to

God is to turn the deity into a callous politician ready to sacrifice millions of innocent people for an ulterior cause.

Others say that the Holocaust proves that there is no God. They would say that the belief in a benevolent divinity is naïve and deluded, a comforting illusion at best. Yet others say that God died at Auschwitz. Powerful as these arguments are, they ignore the experience of those who were there and did maintain, or even find, their faith in the ghettos and concentration camps. They fail to honor the spiritual triumph of those who discovered God in the midst of terror and who died with prayers on their lips.

Some say that the Holocaust happened because God hid the Divine face. Perhaps; but what does this actually mean? God appears to "hide his face" rather often. How frequently can this happen before the explanation loses any meaning? To be considered to have hidden one's face, one has sometimes to show it. I find it hard to believe in a God who, in our day, sometimes steps into history and sometimes, for reasons beyond reason, deliberately refrains from so doing. The Bible does testify that God was "hands-on" and did enter directly into history. But perhaps those really were other times, or perhaps — a more radical explanation — people had reason then to project a different image onto God. For whatever anyone says of God is ultimately only a product of their own perception.

I believe that we have to live without answers. Sometimes what the desire for a clear answer to an unfathomable question actually expresses is the need to evade the pain that lies in the fact that some things simply cannot be explained. God remains inscrutable. But we can draw a distinction between faith and theodicy. The problem of theodicy, the issue of God's justice, is not co-extensive with the question of faith, the issue of God's existence. One can believe in God without being able to understand or justify what happens in the world.

Nevertheless, I do believe that there is a relationship between God and the Holocaust, and future holocausts, to whomever they may happen. This is because that relationship has a middle term — *us*, every human being. The issue, therefore, is not only the relationship between God and history, but also, especially, the relationship between us and God.

Do we mean it when we say that all life is sacred? Or are some lives more sacred than others? Do we really believe that we are accountable for our actions, and, if so, before whom? Does it strengthen our sense of accountability to believe in God? Or do we make God the ultimate guardian of injustice, always, in our minds, on our side whatever we do? And if God should turn to us, not from the top of some mountain but from inside our own heart, and say, "Where is Abel your brother?" what will we reply? Will we, too, turn like Cain and answer, "I don't know and I don't care"? These are the real questions; all theology that avoids them is evasion. The future will depend on how we answer, and our response will be measured by our actions, not only our beliefs.

In the meantime genocide continues; our vow, "Never again!" has so far proved insufficient to prevent it.

The Sanctity of Life

> No, no: they definitely were
> human beings: uniforms, boots.
> How to explain? They were created
> in the image.
>
> I was a shade.
> A different creator made me.
>
> Dan Pagis[3]

There ought to be no question about who counts as human. Nobody should fail to qualify. Are we not all created equal? Yet history testifies that this so-called basic truth is often far from self-evident.

The Torah teaches that on the sixth day of creation God made the first human being in the Divine image. Into this being God breathed the breath of life. That account, coming at the commencement of Jewish teaching about the nature of the world, and of humanity in particular, tells us that every life is sacred. Every single person contains in equal fashion the likeness of God. What this likeness is we are not told. But whether we understand it to mean the capacity to reason, or imagine, or create, or simply breathe, is in this context irrelevant; it does not alter the basic principle.

Rabbinic teaching seizes hold of this key point and amplifies it: "Therefore was the human being created single," declares the Mishnah, "to teach you that whoever destroys one life is considered by Scripture as if they had destroyed a whole world."[4] The context is the adjuration of witnesses in capital cases to testify truthfully, lest an innocent life perish by their word. How much more so should the principle apply in times of moral chaos, when judicial procedures themselves are a vehicle for deceit and degradation. Significantly the Hebrew word for "single," *yeḥidi*, may also be translated as "unique," thus indicating the singularity and importance of each and every life. Furthermore, the Mishnah continues:

> And to declare the greatness of the Holy Blessed One, for people stamp many coins with the same seal and they all look the same; but the King of the king of kings, the Holy Blessed One, stamps every person with the seal of the first human being, yet not one of them is the same as any other.[5]

Hence the sanctity of each life lies not only in the fact that we are all created in the same image, but also in the appreciation that every one of us is a unique manifestation of the divine creativity. Thus, far from being the pretext for denigrating one another, the very differences between us should lead us to contemplate with wonder our common origins in the creative capacity of God.

Against this basic Jewish teaching, Pagis's words resonate dismally: "They were created in the image . . . A different creator made me." Surely Judaism holds that there is no such thing. In Jewish teaching there are no children of a lesser god, because there is only one God. Indeed, the very mishnah quoted above points out that we are all made in the same image for exactly this reason — so that no one can say that there are several gods in heaven.

Further, there is something in the poem that strikes an even deeper discord. What kind of God are we talking about if "they," with their uniforms and boots, "definitely were human"? Pagis specifically says that "they were created in the image." If we can learn about the image-maker from the image, then God is wearing jackboots too. Perhaps, then, the poem is a sardonic commentary about God; that's what God's like these days. Or perhaps it is a critique of man, for remaking God in the image of his own brutality.

This inversion of Jewish teaching is exactly what Hugo Gryn describes when reflecting on his experiences in the concentration camps and on the death marches.

In the intervening years, I have often thought how Auschwitz-Birkenau was the denial and perversion of all the Ten Commandments, which stand for what we have come to call the Judaeo-Christian spiritual tradition and morality — and one of the pillars of Western civilization. In that Nazi empire . . . it was clear that:

1. God was replaced by a Führer and his minions who claimed for themselves the power of life and death.
2. They fashioned countless idols of silver and gold and filled their world with the sight of *swastikas,* the sound of *Heil Hitler!* and the smell of burning corpses.[6]

For many, the desecration of God and of human beings goes together. In the Bible there was a brief way of describing those people from whom one could expect a basic standard of civilized conduct. They were *y'arei 'Elohim* — they feared God. If a person or a people did not fear God, one could only anticipate the worst; violence and exploitation were simply to be expected. Thus the midwives who defied Pharaoh's command and saved the boy babies of the Hebrew women are described as "fearing God." But the Amalekites, who attacked the Children of Israel from behind and killed the old and weak on their way out of Egypt, are described as "not fearing God." In the biblical worldview there is thus no other adequate guardian of the sanctity of human life than the sense of awe and accountability deriving from the knowledge that we live in the presence of God.

Replace God with a dictator, and there is certainly fear, but not the fear of heaven. On the contrary, there is only that pervasive and corrosive fear which corrupts the conscience of all but the most steadfast of human beings. Accounts of life in any totalitarian state are filled with descriptions of the effects of such terror.

We may not agree that faith is the only guardian of the sanctity of life. We may feel that there are other guarantors of decency that are equal, or even superior, to it — strong humanitarian values, a high regard for the dignity of life, a sense of love and compassion. This is borne out in the noble conduct of countless people in whose lives religion does not feature at all.

But put God in jackboots, make God a god of some and not of others, and the desecration of the earth is bound to follow from the desecration of heaven.

Heroism

> In a poverty-stricken neighborhood of that city, on Krochmalna
> Street, a healer of the sick had built up his dream . . .
>
> from *The Last Walk of Janusz Korczak*[7]

Among the many heroes in the Warsaw ghetto lived two great teachers
who, each in a totally different way, exemplified the meaning of spiritual
resistance. One of them, though deeply committed to the Jewish people,
was a great humanitarian who sought to put his ideals into practice uni-
versally. He expressed his vision by creating homes for children, writing
wonderful children's stories, developing the concept of the rights of the
child, and sharing the dream of a parliament of children from all over the
world. The other was a scion of dynasties of hasidic leaders, a rebbe and
the founder of an important yeshivah. His vision was expressed in the traditional language of Torah interpretation and in the particular zest and
insight of hasidic exegesis. In this medium, often abstruse and obscure to
the outsider, he articulated a unique struggle to encourage his followers,
to maintain and deepen faith, and to discover new levels of meaning
amidst the most appalling suffering. Both men were leaders in the truest
sense and, rejecting opportunities to save themselves, refused to be parted
from those toward whom they felt an absolute responsibility. Both went to
their deaths knowingly, as an act of faith.

A report published by the Yiddish daily *Forward* in America in March 1940
read as follows:

> The Piaseczner Rebbe is now left all alone, bereft of his closest family mem-
> bers. The stricken Rebbe, however, is not broken in morale or spirit. He has
> remained in Warsaw, conducts *tish* with his *Hasidim*, learns Torah throughout
> the day and is currently writing a book. The Piaseczner *Hasidim* marvel at the
> remarkable self-control of their Rebbe.[8]

In fact, the rebbe's conduct reflected far more than self-control.

At the outbreak of war, Kalonymus Kalman Shapira was considered among the greatest ḥasidic luminaries in Poland. Rebbe of Piasecz since the age of twenty, he had founded the yeshivah *Da'as Moshe* and was a famed theorist and practitioner of spiritual education. At the same time he provided, in the tradition of Ḥasidic rebbes, support and counsel to the mass of poor and dejected Jews who came to seek his help. He also had a high reputation as a healer known to have a deep knowledge of medicine.

The rebbe was not spared immediate personal suffering. His wife died shortly before the war. In the terrible bombardment of Warsaw through the High Holidays of 1939, his only son was gravely wounded and died in agony a few days later. While waiting outside the hospital where he lay, the rebbe's daughter-in-law and sister-in-law were killed by a bomb. Not long afterward the rebbe's mother, overcome by these tragedies, died. Yet, as the report in the *Forward* said, the rebbe was not broken in spirit and was, in fact, writing a book.

This work, buried by the author himself at the beginning of 1943 and recovered after the war by a Polish construction worker, is one of the most remarkable documents to emerge from the Holocaust. Containing the rebbe's commentaries on the weekly Torah readings from 1939 until the great deportations in the summer of 1942, it is an extraordinary testament to faith, courage, creativity, and spiritual imagination. That someone in such a situation could teach at all, let alone derive new insights into Torah and share them with his followers, seems inconceivable. The rebbe himself addressed this subject after seven weeks of silence following the deaths of most of his close family. "At first," he wrote, "I wanted to succumb and live a life of muteness, but when muteness threatened to prevail, I could no longer bear it so I took hold of myself, crying out to God more." He dramatized this message through a word play between *'ilmut,* muteness, and *'alumah,* a sheaf, as in Joseph's dream. In the dream, Joseph's sheaf stood up and the other sheaves gathered round. Similarly, when the rebbe drew speech forth out of his silence and pain, then, like the other sheaves, people rose up out of their own mute anguish and gathered round him, finding strength and encouragement in his words.[9]

At many points the rebbe noted how difficult it was to study Torah and engage in prolonged intellectual activity amidst the appalling conditions of the ghetto. The burden of suffering was so great that it was difficult to feel in the same way as one had felt in normal times. To a degree, this was a merciful protection against an intolerable burden of sorrows, but the deep engagement and joy that had characterized prayer in the pre-war years were missing. The institutions that would have ensured the continuing strength of Jewish life and which had been the source of spiritual resistance in the past — the houses of study, halls of prayer, and ritual baths — had all been shut down. Nevertheless, he continued to teach and write, grappling with the meaning of faith in the context of extreme suffering at the deepest level of spiritual intuition and with the highest degree of intellectual rigor. He maintained throughout the capacity to perceive the world as the work of God. In February 1942 he wrote:

> The world was made by the Word of God, and the Torah is the Word of God. So in truth — since God is one and His word are one . . . the Word of God in the creation and the Word of God in the Torah are actually one. As that word cascades down the chain of emanations, it branches into two modes. One mode is the divine Speech which summons creation into being. This speech, imprinted in the natural order, causes the sun to shine by day and the moon by night . . .
>
> So when an individual makes the ascent, conjoining in unity with the voice of God in the Torah, such an individual hears the sound of the Torah from the world as a whole: from the chirping of birds, the mooing of cows, the voices and tumult of human beings — from all of these one hears the voice, the unceasing voice, of God in the Torah. . . .[10]

We can only wonder how in the midst of the ghetto he could find the strength to see the world in such a way. He himself endeavored to answer this very question by considering where God might be found amidst the ever-present horrors. Beginning with a familiar passage from the Talmud, he explained that at times of divine concealment God was in his inner chambers and that each person had to commune with him there in accord with his personal situation. In March 1942 he wrote:

> God, blessed be He, is to be found in His inner chambers weeping, so that one who pushes in and comes close to Him by means of studying Torah, weeps together with God, and studies Torah with Him. Just this makes the difference: the weeping, the pain which a person undergoes by himself, alone, may have the effect of breaking him, of bringing him down, so that he is incapable of doing anything. But the weeping which the person does together with God — that strengthens him. He weeps — and is strengthened; he is broken — but finds courage to study and teach.[11]

There, in those inner chambers, new Torah insights were revealed.

Eyewitness testimony described how after the great deportations in the summer of 1942 Rabbi Shapira, together with other rebbes and teachers, was assigned work in a shoe factory:

> Talmudic and rabbinic quotations fly back and forth; soon there appear on the anvil — or, to be precise, on the minds and lips of these brilliant scholars — the words of Maimonides and Ravad, the author of the *Tur,* Rama, earlier and later authorities. The atmosphere of the factory is filled with the opinions of eminent scholars, so who cares about the SS, the German overseers, the hunger, suffering, persecution and fear of death?[12]

In the spring of 1943, toward the end of the ghetto revolt, Rabbi Shapira was deported to the Trawniki labor camp. It was liquidated in November and he, together with all the other Jews, was killed.

Janusz Korczak walked at the head of the procession of children from his orphanage to the train which took them to the gas chambers. Misha Wroblewski was one of the last survivors to have seen him. Years later she commented:

> Everyone makes so much of Korczak's last decision to go with the children to the train. But his whole life was made up of moral decisions. The decision to become a children's doctor. The decision to give up medicine and his writing career to take care of poor orphans. The decision to go with the Jewish orphans into the ghetto. As for that last decision to go with the children to Treblinka, it was part of his nature. It was who he was.[13]

At the age of five Korczak is said to have told his grandmother that he wanted to do away with money in order to make the world a better place. His idealism led him to leave behind the well-to-do but restricted middle-class environment of his childhood and begin his work with deprived children. Serving as a doctor, he became frustrated by the fact that however well he treated the particular symptoms of a child, that boy or girl had no choice but to return to the physical and emotional misery which had occasioned the sickness in the first place. Thus he was led to his life's main task, the founding and running of homes for children. He became the head of a new

Jewish orphanage in Warsaw in 1911 and, apart from his years of service as a Polish medical officer during the First World War, remained at his post till his death. His educational approach, which included providing the children with opportunities for self-government and encouraging them to publish their own newspaper, were so successful that he was asked to develop a parallel non-Jewish orphanage nearby. Throughout his life he cherished the dream of bringing children of different peoples together. Yet in the end he couldn't help but acknowledge the hatred that made this impossible:

> There is an abyss between Jewish children and Polish children. I would like to close that abyss, but it is too late. The workers of the world did not unite during the First World War, nor did they unite afterwards. Now a second world war is coming, and new chasms. Deep trenches are being dug everywhere. It is too late.[14]

During those years Korczak wrote widely. His stories from the vantage point of the child and his books about the care of children, including *How to Love a Child,* became classics. He also broadcast frequently under the title of "The Old Doctor," communicating a mellow but challenging wisdom:

> Who are you? Pilgrim, wanderer, castaway, deserter, bankrupt, out-cast? . . . How have you lived? How much land did you till? How many loaves of bread did you bake for others? How much did you sow? How many trees did you plant? How many bricks did you lay before taking leave . . . While you lived, did you just observe languidly as life flowed by? Did you steer the course, or were you carried along?[15]

During the 1930s Korczak twice visited Palestine and was drawn to settle there, but he would not leave his orphans. It was with them that he chose to be when the German army occupied Warsaw, and it was with them that he went into the ghetto where the orphanage was moved, to the corner building of 16 Sienna and 9 Sliska Street, in 1940.

Despite his severely deteriorating health — by 1942 he suffered from a weak heart, a hernia, swollen feet, and pleurisy — Korczak continued to care for his orphans in every possible way, from the provision of food and fuel to the spiritual needs of children who sensed that they were shortly to die. Mundane, speculative, self-questioning, tender, his ghetto diary reflects the full range of his vast responsibilities. By the end there were over two hundred children, adolescents, and adults in his care:

Yesterday I went to Grzybow No. 1 to collect a donation. The last building before the ghetto wall. A Jewish policeman was killed here yesterday.

They say he was signalling to smugglers.

"That's not the place for wholesale business," a neighbor explained.

The store is closed. The people are scared.

And (possibly some days) later:

A boy said to me when he left the Children's Home: "Were it not for the home I wouldn't know that there are honest people in the world who never steal. I wouldn't know that one can speak the truth. I wouldn't know that there are just laws in the world."[16]

As the state of the ghetto worsened even further and its fate became ever more obvious, Korczak arranged for the staging of Tagore's play *The Post Office* in which a young boy prepares to meet his death. In the play the king's own doctor arrives unexpectedly at the bedside of the child in his poor foster home and demands that all the doors and windows be thrown open. Through the open shutters the boy sees the stars shining in the darkness and falls asleep waiting for the arrival of the king. Korczak is reported to have said after the performance, which was followed by deep silence, that, "he wanted to help the children accept death," which now seemed inevitable.[17]

It is also reported that he refused all offers to save his life because he did not want the children, whose faith in humanity he had so painstakingly cultivated, to have that faith destroyed. To walk to the cattle trucks at their head was not just a heroic gesture but the ultimate protestation that in spite of everything human beings were worthy of trust.

YOM HA-ZIKARON
AND YOM HA-ATZMA'UT

Stones and Dreams

Like a lonely bird on the roof . . .

Ps. 102:8

It is late at night in Jerusalem and the crowds have gone home. The birds cry in the dark from high above the Western Wall and from the tenacious bushes rooted between the stones. Here by this wall the Divine Spirit is said to dwell as, since the dedication of the Temple by King Solomon, it always has. However, that is only part of the truth. It is also taught that the Divine Spirit went into exile with the Jewish people. It followed us to Babylon, to Rome, to Spain, to Northern and Eastern Europe, wherever through the millennia we were allowed in our wanderings to settle. Our journey was therefore also God's journey, for all human suffering is also God's suffering. But at the same time the Divine Spirit never departed from this wall. Here it has remained through the many centuries when Jerusalem was all but forsaken, likened to a lonely bird upon a tumble-down roof. That is why Jews have gathered here for millennia, to pour out our souls, to find comfort and to commune with God.

Here throughout the ages Jews have come with love and longing in their hearts. It was here that Yehudah Halevi yearned to be when he wrote that his heart was in the east though he was in the furthermost corner of the west. Here he sought to kiss the dust on which the ancient prophets trod. It was here that Moses ben Naḥman came when, forced to flee Spain, he found refuge in the Holy Land:

> I left my family, I forsook my house. There with the sweet and beloved children, whom I brought up on my knees, I left also my soul. With them, my heart and eyes will dwell forever . . . But the loss of all else which delighted my eyes is compensated by my present joy in a day passed within thy courts, Oh Jerusalem! visiting the ruins of the Temple and crying over the ruined Sanctuary, where it is granted me to caress thy stones, to fondle thy dust, and to weep over thy ruins, I wept bitterly, but I found joy in my heart. I rent my garments, but I found solace in doing so.[1]

Indeed, it was Naḥmanides who challenged the Maimonidean computation of the commandments and insisted that among the six hundred and thirteen there had to be included the mitzvah of going to live in the land of Israel.

I don't always find it easy to visit the wall. When the place is crowded with people coming to do homage, pilgrimage often turns into gesture. One becomes part of a spectacle and has to struggle to find the privacy in which to listen to one's own thoughts. Sometimes my spirit retreats and I end up more like a tourist than a supplicant in the presence of God. On several occasions I have left bewildered and disappointed, troubled by my failure to experience what I expected to feel. My father remembers going to the wall in the days of the British mandate, before the Old City was captured by Jordan in 1948. It was approached along alleyways, and the space in front of it was narrow and intimate. He preferred it as it was then. The vast open plaza was created after the Six Day War because of well-founded concerns for security.

Late at night, the atmosphere is different. The crowds have gone. The stones glow in the darkness, layer above layer, immense. No other stones have evoked a deeper longing or elicited a greater love. The papers which choke the cracks between them contain the distillations of the prayers of a thousand souls, all hoping to tuck themselves into God's garment. Those who come here at this hour, some standing right by the wall, some sitting meditating on the Psalms or other sacred texts, have the aspect of the unofficial guardians of the spirit. Like the keepers of the study houses of Eastern Europe, who would rise at midnight and open the books of the Zohar, so this place too seems to be inhabited at this hour by those who know the pathways to the presence of God.

For it is here, according to legend, that Jacob, awakening from his dream of the great ladder and overcome with fear, declared, "How awesome is this place! This is none other than the house of God and this is the gate of heaven" (Gen. 28:17). The Jewish people have kept their dream alive and made this their gate to heaven. That is why the place has held the Jewish heart captive and brought it home after so many years.

Promised Land

> I have not sung to you, my country,
> Nor glorified your name
> In deeds of valor,
> With spoils of war.
> There's only a tree my hands have planted
> On the Jordan's silent banks,
> Just a path my feet have trodden
> Across the fields.
>
> from Rachel, *'El 'Artzi*[2]

Rachel is the poetess of the pioneer's dream, of an age of innocence and ideals. Zalman Shazzar, later to become President of Israel, remembered her like this:

> The gate opened and there emerged from the courtyard a flock of squawking, cackling geese who proceeded to spread themselves out across the hillside. Behind them came their keeper, tall and upright, in a white dress, blue-eyed, lithe as a deer and beautiful as the Kinneret. In her hand she held a palm branch and, with such sceptre and her young, warm voice, held sway over the tumult . . . This was the poetess Rachel . . . She made haste to climb an old carob tree and stretched herself out on a branch. From there, in her white dress and golden in the light, she lifted up her voice in song. . . .[3]

Between Rachel and Zalman there developed one of the great literary love affairs of the time.

The land gave Rachel all it could possibly promise, and she gave it her life in return. She was born in Poltava to a father who preserved his Jewish commitment despite twenty-five years in the Russian army and a mother who was both pious and artistically gifted. In 1909 she set sail with her sister for Palestine. They had intended only to visit, but when they saw the land, they determined never to leave it again. They took a room in Reḥovot and learned Hebrew by permitting themselves to speak no Russian except for one hour each day at sundown. They were soon joined by their youngest sister, and, with their music, painting, and grace, "the tower of the three sisters" quickly became the cultural center of the town.[4]

Rachel was not satisfied with such a life, however. She wanted to fulfill her love of the land more actively, to "make music with the hoe and to paint upon the face of the earth."⁵ It was this desire which brought her to her beloved Kinneret, where she spent the happiest days of her life. She was persuaded, however, that she could best serve the needs of her country by gaining a proper, academically based knowledge of agriculture. In 1913 she therefore traveled to Toulouse to study. But when the First World War broke out she found herself repatriated to Russia where she spent, alongside many millions of other victims of the fighting and the revolution, four wretched, cold, and hungry years. She returned to Palestine at the earliest opportunity, with the first ship to sail from Odessa in peacetime, but she carried within her the germs of the tuberculosis that would kill her.

Her life became a slow retraction. Undeterred by her ill health, she went to Degania and took her share of the hardest physical labor. Forced to give it up, she began to work with the children of the kibbutz. After she became too ill to do that, she moved to Jerusalem where she taught agriculture to Yemenite girls. When she could manage this no more, she took a room in Tel Aviv where she remained until she died in April 1931. It was here that she began to write, poetry of the love of the land, poetry of longing and the struggle to maintain her inner grace through the long, slow relinquishment of life:

> I don't complain! From a narrow room
> How sweet to long for broad spaces.
> Sad days and the autumn cold
> They too have their purple and their gold.
>
> I don't complain! From the wounded heart
> Wells the song of its love . . .⁶

Israel is the land of the dreams of generations: "When God returned the captivity of Zion, we were as those that dream" (Ps. 126:1). But there are things no land can promise. Maybe that is why the narrative of the Torah ends before the Children of Israel cross the border into the promised land. For every promise leads to another struggle and every dream yields to the challenges of daily reality. Maybe that is why Rachel's poetry, despite the attainment of her first objective, to live in the land she loved, is nevertheless haunted by the image of the mountain from which God showed Moses the lay of the land he was not allowed to enter:

> Stretch out your hands. Behold from afar.
> Thither — none comes.
> To each his Nevo
> In the land's vast expanse.[7]

In the promised land, we still reach out for the promise.

Were Our Feet as Fleet as the Deer . . .

Early in the morning a fawn comes to the entrance of my hut, curious, eager for its alfalfa and hay. The other deer gather shyly just a little farther away. I go out to fill their trough with water and their rack with food. The view across the valley takes the gaze up the rocky mountainside to the kibbutz of Beit Oren; downward it runs through rough wooded hills to the narrow plain and the sea. This is a magnificent place to recite the prayers that form the prelude to the Shabbat morning service: "Were our mouths as full of song as the sea, or our tongues with joy as its multitudinous waves . . . Were our feet as fleet as the deer. . . ."

My love was strong when I sought to spend a weekend alone with the woods and the hills and the animals. Love for what? For life, for the land, for beauty, for God? I could not say; it was all of those together. The Israel Nature Reserves Authority told me that the Druse keeper of the park in the Carmel above Haifa wanted a weekend off and that it would be useful if I were to relieve him for a couple of days. For a long time I had fantasized about planting trees and working with animals. I could scarcely believe my good fortune. But did I know: I would be on my own; I would have to provide my own food, stay there until the warden returned, take complete responsibility for the animals? These were rare deer, specially reintroduced into Israel as part of a project to restore to the area the original wildlife described in the Bible. Would I take due care? At least, they told me, there was water; I wouldn't have to bring that.

Soon I was following the path from the road below the university buildings on the mountain top and making my way across the fields of scented scrub to the gate and the keeper's hut. In an hour all was explained — how to fill the trough and the urn with water, where to put the hay and the soft grass, what to watch for and what to avoid — and soon I was on my own. What a rich and wonderful isolation! Twenty years later the two weekends I spent there still sustain me. Though I cannot deny the pain of a certain longing. For every life is less than its greatest dreams, and in one's youth one always imagines one will be free with a total freedom that — in this world — only the spirit can attain. I remember the fragrance and the water, the forest, the mountains, and the slope of the decline to the sea.

For a Jew outside Israel there may be little feeling of being at home. We grow up with a double culture; a language, or several, which is not the surrounding language; a long history and an immediate geography in dissonance with each other; a celebration of time out of time with the secular year or the year of another religion; a picture of biblical beasts and trees very different from the European, American, Australian, or African terrain that we see beyond the window. Sometimes, we don't know what to love, or in which language to rejoice. If I sing of the trees here in the Diaspora, I know it is not my song as a Jew. If I sing of trees in another land, which I don't know as well, is it my song at all? For doesn't the landscape of our childhood enter the soul, creating a unique resonance with its colors, mountains, rivers, and skies? Thus we may wonder: When will everything I love ever belong together and cohere? Nor can coming to Israel simply resolve this painful, rich dichotomy for one born abroad. For already from our birth we are more than one person. And in truth, at some level, virtually everyone, born anywhere, always is.

Sometimes, though, our loves do come together. On those two precious Sabbaths, alone with the deer, the trees, the herbs, the hillside, and the sea, they did. There were scarcely any intruders — maybe a single stray tourist seeking directions and glad of a drink, and a friend in the evening who had heard of my crazy plan. Those days had a fullness I have not often rediscovered since.

I remember the pitcher in the shade outside the door of the hut, full of cool water. I drink from it still.

The Kaddish

And in the night there came to me
the child who was not born,
looked into my eyes
and asked, "Where is my father?" . . .

. . . Your father, my child, was borne away by the mountain
wind. In a foreign land
did your father remain, my child.
Someone made a mistake, my beautiful son,
and now you shall not be.

from Ra'ayah Harnick, *Uvalailah ba 'elai hayeled shelo nolad*[8]

Late one night when his wife was in the hospital and it was uncertain whether she would ever return home, the old man beckoned me to follow him into the room. By this time I had lived in their flat for several months, but I had not even noticed the existence of the door through which we now passed. I was there as guest and helper, to assist him on the slow walk to shul on the Sabbath and by cooking, shopping, and providing company in those weeks of his aloneness.

The study was dark. From a heavy European desk he took out an envelope and told me it contained his will. I was afraid, caught between a feeling of unworthiness, and honor for the trust so simply and immediately bestowed. He picked up a photograph from the desk. It showed a cheerful and attractive woman in her early twenties standing next to a young man whose face communicated kindness and reliability. "This," he said, "was my daughter. And this is the man she was going to marry. They were both killed at Kibbutz Kfar Etzion in the War of Independence." He wept. They had died in 1948 when the Egyptian army had attacked from the south and occupied the area known as the Etzion block. It was 1980 now, but grief does not obey the laws of linear time.

Outside the rain was pouring down, and he was too unwell to manage even the short journey to the nearest synagogue in such weather. So he asked me to listen while he recited the *Kaddish* which, as an Orthodox Jew, he knew full well should only be said in the presence of a *minyan*, a quorum of ten. I did so, and made the traditional responses. This formed the signature to a kind of testament between us, which I have never foregotten. Sometimes God, represented by a scroll of the Torah or by the Holy Ark in the synagogue, may be considered to make up the final member of the *minyan*. In this case it felt as if God were rather more, a presence that unified the living and the dead and rendered numbers futile.

He shut the door behind us. Though I stayed some further months with him and his wife in that flat, I don't think I ever went into his study again, or saw him do so either.

What do we know of the absent people in another person's life? We do not behold the remembered presence which renders for them the room empty, the street desolate, the heart a hole impossible to plug, constantly leaking pain. However short a war, it always leaves parents who ask for a lifetime: Where is my child? Where is the child who ought to have been?

Whose Dead?

Slowly, slowly retreated
The repugnant image of vengeance
And joyous worlds of hope were revealed
And the delights of springs rich in water.
. . . On this island, in one of its caves,
Peace opened its eyes.

from "Truce" by Zelda[9]

The road to Neveh Shalom — Waḥat al-Salam — climbs past the beautiful monastery of Latrun. They make and sell wine there. But I was more impressed by the fine buildings and gardens, and the silence which encompassed this peaceful place of devotion.

When I thought about the wars in Israel, I used to think of "our wounded" and "their wounded," of "our dead" and "their dead." In my mind the latter definitely counted for less. This was no conscious decision. It was just that the former were part of my side, belonged to families I might know, were part of a grief which I, albeit at some distance, had grown up to share. Their death was, and is, the suffering of my extended family. My father's uncle was burned to death on the ill-fated convoy to the Hadassah Hospital on Mount Scopus in 1948. That is why, like countless Jews, I listen intently, desperately, whenever anything happens in Israel, whenever we even hear its name mentioned in the news.

This feeling remains, but I gained another insight that day when I climbed the small road that leads past the monastery up to Neveh Shalom.

Neveh Shalom, Waḥat-al-Salam, is the village in which Jews and Arabs live together and educate together for peace. There are homes, school, communal halls, and a place of silence for those of all faiths to come to reflect and seek God. Soon after I arrived I was asked if I wanted to join a small group for a walk in the surrounding hills. Descending through the valley, we were soon back at Latrun. Here some of the worst fighting in the War of Independence took place. One can still see the shell of the old British police station, which, by virtue of its elevation, controlled the road to Jerusalem from the coastal plains inland until it entered Sha'ar Ḥagai, the Gateway to the Valley, and began to climb through steep ravines toward the then beleaguered city. Few roads could be more vulnerable to attack, the stony hills offering ample shelter from which to ambush the slow convoys as they crawled up the steep incline below. The rust-colored remains of burned-out cars still stand as memorials along the route.

Some thirty or more years later we stood, a mixed group of Israelis and Arabs, by the sides of the same trenches. Our guide was an Arab, though I don't think his or her identity would have made any difference to the impact of the experience. "Here," he said, "were the Israeli trenches, and here were the Arab positions." Looking at them so near to one another, both presumably filled with the same fears, the same blood, the same dying, the words "ours" and "theirs" hung suspended in my mind and ceased at some basic human level to have meaning. Did it hurt parents less when their son died just because they lived in a village somewhere in Egypt or Jordan or Syria, rather than in a kibbutz or a flat in Tel Aviv?

Of course we care most for our own. But we should remember that beyond our differentiation of them into "our dead" and "their dead," the dead are simply all together dead. And beyond "our land" and "their land," and "our peace" and "their peace," one hopes that one day there will simply be peace.

In the Courtyards of Jerusalem

Sorrow rather hollows out
Some hidden inner concave
Which I hitherto knew not . . .

. . . And it hurts that you should haunt me
Like the entrance to a different world
That nowhere else is found.

J. T. W.

Everyone has streets and vistas, haunts and corners, that they love. These are some of mine: the road to Jerusalem as it climbs through the hills past Sha'ar Ḥagai; the first view of the city on the hilltops; the first streets, which soon enfold the approaching traveller in an entire universe; the lanes of Reḥavia, the Moshavah, Emek Refa'im, and Bak'a, with their narrow pavements, stone walls, dark cypress, pine, and jasmine; the courtyards of the old, rundown Bukharan quarter; the ancient piety of Shabbat nights, the singing, and the silence; the climb up the path lined with rosemary to Mount Zion and the high walls hiding the gardens of the Domition Abbey and other holy places; the road that runs along the sea toward the north of Israel past beaches where illegal immigrants disembarked to be swallowed up in a land they learned to love; the central station in Haifa where I would wait for a bus up the mountain or out into the hills and fields, and from where I would ring my aunt (thrice removed, but very close) and tell her all that was happening in those difficult days when I struggled with absolutely everything; the view over Haifa bay at night, the lights around the shore, the ships at anchor, the long road climbing the mountain at an angle past Stella Maris, far out from the city; the first flowering of an orchard when the ground was sodden and the trees a contradiction of blossom and icy bark; the call of an owl, close but invisible in the scrub of the Carmel Mountains. All these I have loved, and by virtue of that love, appreciate the longing in every heart for the smells, sights, branches, and bricks of the land that is home.

My love for Israel did not grow swiftly or easily. I remember the terror I experienced on my first visit; fear was a subliminal presence throughout the months I was there. I was afraid of the colors yellow and brown. I was afraid of the dryness and the heat. I was afraid of the broad blue sky, which turned every day into a cloudless and desolate white. I was afraid, because I felt as if this stony land were somehow more inimical to life than the greener, damper climates that had surrounded me since birth. Perhaps, on reflection, what I sensed, but did not then understand, was the sheer mortality with which this land contends, its survivors from the Shoah, its refugees from persecutions, its mourners from the wars, its bus bombs, its bloody battles to survive.

I do not know how it was that I found my love for Israel, as one finds a secret bower with a hidden spring in a desert. But find it I did. It was partly persistence. It was partly that the radically different beauty of this land came to overwhelm me, and I began to experience it as ancient, passionate, painful, joyous, and profound. Nor was what I discovered just one single love, but rather the threads of many loves intertwined. I found in myself a longing, seeking to be woven into belonging.

I experience those loves otherwise now from how I did then, some twenty years ago. What were they? A part of me unfurled that could respond aesthetically to the different beauty of this extraordinary Mediterranean land. I remember and experience again the rich, vital smell of earth on a warm winter day, the blooming of hundreds and hundreds of cyclamen, the broad green leaves of nut trees in the Galilee, the smell of wet pine, the intense, sensuous generosity of the scent of orange groves, of jasmine in the gardens of Jerusalem. In short, I began to understand the tenacity and fertility of life within this soil that dehydrates each summer.

I also began to discover and explore my love as a Jew for the place where Judaism began. I do not believe that God is closer to, or farther from, a person just because he or she prays in this country rather than that, or speaks this language rather than another. I do not believe that God's presence is intrinsically spread more thickly in any particular location. Nor do I believe that a Jew, a Christian, or a Moslem, or anyone in sincere devotion, prays to a different God. But I do believe that there are places where the search for God has been more intense and that this leaves traces that can be rediscovered, even after centuries of intermission. And I do believe that in Israel the ancient and persistent presence of Judaism is greater, that both history and contemporary reality have created what might be described as a collective unconscious which is Jewish and which carries Jewish prayers and meditations swiftly upward on paths familiar with the language and the words. Here Hebrew prayer and the study of the Torah are not strangers; they belong, they are expected — as the nine await the tenth to form a quorum.

Then there is my love of family, friends, and teachers. I include among them all the people I have met in the countless encounters with familiar strangers which characterize life in this extraordinary land. I think of my teacher Reb Dovid of the Yeshivah of Ḥasidei Sadegora who would reply whenever I asked him why a passage of Talmud was so difficult, "Because it's fun and God likes it that way!" I think of the man I met on a bus north of Haifa who, having run for his life from the British as an illegal immigrant in mandate days, promised to hide me in his factory any time I wanted. I think of the friends, formerly from Scotland, who supported us so well there, in whose small Jerusalem garden I planted a sapling lemon tree and who now send me fruit every year. I think of the Arab man who taught me from the Bible and the Talmud while we dug holes to plant trees together. I think of the person I once heard outside in a thunderstorm whistling an aria from *Carmen*. Israel is a land of proximity and kinship, of immediacy and passion. Like it or not, the skin between yourself and your neighbor is thinner here.

And with these reflections I know that through not living in Israel, in part a conscious decision to contribute to Jewish life in the Diaspora, a portion of my heart has lost, too. But we cannot be in two places at once, and we cannot live without mourning.

Bus Bombs and Hopes

The State of Israel . . . will be based on the precepts of liberty, justice and peace, taught by the Hebrew Prophets; will uphold the full social and political equality of all its citizens, without distinction of race, creed, or sex; will guarantee full freedom of conscience, worship, education and culture . . .

from the Declaration of Independence

Sometime in the 1930s my grandfather stood outside the Mosque of the Dome of the Rock and recited in fluent Arabic the opening verses of the

Koran. Moslem worshipers embraced him, a rabbi declaiming from their scriptures. This could hardly happen now.

"Jerusalem built as a city that is compact together," says the Psalms (122:3). But what is it that this city, famous for its great divisions, has joined? Is it not rather a place where the illusion of unity ends in a blind alley, like the streetscape Amos Oz remembers from his childhood — intriguing archways ending in barred and bricked-up passages? Yet Jerusalem is not a city in which one succumbs to cynicism. Here ideals may seem vain, but they do not vanish. They come from the tongues of prophets and have been absorbed into the stones; the very birds of the air seem to carry them.

There are countless legends about the origins of the city, but the well-known story of the brothers is perhaps my favorite. Two brothers, it is told, went home after the harvest, each to his house on opposite sides of a steep hill. Neither could sleep. One of them was thinking: "My barn is full and I have plenty for my family. My brother is on his own; he has the blessings neither of wife nor of child. His needs are therefore greater than mine. I shall load my cart and quietly fill his barn with more grain." The other thought, "My barn is full and I have plenty for myself. My brother has a wife and children to feed. He needs more than I do. I shall load my cart and secretly add to his stores." So both brothers rose in the middle of the night and drew their laden carts to the top of the hill. There they met and, understanding each other at once, embraced. And there, in a future generation, the first stone of Jerusalem was laid.

It was with ideals like these of sharing and equality that the Declaration of Independence was written and signed.

In the light of all that has happened since, we should remember that Hillel and Jesus were virtually contemporaries and that their most famous teachings are based on the same commandment to love your neighbor as yourself (Lev. 19:18). Each of them formulated his belief with the pragmatic aim of teaching a simple, basic, and practicable morality. The rabbis who lived through the destruction of the Second Temple some two generations later had the courage to explain the reason for this calamity as causeless hatred, precisely the failure to live by that key commandment. Causeless hatred, they explained, drives even God away.

We should also remember that historically the relationship between Islam and Judaism has often been close and positive and is not a tale of constant conflict.

Where did the trouble begin? Was it endemic in the very concept of the return to a land which belonged to the heart and history of a people, yet had an indigenous population too? Was it part of the colonial heritage, that has almost everywhere left ethnic strife in its wake? Did it begin with the hostility of the Arab nations toward a Jewish neighbor, their rejection of the 1947 United Nations plan and their remorseless attempt to destroy the fledgling state the following year, and again in 1967? However it started, it was subsequently exacerbated by many factors: the inability of any party to resolve the terrible humanitarian crisis of the Palestinian refugees, who require justice and a home, but have been used as a political pawn; the inevitable wrongs of the Israeli occupation, bound to involve violence; the dangerous mixture of theology and nationalism that created an expansionist and messianic Judaism; the hatred preached by Islamic militants; Israel's well-founded fear of the intentions of its neighbors, who outnumber it massively, and, following the long history of anti-Semitism, its distrust of the good faith of supposedly impartial nations; the bombs planted by Ḥamas and Ḥizbollah partly to kill as many people as possible, but mainly to blow whatever trust there may have been to smithereens. Like many Jews, I often cannot tell with what or whom I feel most angry.

Most of my — mercifully few — experiences of hatred have occurred in Jerusalem. As a teenager I remember being stoned in the Old City. I can recall, from over the years, the look of people whom I knew would be glad to have killed me had there not been consequences. I remember how I became caught up in ugly demonstrations between Jew and Jew, as well as between Jew and Arab. These are no more than the stray experiences of a person who has lived in Jerusalem, all in all, for approximately three years, but they were enough to teach me that I hate the experience of hatred and that the reliance on force — currently essential — to defend Israel's right to exist, is fearful.

This is how Amos Oz recalls his first visit to the Old City in 1967, three days after its capture in the Six Day War:

> The Bible came to life for me: the Prophets, the Kings, Temple Mount, Absalom's Pillar, the Mount of Olives . . . I wanted to be part of it all. I wanted to belong. Were it not for the people . . . I passed through the streets of east Jerusalem like a man breaking into some forbidden place. Depression filled my soul. City of my birth. City of my dreams. City of my ancestors' and my people's yearnings. And I was condemned to walk through its streets armed with a sub-machine gun . . .[10]

If Amos Oz could hardly bear to walk through the streets of east Jerusalem then, I wonder what he feels about it now. There is such an obvious differential between the realities of life for the different peoples; one only has to walk the few yards from the Jewish to the Moslem Quarter of the Old City. The difference, and the hatred, are palpable.

Yet, for all that, we cannot abandon our dreams and ideals. Jerusalem will not let us. For we need them; our dreams and ideals are an essential part of our equipment for facing every day. Without them we lose the capacity to make decisions about today and tomorrow in the light of ultimate objectives. We have to continue to believe that Jerusalem will be the city that brings faiths and peoples together, that one day a Jew will be able to recite the Koran in a mosque, and a Moslem, the Torah in a synagogue, and no one will seek to kill them because everyone will recognize that we pray to the same God.

SHAVUOT

God's Voice

For thus it is said, "Face to face did God speak . . ." for the whole of creation was directed upward toward the root of its vitality; and . . . when God said, "I am the Lord your God," every single particle of creation thought it was to itself that the divine word was addressed.

Rabbi Yehudah Aryeh Lev of Ger, *Sefat Emet*[1]

For lovers the question is almost never, "Did you love me then?"; it is, "Do you love me now?" The same is true of our relationship with God; the crucial question is not about the past but about the present. If a couple are chiefly concerned with whether or not they loved each other once, it is probably correct to infer that they doubt that they do so now. Similarly, the issue is not whether we once heard the voice of God in the Torah, but whether we hear it and feel the love of God today.

When I teach children I try to communicate to them something of the love of Torah. I show them my mother's father's Torah scroll. I tell them how my grandfather was a chaplain in the German army for the duration of the First World War. I speculate with them as to whether this was the reason why his Torah scroll is so small — little enough to fit into a kit bag. I tell the class how, when my grandfather was sent to Dachau after Kristallnacht, the Nazis came and made my grandmother, my mother, and her sisters throw all his books out of the window of their first-floor flat, this scroll perhaps among them. I show them the letters, indicate the care with which each one is drawn, the crowns upon them, the exactly etched lines from which they hang, the evenness of the columns, explain the trouble taken so that every single word should be absolutely accurate. I talk to them about *ḥiddur mitzvah*, the principle of keeping the commandments in a graceful manner, and trust that this will convey to them some small portion of what the love of Torah means for the Jewish people who have nurtured it with so much dedication through the ages.

Yet, these are only the outer garments of Torah. To the spirit it is not the outward form so much as the inner voice that matters. It is to this part of the self that the mystics spoke, in the Talmud, the Midrash, the Zohar, and, above all, in the writings of the ḥasidic masters, declaring that that call has never ceased. For God speaks to every person all the time in a voice limited only by the capacity of each one of us to apprehend it. "We translate *velo yasaf* as *that never stopped*," explains Rashi, on the verse in Deuteronomy which teaches that God spoke at Sinai in a great voice out of the midst of the fire, the cloud, and the thick darkness, "because God's voice is strong and established forever."[2] Therefore it is this same voice that a person hears today who experiences, arrested for a moment by some unanticipated glory, the sudden descent of awe. The Talmud says poetically that when each commandment was spoken the whole world filled with the aroma of spices. Ḥasidic literature repeatedly affirms that the residue of this fragrance is still present now and that, year by year, God is revealed again on Shavuot.

From where does God's voice come? Its source and origin lie within the ultimate freedom that it heralds. The Torah tells us that every fiftieth year the shofar is to be blown on the Day of Atonement to proclaim freedom throughout the land. If, then, God's voice was heard in the midst of the sound of the shofar on Mount Sinai, it too must be calling the world to freedom. The shofar itself, according to the Zohar, acquires the sound from what it describes as the original treasury of freedom. And it is this freedom that we taste when we hear God's voice, feel God's presence, and experience ourselves as spiritually alive. For when we are stirred by the awareness of God, whatever oppresses us releases us temporarily from its dominion, and we *are*.

Ancient tradition connects God's voice in the commandments with the divine utterance by which the world was made. All creation is therefore only a reification, a thickening into material substance, of the word of God as it travels through all the worlds. For everything, were we capable of so perceiving it, is only God's voice and being, embodied in the form of something else apart, a tree or a bird, a boy, a girl, or a cloud. When God said, "I am," then everything for a moment recognized its own essence and was reconnected to the source of its spirit, before the laws of nature by which the world is ordinarily governed came back into force and the Divine was once again concealed behind the clothes of its manifestation.[3]

In moments of inner concentration we may become aware of the very essence of a thing. We perceive it not only according to its external form but feel ourselves to be communing with its inner being. Such moments become for the artist an image in a poem or a vision translated on to canvas. According to the mystical tradition, when God spoke at Sinai all the world was manifest with such intensity and we all had the capacity to perceive it in that way. God still speaks today; God speaks in all creation all the time. Now, however, the task of seeing the world like that is up to us.

What does God's voice say? On the one hand it speaks with redeeming beauty; it restores the soul. But on the other, it speaks in questions, it never fails to interrogate, piercing to the essence of who we are. It is as if the sequel to, "I am the Lord your God," were, "And who are you? What are you doing in my world?"

The questions are always the same, but no two of us hear them in the same manner, and no one of us experiences them in the same way at two different points in our life. Sometimes, in the rush of all we do, in the middle of the tasks that occupy our time, the questions merge with the voice that asks us what the point of all this running around really is. Sometimes the questions ask themselves in the silence before the consciousness of a great decision. Perhaps the people who brought Anne Frank food during those two years of hiding heard those questions and knew that they could live with them. Perhaps the unknown person who phoned the Gestapo and gave the family away smothered himself with constant noise because he was afraid to hear them. Perhaps the questions will reach us at the end of our days; perhaps we will attain the wisdom to answer, "Here am I," content to return to the eternity out of which our atomized consciousness was drawn forth at our beginning.

While we live, the voice, and the questions which follow it, command us. That is why the simple statement, "I am the Lord your God," stands at the entrance to the Ten Commandments. We may or may not believe that in the formulation in which we have them the commandments are literally God's word, unsullied by human intervention. We may prefer to think, like Franz Rosenzweig, that everything that follows the basic declaration of God's presence is interpretation. But the command is real either way. "Nature itself prevents a person from sinning," teaches the Sefat Emet, for when we experience the presence of God in anything, in our fellow human beings, in animals, plants or even things, what can we feel but utter respect, what can we do but strive to honor it?[4] When we are touched by the knowledge of God, how can we really want to hurt or to destroy?

God's Presence

> Finer than finest particles, you cannot be found out,
>   your wisdom knows no sounding;
> But you, awesome God, with a single glance, distinguish
>   good from evil.
> The Lord of hosts, with how many wonders he holds
>   together his tent!
> By the paths of the heart he plants the heart's growth, the
>   Rock whose work is perfect!
>
> *Yah 'Eli veGo'ali*[5]

Everywhere bespeaks a presence, frightening and far, gentle and close.

We enter a room and have to wait a few moments before our friend comes in. Immediately we absorb an atmosphere, observe a pile of books on a desk, books on shelves to the very ceiling and all around the walls, a dampness of old books. Or we note just one volume placed open on a shelf, or plates arranged on a table with small flowers in the middle, unobtrusively graceful. Or we are drawn to the family photographs where we see a picture of our friend's parent as a little child. Standing in the fullness of the unoccupied room we engage in the discovery of who it really is that lives there.

In a similar way, we watch a candle burn, or the expanding and contracting flames in a wood fire, or the many stars on a clear night, and are drawn into the consciousness that these illuminations manifest an invisible but perceptible presence. The Divine name *Hamakom*, literally, *the Place,* the All-Present One, denotes this "being there" of God, intimate and immense. In the panoply of stars, God appears unknowable and uncaring; in the light of a candle, close and searching.

Perhaps we enter into a conversation. This needs time, and not the constant rush which so often stunts communication. It needs a certain sympathy, which allows the recognition of congruity of feeling. Then we hear not only the unspoken words within ourselves before we give them voice, but also those we attempt to intuit in our partner. Words that come from the heart enter the heart, teaches the Talmud; attentiveness and companionship that come wordlessly from the heart enter the heart even more. Then, in such special moments, we may also apprehend the presence of a third partner, who is both witness and conduit, surrounding and protecting the developing relationship. Perhaps this is the One who is in between and all around us, God by whom we are given understanding.

Maybe we are alone. In the vitality of a garden with fresh buds and leaves, on top of a hill above the flight of a bird of prey, by a cliff where the sea smashes into the rocks and contradicts the import of the meager, single life, we are halted by an inner chastening. Here is God, awesome and eternal. We are caught between heaven and earth, minuscule and mortal, yet alert, a participant in knowledge that searches the heart and marrow:

But you, awesome God, with a single glance, distinguish good from evil.

Perhaps it is joy that brings us the feeling of being close to God. The Divine Presence resides only in the midst of joy, teaches the Talmud. The very awareness, however momentary, however limited, of God's presence brings happiness in the very fact and privilege of being; though it is not right that God is only present in joy. May God not also be there in the aloneness of a person who prays for help in stemming the flow of pain that oozes from an aching heart?

This is the meaning of the first commandment: to make ourselves available to such moments, to expose our being to God's presence and to be penetrated by it; to submit before it; to treasure the knowledge of that experience; to put nothing before it or even beside it, even if such moments of awareness do not recur for years. For they refine and elevate our heart and soul, reminding them of the invisible world to which they ultimately belong.

Such moments are intensely personal. No one finds it easy to communicate their understanding of the spiritual dimension of life. Perhaps that is why the Rabbis taught that six hundred and eleven of the six hundred and thirteen commandments (as traditionally counted) were communicated to the Children of Israel through the mediation of Moses. Two of them, however, "I am the Lord your God," and, "You shall have no other gods beside me," were heard *mipi hagevurah*, straight from the mouth of God. Some things can only be apprehended immediately, by every person each in their unique way.

Of course, there are many arguments against faith in God, and it is wrong to ignore them. It is wrong to claim that the world is sweet and wonderful, disregarding the poverty, misery, ugliness, and exploitation that constitute the overwhelming experience of life for countless people. It is lazy to turn a blind eye to the steady erosion of the world's beauty and the destruction of species. True, these things can be blamed not on God, but on us for misusing God's world. But why doesn't God stop them? Where is God's justice? The world reveals no apparent vindication of right, while everyday violence and cruelty make victims of millions of people. Things that "shouldn't be allowed to happen" happen all the time. There are many things worse than death.

These facts render facile comments about God's nature absurd, and sometimes, when used to justify the agony of others, obscene. But just as faith in God does not negate the reality of suffering and horror, so suffering and horror do not negate the reality of the experience of God's presence. We live, therefore, in the paradox of commanding contradictions. On the one hand, we face a world which cries out in denial of the universal justice and compassion said to encompass it, and which requires us to cry out with it. On the other, we encounter God; we hear God's voice, we intuit God's presence, we listen to the silence in which God simply is.

Perhaps these contradictions are ultimately similar to the impossibilities confronted by Job when he says of God, who has not and will not answer a single one of his questions about his unjustified suffering, that his eyes have seen his maker and now he truly knows. For when God speaks to him out of the whirlwind and describes the sheer abundance and magnificence of creation, he realizes that though God has not answered his questions, God has responded to *him* — in the song of the stars, the power of the sea, and the path of the light at dawn.

"I am the Lord your God . . ."

. . . It is the turning
aside like Moses to the miracle
of the lit bush, to a brightness
that seemed as transitory as your youth
once, but is the eternity that awaits you.

R. S. Thomas, "The Bright Field"[6]

There comes a point where one can exist, but cannot live without "it." Explaining what I mean by "it" is something with which I struggle. To say "God" would be too pious. Perhaps it is a glimmer of the refraction of God's light, an echo from the silent reverberation of God's speech.

I am the Lord your God . . . (Ex. 20:2): The question posed by the first commandment is not a theoretical one. The issue of whether God spoke in a certain way, on a certain day, at a certain place, is important in the context of the argument about the history of the Torah. But its significance is in no way comparable to the question of the impact of the simple words, "I am the Lord your God," on the way we live our lives each day. As Harold Kushner has written, "For the religious mind and soul, the issue has never been the *existence* of God but the *importance* of God, the difference that God makes in the way we live."[7] The reality we do, or do not, experience in the words of the first commandment forms our values and determines how we relate to life and death. It commands our moral being.

Classically, Judaism has spoken of two aspects to the encounter with God: the love of God on the one hand and the fear of God on the other. Between them, as Maimonides taught in the *Laws of the Foundations of the Torah*, is a constant dialectic — as if love were a step out into the wonder of the world and fear a step backward in awe.[8]

Human love accompanies life, should accompany every life, from its inception till its close. During the months when my wife was pregnant with our first child, I was, like many men, apprehensive. "Don't worry," said a friend, "the child will cry when you want to sleep and scream when you want peace and quiet, but you will love it nonetheless." He was totally right. As my mother-in-law is fond of saying, babies bring the love they need with them. One hopes that all through their childhood, it grows. When death cuts a person out of the network of love's bonds, it is impossible to measure what has been lost. Recently a man who lived on my street died. He often used to stand in his front garden and say hello; since he is gone I miss my greeting, the dog misses his pat, and the trees are appreciated less. Every person is part of a living filigree made from the threads of love.

God's love can be seen as something entirely different, as the pure relationship of spirit to the absolute. But in the Jewish mystical tradition, God's love has not usually been understood in such an abstract way. On the contrary, all love, including the love of one human being for another, the love of nature, the love of Torah, and the love of beauty, is seen as a reflection of God's love. For all love has its source in God, in the "love that moves the sun and the other stars."[9]

What this means to me is that all beauty, all joy, all wonder, and all love are, by their very nature, connected to the creative power of God. For it is through beauty, joy, wonder and love that we discover a greater and more harmonious presence within our ordinary, and often painful, world. The consequence of this is that everything matters. Every perception, every word, and every relationship has the potential to be illumined by that refracted light of God. That is why:

> . . . Life is not hurrying
> on to a receding future, nor hankering after
> an imagined past. It is the turning
> aside like Moses to the miracle
> of the lit bush . . .[10]

For there is no bush which may not burn, just as there is no moment which cannot become a revelation.

Fear accompanies love. *Fear,* though, with its punitive connotations, is a poor translation of the Hebrew term *yir'at shamayim,* which really means *awe in the face of the Divine.* Such awe is occasioned by the awareness, within our limited comprehension, of standing in the presence of a transcendent being. It brings a feeling of humility and inner silence. This is followed by the sensation of immense privilege that we are allowed to be part of creation, to intuit the Presence which fills it and to know that it flows through our own heart, too. To experience the fear of God is therefore to receive a great blessing. It is one of the few sensations strong enough to purge the mind, leaving it like a dusty garden washed clean with dew. Afterward, all the degradation we witness every day, and in which we often participate, seems utterly unacceptable, and our deepest wish is to hurt or injure nothing.

Of course we can *exist* without such experiences, but, deprived of them, we come to realize that we are less than fully alive. Much of the time we do, in fact, just exist and feed off recollections. Sometimes we lose even the memory of them and are not conscious that anything is lacking in our lives. It is better, however, to yearn, than not to have anything to yearn for. And mercifully there are times when we break back through into deeper life, or rather it breaks back through into us. Such moments do not have to be many; it would be greedy to ask for them often. Sometimes I think of them as if they were those few stars in the night sky that suffice to tell the lost traveler which way to go. They may be sparse, there may be long distances between them, but they are enough to give our life direction. For who, having known the presence of love and awe, would want to do anything that would make us, gross as we often are, less permeable to their power, less worthy of their visitation?

Return to Sinai

> Evil is real. So is good. There is a choice. And we are not so much chosen as choosers. Life is holy. All life. Mine and yours. And that of those who came before us and the life of those after us.
>
> Hugo Gryn[11]

Rabbi Hugo Gryn had not visited his home town in the Carpathian mountains since leaving it after the war, but some forty years later he was persuaded by his daughter to return. In the beautiful film she made of this journey there is one scene which I find especially haunting. Rabbi Gryn describes how, when in the spring of 1944 the family knew that they were shortly to be deported, he and his mother each buried their most precious possessions in the family garden.

I prayed and even wrote a pledge. It ran something like this: "I, Hugo G, solemnly promise to offer myself in the services of God, should my entire family in five years' time meet together."

Reflecting on this much later, he added:

How strange, that one way or another I did try to make much of my life something of a life of service to God's cause and the cause of my people and how I wish that God would also have kept my bargain with Him.

Rabbi Gryn's father and brother both perished and Hugo came home alone, bringing the news to his mother that her husband and younger son were dead.[12]

In the Torah we are presented with a God of justice, a God who fights for the oppressed, a God who will not tolerate tyranny, a God who brings us out of the house of bondage with a strong hand and a mighty arm. Yet it is immediately obvious that life doesn't work like that and that such a deity, if not entirely illusory, at the very least fails to make his presence felt. If little justice appears to descend from heaven, there often does not seem to be much of it on earth either. So the question arises: What does God actually do?

The story is told that the raven and the nightingale once had a competition to decide which of them had the sweetest voice. All the animals gathered to listen and the pig was appointed judge. The nightingale sang sweetly, the raven cried out hoarsely, and the pig, whose decision was final, ruled that the raven was the winner. As agreed, the raven pecked out the nightingale's eyes and flew away triumphant. A lion used to rest beneath the tree where the nightingale had its perch. Every night after losing the competition the bird sang so poignantly that the lion couldn't sleep. "Your song is so sad that I can't sleep," he said to the little bird. "Is it because you lost your sight that your heart aches so terribly?" "No," answered the nightingale, "that's not why I'm sad. What really hurts me is that it had to be the pig who was the judge!"

In life the pig is often the judge. *Tzedek, tzedek tirdof — Justice, justice shalt thou pursue,* commands the Torah (Deut. 16:20), requiring us to do right and behave justly because God is holy and just. But I sometimes think that what the words really mean is: If you want a fair hearing in life before other people, and even before God, who is supposed to be entirely just, then you'll have to look for it extremely hard because it isn't going to be easy to find. This was King Lear's insight, when he cried out in his madness:

> Thou hast seen a farmer's dog bark at a beggar? . . .
> And the creature run from the cur?
> There thou mightst behold
> The great image of authority —
> A dog's obey'd in office.[13]

If people are often unfair, so is fate. Like all my colleagues in the clergy, it often falls to me to officiate at funerals, sometimes of the young, sometimes even of babies. At the service we say the words, "Righteous are thou, O Lord, who causes people to die, and brings them to life." This prayer, called *Tzidduk Hadin,* accepts the righteousness of the judgment, but the "judgment" often doesn't feel just at all. For fate can be notoriously cruel, and reconciliation to it — which is what the prayer is really about — is possible only through prolonged courage and at the cost of much pain.

This, therefore, is where many people reach the parting of the ways. For some, God and religion simply cease to have meaning; they fail the reality test. Either God is dead, or God was a fiction in the first place. Others try to find a way of relegating the problem to a place where it can safely be ignored. But if we care about our faith we can't really ignore the problem for long. We have to consider a third possibility, that we can go back to Sinai and speak to God, or rather listen to God, again.

Fortunately the Bible contains an account of just such a return. The Prophet Elijah lived in an age of great cruelty. Ahab was a despotic ruler and his wife Jezebel had a particular hatred for the prophets of God, whom she put to death remorselessly. Elijah knew that there was nothing idle in her threat to feed his body to the dogs. He therefore fled to the desert and hoped to die, but an angel brought him food and, telling him to eat and be strong, led him on a forty days' journey through the wilderness back to Ḥorev, the mountain of the Lord. There, he heard no Decalogue, no mighty voice of God declaring, "I brought you out of the land of Egypt." All that stuff he already knew. Instead he was simply asked a question: "*Mah lekha fo Eliyahu?* — What are you doing here, Elijah?" Instead of the great declaration by the Almighty of his own credentials, a voice asked him, "Who are you?"

The question is asked of Elijah and it is asked of every single one of us.

It is asked of us in all the small details of our lives. I remember what it felt like when my wife and I moved into our new house to establish a home together. It was an exciting but frightening experience. We wondered: will we rattle in this building like dried beans in a box? (Ten years, three children, one dog, one rabbit, and two gerbils later, the question of space seems rather different!) Will we manage to make it into a real home, or will it be too much for us so that we never succeed in filling it with love? The previous owners had lived there for forty-one years, so that we naturally thought in terms of a similar duration. What will happen to us in such a long time? Will we leave here old? What will we make of life in the meanwhile? Then, amidst all these thoughts, we realized that we were being asked a question: "What are you doing here?" it said, just like the voice at Sinai. There came a sense of being extremely small, distinctly mortal, subject to chance; yet of being privileged to be asked this question in the face of infinite and absolute being: "So what about your life?"

I remember meeting a lady who used to live near my parents. She had recently lost her husband and was full of grief. "I've been crying a lot," she said, "but the other day when I took my handkerchief out of my pocket I noticed how the petals on it were beautifully embroidered. That forced me to look out at the world again." The thought had given her pause in her grieving, and in the interstice she had heard the question, "What are you making of this world? How are you living your life, now?"

One comes away from hearing such a question with no bold convictions or dogmatic declarations. Elijah did not hear commandments on God's mountain. When all the Children of Israel stood at Sinai there was lightning and thunder; for Elijah, God was not in the whirlwind or the fire. At Sinai the earth shook; for Elijah, God was not in the earthquake. At Sinai there was the all-powerful call of God; here, there is only the small voice of fine silence. The only commandment is, "What are you doing here?"

Yet just that is the question through which the historical memory of Revelation, of the grand theophany at Sinai, becomes significant in the life of each person. We go away from the experience with a sense of awe, but also with a feeling of privilege that the infinite silence should address us — even us — in the limitations of our minuscule being.

This isn't an answer to the problem of God's justice. It can't be. But it is an experience that changes the nature of the questions we ask. We no longer say in the same manner, "What are you going to do about it, God!" or, "Why did you make the world like this?" Our questions are more likely to be addressed to ourselves and to each other now: "What can I do with my life?" "How can we respond to you, God?" For the feeling that life owes something to us, if only an answer, is replaced by the understanding that it is also we who owe something to life. God's justice is now seen to depend on our deeds, on how we treat each other and the world, on how *we* answer the question.

Perhaps this was true of Rabbi Gryn: his real response was his life. God wasn't fair; God didn't respond to a bargain that God never in fact made. But what really came to matter was not that. What mattered was how his own life could be an instrument of God's work.

Images of Torah

The tablets and the fragments of the tablets lie in the Ark.

B. Berakhot 8b

Songs have your statutes been to me in the house of my sojourning.

Ps. 119:54

To the Jew the Torah scroll is the most precious object in the world. "Object," because in the end the Torah scroll is only a thing, and if there should ever be a choice between saving a scroll and saving a life, life basically comes first. With that sole proviso, the Torah remains of all things the most sacred and the most beloved.

Three images of the Torah are fixed in my mind; between them they express the different facets of what that love and sanctity mean.

The first is connected with a ceremony which was originally a tradition of the Jews of Alsace. When a baby boy was thirty days old, the parents would present a *wimpel*, or Torah binder, to the synagogue. We have two of these in my community. One was given to us just recently. It is over thirty feet long; when unrolled it stretched right across the synagogue. On it was written in traditional fashion the name of the child and the names of his parents, together with the prayer that they should have the merit to bring him up to receive the blessings of Torah, marriage, and the performance of good deeds. The other *wimpel* belonged to a scroll discovered after the war in Czechoslovakia, part of a vast hoard of loot including over fifteen hundred Torah scrolls assembled by the Nazis as part of their projected museum of the defunct culture of Judaism. We do not know the name of the community from which that Torah scroll came, nor the fate of the descendants of the little boy whose parents desire that his life should be blessed was recorded in red stitching on the binder some hundred and fifty years ago.

These *wimpels* are traditionally made of the swaddling bands in which the baby was wrapped. Transferred to the Torah, they express the tender love in which its teaching is held and the desire to bind them into our lives and those of our children with the same compassion with which we nurture our own flesh and blood. For Judaism speaks not only of keeping the Torah but, more profoundly, of *'ahavat Torah,* of loving the Torah. This is evidenced in the whole process of its study and transmission. One of my earliest memories is of my mother teaching me how to draw an *aleph*. Now a parent myself, I experience a special joy when my children say, "Print me an *aleph-bet* from your computer, daddy." The link goes further than these two generations. I have often seen the tenderness of the contact between grandparent and grandchild that the Torah has the power to occasion. Rachel Naomi Remen remembers how, brought up in a secular Jewish home, it was her pious grandfather who would respond to her queries about God and the Bible by sitting her on his lap and saying, "*Neshume-le* [little soul] . . . this is a most difficult question, a question worthy of much thought."[14]

These *wimpels* represent the love which, in defiance of history, the Jewish people have always wrapped around the Torah.

The second image I owe to Rabbi Avraham Soetendorp, who told me the story when I visited his synagogue in the Hague. He was born during the German occupation of Holland. Soon after the rabbi's birth, a Nazi officer entered his parents' home, and seeing the baby, declared, "What a pity he's a Jew!" Avraham's father, a rabbi, must have been a man of exceptional courage; he replied: "No! It's an excellent thing that he's a Jew. He won't have any blood on his hands!" The man was evidently stirred by this comment. He beat Avraham's father — the presence of other Nazis meant that he had to do this — but the rabbi noticed that his assailant was weeping. Instead of deporting them there and then, he told the family that he would be back the next day to take them away, thus deliberately giving them an opportunity to escape. The parents arranged to have their baby hidden, and they went underground. All three survived and Avraham grew up to follow his father into the rabbinate.

One day many years later Avraham, now Rabbi Soetendorp, received an unknown visitor at the synagogue. The man brought with him a parcel to give to the rabbi. He was an artisan and worked in leather. During the war a Nazi had called at the workshop and ordered his father to repair the torn skin of his drum. The man protested that it was wartime and he had no materials with which to do so. "But I have," insisted the Nazi, producing a roll of thin leather. "Use this!" The Hebrew writing betrayed its origins; it was parchment cut from a Torah scroll. Visitors to Yad Vashem will be familiar with a whole host of items, lampshades, shoes, and so forth, all products of similar acts of profanation. The man was taken aback, but this was war and what could he do? Years later, his son brought the remnants of that section of parchment, marked by the circle cut out to repair the drum, back to the place where he felt they belonged. Rabbi Soetendorp welcomed the portion of Torah home. He decided to keep it in the Holy Ark with the other scrolls, recalling the ancient tradition that the fragments of the first tablets, smashed by Moses on seeing the golden calf, were kept in the Ark alongside the second, complete set of the Ten Commandments.

This story reminds us to have faith. There is a limit to the power of evil. What is sacred may be repressed and disfigured, but not totally destroyed. "God has planted eternal life in our midst," says the blessing over the Torah. A way of life based on justice, compassion, and the value of every person will ultimately outlast the onslaughts of those who try to destroy it.

The third image is Chagall's painting, *Solitude*. In the background of the picture stand the buildings of a small town, houses, domes, and turrets. The sky above is dark and the figures in the foreground are wrapped in swirls of black cloud, except a small angel flying upward in a drift of blue, but it is the two main characters in front who attract the most attention. On the right is a young calf, all white, lying down with a violin beneath its neck, as if it were making music. Its gaze is directed elsewhere. To the left of the calf sits a Jew in a dark mantle covered by a large white cloth or *tallit,* his head resting on his hand, his other arm encircling a *sefer Torah.* The calf and the violin, the Jew and the Torah, balance one another; each has their solitude, each their undisclosed thoughts, and each their instrument of music.

I have few memories of my grandfather's actual preaching, but I know that he loved the Psalms and liked the verse, "Songs have your statutes been to me in the house of my sojourning" (119:54). He loved the song of Judaism, both literally and in the sense in which the spirit of a way of life is its music. As a refugee, an exile, he also knew what it meant to inhabit "the house of sojourning," the house of estrangement, where home lies not in the villages and valleys, but above all in the music. For statutes create a way of life that is familiar, that is music. Judaism, throughout its many exiles, has travelled nowhere without that music and its instrument is Torah.

The calf sits in the foreground of the picture next to the Jew as if she were an analogy, an interpretation of his existential state. I do not know if she is "a calf to the slaughter," representing the innocence of victimhood, or simply a being in her own right, immersed within herself, her large eyes focused elsewhere. She does not look as if she were still playing the violin; the music appears to have stopped, but she continues to contemplate the sound. It is because of her that the picture is so tender, counterbalancing a harshness it would otherwise convey; transmuting loneliness into solitude, and exile — from that small town in the middle distance behind them — into the habitation of another world.

For, "Songs have your statutes been to me in the house of my sojourning." Your songs, the songs of Torah, have made me feel at home.

The Story of a Scroll

One very special Thursday morning we had the privilege of reading from a Torah scroll that had not been used in sixty years.

The story of the fortunes of that *sefer Torah* involves at least five generations and epitomizes the fate of the Jewish people in our century. It begins, insofar as we can reconstruct it, in 1937. It was in this year that my paternal great-grandfather, Rabbi Jakob Freimann, died suddenly while on holiday in Moravia. Although he was *av bet din*, head of the rabbinical court, in Berlin, it had been his express wish that he should be buried in

Holleschau, Czechoslovakia, the place where he had begun his rabbinical career. We have pictures of the long procession that accompanied him to his final resting place.

Soon afterward his library, including the *sefer Torah*, was packed in some thirty crates to be sent to his son Alfred, my father's uncle. Alfred Freimann was a judge and had been living in Germany, but two years previously, when the Nazis prevented him from even entering the court over which he had been used to preside, he and his wife had left for Rome. There, a family member who was researching the Jewish section of the Vatican library was able to help him obtain employment. But before his father's books could reach him, he was once again obliged to flee; he left fascist Europe behind him and settled for good in the ancient homeland of the Jewish people.

The crates would duly have followed, except that by the time they reached Italy, Mussolini had declared war on Ethiopia and the Mediterranean was blockaded. The books and the *sefer Torah*, along no doubt with the possessions of countless others, were lost in Italy, victims first of a regional, and then of the global, conflict that engulfed most of the world and devoured over a third of the Jewish people.

Once the British had realized that those Jews who had fled Europe for the safety of its shores were not enemy aliens but passionate foes of Nazism, they allowed them to enter the forces and eventually permitted the formation of the Jewish Brigade. Among the chaplains to this force, as it fought its way through Italy with the British army, was Ephraim Urbach, later to become a renowned author and professor at the Hebrew University. In his youth he had frequented my grandparents' home in Breslau, where, as a young rabbinical student, he had taught Hebrew to the children, my father among them. One day a soldier in the Brigade came to him with the report that he had found some boxes of Jewish books in a cave. Urbach's curiosity was immediately aroused, and one can only imagine his surprise when he found on the crates the familiar name of Freimann. Thus nine years and a world war later, the books finally reached their destination; Alfred Freimann was at last in possession of his father's library .

Around this time Alfred was offered a professorship at the Hebrew University. This honor was to lead to his tragic death. Situated on Mount Scopus, the university, together with the Hadassah Hospital, was cut off from the Jewish sectors of Jerusalem in early 1948. By agreement with the

British authorities, a convoy of doctors and nurses, students and academics would travel fortnightly under their protection to relieve the beleaguered personnel of those institutions. Thus it was that my father's uncle came to be among the seventy-seven Jews who lost their lives when, shortly after the bombing of the King David Hotel, the buses carrying them to Mount Scopus were attacked and burned — within sight of the watching British army.

Alfred's books were eventually given by the family to the Hebrew University in his memory. The *sefer Torah,* which was seriously damaged and unusable as a result of the time it had been left in the cave, passed to Alfred's sister, my father's mother. With her death it went to my aunt; eventually it came to my father.

My father brought it with him to England. When one day he heard that a scribe would be coming to my home to examine some letters in a scroll belonging to my congregation, he brought his *sefer* along to gain an expert opinion. Passages in the book Bereshit were entirely black, sections in the book Vayikra were pale, bordering on the reddish; it was "a law given to Moses at Sinai" that every letter of the Torah should be black. The situation did not look hopeful. But when the scribe, a wonderful, warm-hearted man and a true *ḥasid,* saw how much the fate of this *sefer* meant to our family he determined to take it with him. He considered it to be some two hundred years old, and it aroused his keen interest. Even though some parts were irreparable, he would see whether on his travels he could not discover usable sections of other fading scrolls, compatible in their small size, by means of which he could reconstruct and render kosher our Torah.

There followed almost a year of hope, inquiries, and waiting. One Sunday night the phone rang at my home. "I've finally done it! Can I bring the *sefer* round and show it to you now?" Unfortunately my father was away that day, so the scribe unrolled the scroll across my table and explained how here he had amended a fading section, there found a parchment of three or four columns that fitted, here inserted just a column. It was all done — except that when he unrolled the Torah in full, there was not one scroll but two: he had foregotten to sew the last of the new parchments together. Off he went in search of the ritually suitable thread to make the stitches.

Although it was half-past-ten at night, my wife and I, moved by what was unfurling before us, woke our then five-year-old son to watch. Mossy

232

has always loved to draw the Torah and play with a scroll he has made for himself; we wanted him to witness and remember this final act of restoration. The scribe came back and Mossy watched, but not in silence. "Is that the same kind of thread," he asked, "as mummy uses when she sews?" How do you tell a child that actually it's not a thread but animal gut? It was then that it occurred to me that the question pointed to a metaphor, and a richer response. The Torah is stitched together with a living substance; life, the living of it, is what transforms it from withering columns awaiting burial to sacred testament. That is why the young must be witness to, and of, the rededication of the old.

The next Thursday my father was called up to this *sefer Torah*. For once it was fortuitous that there was no *Kohen* at the minyan — my father could be given the very first *aliyah*. He quietly said the *Sheheheyanu* blessing to God who has preserved us, kept us alive, and brought us to this time.

The Book of Ruth

"God doesn't make strangers."

In *Kitchen Table Wisdom*, Rachel Naomi Remen describes how Yitzak, a concentration-camp survivor, came to a retreat she ran. Initially, he was wary of the affectionate spirit of the meetings, but his attitude gradually softened. When asked what had brought about this change, he replied that he had had a conversation with God: "I say to Him, 'God, is it OK to luff strangers?' And God says, 'Yitzak, vat is dis *strangers*? *You* make strangers. *I* don't make strangers.'"[15]

The Book of Ruth describes a similar movement from being a stranger to finding companionship and compassion. Ruth is a foreigner, a Moabite, the descendant of a people who refused to provide the Children of Israel with bread and water on their journey to the Promised Land. She stands on the wrong side of all those divisions that so often set us apart and make us enemies — religion, history, and race. Unfortunately, making strangers is easy, removing estrangement hard. That is surely why her mother-in-law Naomi presses Ruth and her other daughter-in-law Orpah not to accompany her back to Israel but to remain behind in Moab and return home to their families. They will find new husbands there, they will be among their own people. Naomi invokes their love, the faithful kindness they have shown "to the dead and to me," in order to persuade them to stay.

But Ruth refuses in the name of that very same love and utters perhaps the most famous words in the long history of companionship:

> Wherever you go, I will go;
> and where you lodge, I will lodge;
> your people shall be my people,
> and your God my God;
> where you die, will I die, and there will I be buried.
> The Lord do so to me, and more also, if even death
>   parts me from you.[16]

Ruth and Naomi return together. When they reach Bethlehem, Naomi's former acquaintances surround her and stare in disbelief: "Can this be the same woman we used to know?" (1:19). Naomi cries out in response, "I went forth full; empty has the Lord brought me back" (1:21). She has lost her husband, her sons, her wealth, her social standing and her self-respect. Yet what she says is not the whole truth, for she has brought back with her a love which has already crossed borders, and which will make the crossing of further borders possible.

The Book of Ruth illustrates many actions through which friendship and love are formed. That is why it is described as "entirely *ḥesed*" — pure loving-kindness. A key scene in the Book, which particularly demonstrates the movement from being a stranger to finding friendship, occurs when Boaz sees Ruth reaping in his fields and promises her his protection. These are pained and stressful moments for Ruth. Although the narrator paints a charming pastoral scene, Ruth is in fact on her own amidst a foreign people in a foreign land. Keats is surely right when he describes her as "sick for home amidst the alien corn."[17] But Boaz senses Ruth's loneliness and vulnerability, and his words, offering welcome, blessing, and protection, soothe her spirit and take some of the strangeness away.

"Why have I found favor in your eyes that you acknowledge me, when I am a *stranger*?" asks Ruth in response (2:10). Pointedly, the Hebrew words for *acknowledge* and *stranger* are both formed from a similar, perhaps the same, root, one from the simple and one from the causative form, as if to show how thin the division can be between recognizing or ignoring the humanity of another. The careful play of forms and sounds — *lehakireni ve'anokhi nokhriah* — demonstrates how readily the transformation from alienation to welcome can be made. Kind words, food, and water, the offer of protection, and a person is no longer a stranger on earth. If we could always respond to other people like that, how much less hatred there would be. But all too frequently the heart doesn't soften, and the words which could have meant recognition and friendship remain unbending or unspoken. The stranger remains outside.

Maybe this is why we read the Book of Ruth on the day after we celebrate receiving the Torah. We know all too well how we can misuse Judaism to set Jew against Jew and abuse religion to generate hate in God's name. The Book of Ruth reminds us that the Torah was given to us for precisely the opposite purpose, to help us discover each other's humanity and to enable us to see God's image in every person. God does not make strangers and we shouldn't do so in God's name.

Three Choices

> Therefore was the human being created single, to teach you that whoever destroys a single life is considered by Scripture as if they had destroyed a whole world, and that whoever saves a single life is considered by Scripture as if they had saved a whole world; and for the sake of peace among all beings, so that no one should say to their fellow: "My father is greater than yours."
>
> M. Sanhedrin 4:5

If I were asked which commandment most urgently needs to be put into practice if we are to survive, high on the list would come, "And you shall love him as yourself, for you were strangers in the Land of Egypt. . . ." (Lev. 19:34).

The twentieth century, perhaps the whole of human history, has shown us three models for different peoples to relate to each other. The first is the way of ethnic purity. Only the racially pure are allowed to live in our land; others, if they are tolerated at all, must go elsewhere. The second is the way of absolute sameness. All ethnic and religious difference must be erad-icated. The third is what I would call, for want of a better name, the way of compassionate coexistence.

We know all too well what the first approach entails. My family were its victims. My grandfather would never speak about what happened at Dachau. He was one of the few people fortunate enough to be released, on the strength of emigration papers obtained by my grandmother at the cost of much courage. My grandparents and their children survived, but other relatives did not.

We say, "Never again." But the past has proved an unsuccessful teacher, and hate appears to spring eternal in the human breast. Its victims have committed no further sin than that of existing, as Jews, Kurds, Cambodi-ans, Rwandans, Bosnians, Kosovars . . . Not in exactly the same way, not with precisely the same intent, but the evil of ethnic hatred continues.

Quite apart from the fact that it is morally abhorrent, the ideal of eth-nic purity is vitiated by two pragmatic considerations. The first is that such purity is a fiction. If I take myself for example, I am the descendant of Jews on all sides of my family for as far back as we are able to trace. (Some Jews today of course are not — but they are, for all that, no less Jewish. Judaism is not a race.) This, however, is only part of my story. I was nurtured by the rains, rivers, hills, and heather of Scotland. Prior to that my family was central European, my various grandparents delighting in the poetry of Goethe, Schiller, and Heine. Before that, my ancestors probably lived amidst Russian plains and rivers, suffering the Cossack pogroms, poverty, and famines. Earlier than that, they may have lived in Spain. In all of these phases, their Judaism was influenced not only by the strong currents of its own past, but by the philosophy, literature, and faiths which it encountered and which overflowed into it to mix and be carried along amidst the waters of its primary beliefs. When someone speaks, therefore, of the "true, pure Judaism," I wonder to what they can possibly be referring. "Purity," in this context, is a fiction. The Rabbis of the Mishnah noted that when accusing Cain of murder, God said, "The voice of your brother's bloods cries out to me from the earth." They ques-tioned why the Torah used the plural, "bloods."[18] My own answer would be that no one contains just one pure kind of blood, or one pure kind of culture or belief.

The second consideration is that the very motives that lead to "ethnic cleansing" ensure that the process is never complete. For the leaders, and the people, who need an *other* to hate, will still need an *other* to hate when all the initial *others* are banished, imprisoned, or dead. Once the "foreign element" has been purified, there is bound to emerge a further reason for discrimination and a successive cause for purges after that. Secret police don't run out of work, for the state, or the religion, or simply the group which cannot tolerate diversity is wedded to a philosophy of everlasting hate. It is bound to destroy just as it is ultimately bound to self-destruct.

But pragmatic grounds only furnish a secondary reason for opposing such systems. They are in principle a profanation. They are an offense against the Torah's declaration, the touchstone for the Jew on all issues of human rights, that every person is created in the image of God, together with the basic rabbinic assertion deriving from it, that those who destroy a single life are considered as if they had destroyed the entire world.[19]

The second way is that of radical sameness. This appears to be a response to the evils engendered by the exploitation of ethnic and religious difference. It seeks to put an end to diversity and a full stop to the long history of racial hatred which has bedeviled humanity. This can seem attractive. It is known that Jews who survived the *Sho'ah* and subsequently found themselves under Communist rule saw it as a cure for anti-Semitism and a canopy of protection. But the ideal is misguided. It is not surprising that it has failed the reality test. For differences are neither capable of being eradicated, nor should they be. Thus Soviet propaganda never quite succeeded in emptying the churches, mosques, and synagogues, and the resurgence of religious practice proved an important factor in that system's collapse. For it sought to impose not equality but sameness; and sameness and equality are very different things.

When I was studying to be a teacher, we were taught that all children were born equal. Nurture alone was responsible for the differences in intelligence and behavior which were to be observed in children as they grew up. Few, if any, parents will agree. Within hours of the birth of our second child, my wife and I could see how different, and therefore how unique and special, each of our children was. The same applies in culture and religion. It is to be doubted whether anyone's soul sings in Esperanto. Some years ago my wife and I were in Budapest and were privileged to participate in a discussion with a group of Jewish people in their thirties and forties about how they had been given their names. Their parents had been afraid to give them obviously Jewish names. One man said that his parents had wanted to give him an international name, a name which would not mark him out as coming from anywhere, lest during the course of his life he should be obliged to flee and make a new home in another land. One woman said that she had indeed been given a Jewish name, but only because it was that of the heroine of a popular novel, so that everyone would presume that this was its source. There was something sad about this testament to the repression of identity. Suppression does not lead to equality; it simply pushes people's real feelings underground. Equality cannot be achieved by force.

Judaism teaches that God rejoices in difference. God, we are told at the very beginning of the Torah, is a creator, an artist. To the creative mind the perception and valuing of difference is essential — a drift of grey and blue, as many kinds of green as a garden in spring, the grain and knotting in a piece of wood that make it the right, the only, piece capable of being carved. The artist rejoices in the specific. In the same way God makes many people, all in the same human mold, but each unique and different. "Therefore," teaches the Mishnah, "everyone is obligated to say, 'For my sake was the world created.'"[20] Take any one person away, suppress his or her identity, and an irreplaceable portion of creation ceases to exist.

There remains therefore no alternative but the way of compassionate coexistence. This involves neither the abandonment of our personal identity nor of our particular community. At the same time it does not mean that people from different faiths should share everything. There are good reasons why they cannot and should not.

We do not all need to express our values in the same way, though we do need to realize that there are values to which we all either assent or perish: the sanctity of life, the integrity of relationships, the preciousness of the earth. We do not need to pretend that we can all care equally deeply for every single person or every group of people. But we do have to be clear that every single person and every community is worthy of care and that in times of crisis everyone and every group has a call on our conscience. We cannot share the same liturgies, festivals, names for God, but through the very particularity of our practice, we must perceive and affirm that it is the same God whom we all address. Indeed this realization, which has sometimes struck me with the greatest force precisely in the places of worship of other religions, has led me at once to my deepest affirmation of Judaism and to the most humbling sense of the universal presence of God, manifest in an infinite multiplicity of ways.

This issue — how we live, different, yet together — is basic and definitive. As we manage it, so we make peace or war. As we resolve it, so we live or die.

TISHAH B'AV

Helplessness

. . . because the children and babies faint in the streets of the city. They say to their mothers, "Where is grain and wine?" They collapse like the wounded in the streets of the city; they pour out their souls and die in their mothers' laps.

Lam. 2:11–12

Of Gabi — such a splendid brother and I grieve because when it mattered — I could not protect him . . .

Hugo Gryn[1]

I often think of that letter sent from Ida Goldis to her sister Clara on November 4, 1941, and of little Vili, aged two, and the scarf his mother made for him:

My darling, the things and the money which you have sent helped me greatly and arrived at the proper time. From the wool that you have sent me I have made a thick shawl for Vili's neck, because who knows how many days he will be on the way; at least may God give us fine weather . . .[2]

But she was unable to prevent him from dying of cold on the long march to Transnistria.

When I read something like that, I go into the children's rooms and sit on the floor to watch them breathe and silently assure myself of their safety. What does anyone know about the future? What can be worse than finding oneself unable to protect the life of one's child?

Helplessness is terrifying. Today in the Western world we are accustomed to thinking of ourselves as powerful and capable. We do not like to be made aware that there are matters about which we can do nothing. That is part of our arrogance. For there are many situations about which there is absolutely nothing we can do and which all our efforts cannot remedy. Other generations knew that better and were more familiar with suffering. For what we cannot do, as much as what we can do, is implicit in life itself. My sister-in-law was once in the hospital in a bed just next to the children's ward. From time to time she would hear a child cry out, "Mummy, mummy, help me!" But the mother could take away neither all the pain nor all the fear. And that was in peacetime, in the absence of persecution.

My wife and I were thrilled when each of our children was born. What I had not anticipated was the awareness of ending that the beginning would bring, the mortality implicit in birth. I had not understood that in the very moment that was filled with the wonder of entrance, the phantom of departure would already appear. But as our first child was born, when his head and body emerged and he took his first breath of outside air, I felt I could hear a stopwatch starting to tick, the sound of the sand commencing its course through the glass. Our child was embarked on his journey through finitude, time was already counting his breaths. The wholeness of his pilgrimage appeared before me, its extent unknown but its end certain, and pained me like the consideration of my own death. These thoughts never struck me while he was in the womb, where his life truly began; it was the wonder of birth that brought its companion with it, the mystery of death. Then I understood the rabbinic tradition that for the first days of its sojourn here the baby mourns the loss of the sense of eternity its soul had formerly known. That is why, when we share the meal of welcome around the cradle on the night before a child's naming, we eat the foods of sorrow.

Our third child was born on a weekday morning, the hour when the first patients were arriving for their routine appointments. Returning from a rushed errand, waiting for the lift, I watched the various people follow the colored lines along the hospital floor to their departments — physiotherapy, radiology, oncology. To be born, I realized, is to enter a universe of vulnerability and become subject to the laws of flesh. I was struck again by the mystery of life, its tenderness, its susceptibility to pain. Our baby was born so swiftly that my wife literally had to catch her; she slid for her first day into a long, soft sleep. So may she be held always, safe from sickness, pain, and anguish. But it will not and cannot always be. For history bears out this basic fact, that there are many times when we cannot protect one another, not even our children.

One and a half million Jewish children died in the Holocaust, and hundreds of thousands of children of other peoples. But the Nazis were not the first persecutors to target children. The tyrants of the ancient world did exactly the same. In the long history of cruelty, the punishing of parents by hurting and killing their children has been common practice. The Torah knew this well when it included this curse in its terrifying list of imprecations: "Your sons and daughters shall be given unto another people, and your eyes shall look, and fail with longing for them all the day; and there shall be nought in the power of thy hand" (Deut. 28:32). It is irrelevant whether the passage was composed in advance as a threat and a prophecy, or afterward with hindsight, when Jerusalem was in ruins and all those terrors had already come to pass. The writer is describing the worst that can possibly happen in the knowledge that it has happened and will continue to happen. Such horrors were real enough when the Book of Deuteronomy was written, and they are real enough today.

The Book of Lamentations is terrifying. An elegy, an outpouring of grief, an attempt at explanation, its acrostic form keeps measured the immeasurable. It is a work of witness and of struggle. Its opening question "How?" is its keynote and refrain; How do such things happen? Why does Jerusalem sit solitary? Why have her friends betrayed her? How is it possible that the city which we thought impregnable, the city that was the crown of beauty, has been invaded and laid waste? How can those who grew up amidst plenty now be dying in its streets? But of all the terrifying images, it is those relating to children that I find the most painful:

> . . . because the children and babies faint in the streets of the city. They say to their mothers, "Where is grain and wine?" They collapse like the wounded in the streets of the city; they pour out their souls and die in their mothers' laps (2:11–12).

"There shall be nought in the power of thy hand," wrote the author of Deuteronomy (28:32), and the author of Lamentations knew exactly what that meant.

Tishah B'Av is a terrifying day; death rushes past us in waves, breaking ever nearer on the shore. We sit silent on the ground, helpless, and overwhelmed. We remember the sacking of both the first and the second Temples, the crushing of the Bar Kokhba revolt, the destruction of whole communities by the Crusaders, the expulsion of the Jews from France, England, and Spain, and the Shoah itself. On no other day do the laws of fasting and of mourning both apply. On Yom Kippur we observe the former — no food, no drink, no pleasurable washing, no leather sandals, and no intimate relations. Yet, for all its deprivations, it is a rich day, a day of joy and beauty, of community without and communion within, of restoration of heart and soul. But on the Ninth of Av we do not greet one another with a friendly greeting, we walk head bent "as those reproved by the All-Present God," we study only the most painful passages of the Bible and we fast to starve the body, not to sate the soul. For we remember how our people starved and perished in the streets of Jerusalem, on the streets of many other cities.

On the Ninth of Av we share the experience of being powerless. "These things do I remember, and pour out my soul within me . . ." (Ps. 42:5). May God save us and everyone from living through such times!

God's Helplessness?

The three weeks before the Ninth of Av are the most painful in the Jewish year, and the fast itself is Judaism's most painful day. Here we re-encounter our worst tragedies, but we also encounter the courage and passion with which Judaism has kept faith with God.

Keeping faith in spite of tragedy means asking painful questions, both of ourselves and God. It means having the vision to see God differently and the humility to relinquish expectations. This is not to suggest that God becomes different. But the way we think about God does change, as our people attempts to understand the trials and terrors of history, and to make sense of what God did or did not do for us, and why. For we have both a need for faith and a need to try to explain, even if one or both appear impossible. It is the interaction between these two basic human requirements that is reflected in the history of Jewish theodicy, of how through the generations we have attempted to understand why God lets tragedies happen. Indeed, the very courage and creativity with which Judaism has grappled with these problems are powerful testaments both to its own tenacity, and to God.

Jeremiah's contemporaries at the beginning of the sixth century B.C.E. expected God to protect the Temple. It was to them not only a bastion against national disaster but a stronghold of the divine. God was powerful and would not allow Jerusalem to be sacked. If God did, in their eyes it might mean God's defeat, just as when a pagan temple was destroyed and the invaders replaced the statue of the local deity with one of their own divinity. God could not let the Temple fall, for God might then be gone forever. God, in the idiom of the twentieth century, would be dead.

When the First Temple was sacked, Jeremiah challenged that assumption and presented a different understanding of why God lets bad things happen. According to this view, rooted in the theology of the Torah but expressed most poignantly in writings attributed to Jeremiah, God is not bound to buildings or even to countries. In our relationship with God, geography comes second to morality. God's protection of the people in the Land of Israel is contingent on their conduct, and even God's forgiveness has limits if we persistently and repeatedly ignore what God requires of us. Thus Jerusalem falls because its citizens are unworthy and the destruction of the Temple has to be understood not as God's fault but as our own. Jeremiah thus popularizes a theology which we echo to this day when we say in the additional prayers on festivals, "On account of our sins have we become exiled."[3]

When the Second Temple fell some six hundred and fifty years later in 70 C.E., the theology of "*mipnei hato'einu* — on account of our sins," was not superseded. Indeed, in placing the cause for disaster in the human, rather than the divine, sphere, the "for our sins" theology proved to be spiritually empowering. It engendered soul-searching, repentance, and a commitment to responsibility. The Rabbis of the time blamed themselves and the society in which they lived for what had happened. They taught that Jerusalem fell because of *sinat hinam*, groundless hatred.

Yet, as the persecutions continued through the subsequent generations, culminating in the ruthless crushing of the Bar Kokhba revolt in 135 C.E., a new note of challenge entered the discourse about God. No longer was it only the idolatrous enemies who said, "Where is their God?" God's silence prompted questions closer to home. Self-blame could not explain either the cruelty of the enemy or the suffering entailed by the "punishment":

In the school of R. Ishmael it was taught: [Read not] "Who is like thee among the gods [*'elim*]?" [but], "Who is like thee among the dumb [*'ilmim*]?"[4]

God was experienced not as powerful, but as silent. Behind the anguish in this subversion lay a shrewd, if painful, reasoning: God's might lay in the divine self-restraint, which enabled God to watch the Romans triumph and keep silent.[5] God's power was expressed precisely in the painful policy of non-intervention, which allowed human beings to do both their best — and their worst. Here we anticipate Rabbi Hugo Gryn's penetrating observation that the question is not, "Where was God?" but, "Where was man?"

During the same period, there were dramatic new developments in Jewish thought. Indeed this is the time when the foundations of rabbinic Judaism were established as we know it today. There is a deep and thorough democratization in the approach to God. God is present wherever the sacred community establishes the framework of Jewish life and observance. Where the congregation prays, there God is. Where a group, where a single person, studies Torah sincerely, there the Divine Presence rests. "I am with him in trouble," says the psalmist (Ps. 91:15); where there is suffering, there the All-Present One dwells. Where we go, God's abiding presence, the *Shekhinah,* goes too. God, in other words, is to be thought of less as the cause of our tribulations than as the comforter when they happen. God, furthermore, suffers with us, weeping at the effects of a history in which even the Divine is vulnerable, a victim like ourselves. Hence the story of Rabbi Yossi, who enters a ruined building and hears a voice moaning like a dove. When he emerges Elijah tells him that every day this voice can be heard saying, "Alas for the father who has exiled his children and alas for the children exiled from their father's table."[6]

The expulsion of the Jews from Spain in 1492 had a cataclysmic influence on the whole house of Israel. Where was God now, when his people were scattered across the wide seas? Isaac Luria, who died in Safed in the middle of the sixteenth century, taught in his immensely influential interpretation of Kabbalah that God could be seen as somehow scattered, too. There had been a disaster in the very process of creation, as a result of which sparks of divinity were flung far and wide, and lay lost and concealed in every husk and kernel of creation. The spiritual task of each human being was to remove the material garb in which they were hidden and uncover their illumination. Only then could they be reconnected to the source of all light.

Surely one can glimpse in these scattered sparks of God an image of the dispersed and wandering families of Jews, seeking to be reunited with their people. In a haunting poem, Yehudah Halevi compares the lamps of the hapless refugees with the reflected lights of the night sky in the dark ocean:

> And the stars will be bewildered in the heart of the seas
> Like exiles driven from their own homes.[7]

God, too, was seen to be driven from home, little flames of the divine floating on the waves and waiting to be rescued.

To our generation, the Shoah brings the question, "Where is God?" with renewed force. What shall we say about God's justice now? God is not dead, as those who testify to God's presence even in the death camps surely assert. But what kind of god is God? Can we change our expectations once again and still retain the sense of a transcendent being of whose power it is meaningful to speak, who is still "mighty to save"?

As after other disasters, there is, and will continue to be, a theological reaction. We stand too near in time to perceive the general trends of a new response, but it is likely that we will find fresh ways of reaffirming our faith, according to our own experience and in our own idiom. This is surely part of our national recovery, of our reaffirmation of spiritual creativity, in spite of everything. Why should our enemies take this from us? After all, we never allowed them to do so in the past.

One of the ways in which we will reaffirm our faith may be through valuing the stirring literature of personal testament that has come into our hands and which is still in the process of being recorded. Perhaps we can find God in a new way through the experiences of each "ordinary" individual — as "ordinary," that is, as each and every unique human being. Consider, for example, this extract for July 1942 from the diary of Etty Hillesum as she faced the prospect of deportation from her beloved Amsterdam:

> I shall try to help You, God, to stop my strength ebbing away, though I cannot vouch for it in advance. But one thing is becoming increasingly clear to me: that You cannot help us, that we must help You to help ourselves. And that is all we can manage these days and also all that really matters: that we

safeguard that little piece of You, God, in ourselves. And perhaps in others as well. Alas, there doesn't seem to be much You Yourself can do about our circumstances, about our lives. Neither do I hold You responsible. You cannot help us but we must help You and defend Your dwelling place inside us to the last.[8]

On the day we mourn the destruction of the Temple, we should consider that every single life is God's sacred Temple and that God's power in this world lies substantially in what each of us chooses to do with that part of the spirit which is delegated to us.

THE SEVEN WEEKS OF CONSOLATION

Maybe I am Needed

Rabbi Yehoshua ben Levi asked Elijah, "When will the Messiah come?" "Go and ask him directly," was his reply. "Where is he sitting?" "At the entrance." "And by what sign may I recognize him?" "He is sitting among the poor lepers: all of them untie [their bandages] all at once, and rebandage them together. But he unties and rebandages each separately, thinking 'Maybe I am needed and I must not be delayed.'"

B. Sanhedrin 98a

According to tradition the Messiah is born on the Ninth of Av. Out of destruction comes redemption; out of disaster emerges hope. But the road between them is not easy to travel.

Elijah tells Rabbi Yehoshua ben Levi (they seem to meet on a fairly frequent basis) that if he wants to know when the Messiah will come he'd better go and ask him directly. Perhaps the meaning of this surprising turn in the conversation is that other people can help us in our search for hope and consolation, but in the end no one can find them for us. We have to travel that road for ourselves.

Rabbi Yehoshua ben Levi is told to go to "the entrance," an allusion to the gates of the great city of Rome. Why should he have to go there? Had not the Romans just recently destroyed Jerusalem, crushed Betar, imposed an unbearable burden of taxation on its people, and laid half the land of Israel waste? Why should the Messiah be there of all places? But that's the point: unless we can face our troubles, unless we can bear to acknowledge our wounds, there can be no proper healing. Nevertheless, it is a courageous journey to go back to one's own Rome.

I once saw a film about a woman who went to look at the isolated house where the man who killed her daughter had imprisoned, abused, and finally murdered her. I found it almost incredible that she could bear to visit the place. But when she was asked that very question, she said that she had to see and had to know. That was the only way she felt she could ever live with what had happened, the only way she could begin to come to terms with destiny for robbing her of her child. As I remember, she even spoke of her hope that the visit might help her to understand, and begin to find forgiveness for, the man.

Rabbi Yehoshua ben Levi asks Elijah how he is supposed to recognize the Messiah. It's not enough to be told that he's among the sick; at the gates of a city the size of Rome there are countless poor and wounded beggars. Which one of them is supposed to be the Messiah? Elijah tells the rabbi that there is a crucial difference between the Messiah and all the others. The rest of the sick spend their time taking off and putting on all their bandages at once. In other words, they are totally preoccupied with their own wounds; they are not just physically, but psychologically, wrapped up in their bandages. The Messiah, however, unbandages only one wound at a time because he knows that at any moment he may be needed and he doesn't want to be delayed. He doesn't want to be in a position where he is so preoccupied with his own needs that he is unable to respond immediately to those of others.

But what is the Messiah doing among the wounded in the first place? Coming from a different, but closely related, tradition T. S. Eliot wrote:

> The wounded surgeon plies the steel
> That questions the distempered part . . .[1]

Often it is our very pain that guides us toward the contribution we can make. For it is not infrequently out of understanding our own wounds that we acquire the ability to heal. The person who actually knows what it means to be bereaved, or to go through a hostile divorce, or to have chemotherapy, responds quite differently to someone else who is confronting the same difficulties. They know. It will almost certainly be a long, and perhaps a largely unconscious, process that leads us from our own struggles to the position where we can help others. Not everybody travels that road. Just as the poor and sick in the parable spend their whole time preoccupied with their own wounds, so some people can only view life from their own angle. Everything else is seen as a reflection of their own crisis and is measured by its standards. People at that stage may provide the very worst company for someone else who is suffering, but they may later go on to acquire a remarkable generosity of spirit.

The Messiah removes only one bandage at a time, while everybody else puts all their bandages off and on the whole day long. I don't think this means that the Messiah is generically a different kind of person, created from the first to occupy a higher plane. Rather, the others are as yet on a different stage of their journey. Perhaps they are still too close to their own suffering to see anything else. How can it be otherwise? It takes time to come to terms with ourselves and our pain, and we can't say the crucial words, "Maybe I am needed," until we have done so properly. Understanding and wisdom often come from living with our wounds over a long period and are won by experience. If at the time of our suffering we don't feel our pain, if in the season of our mourning we feel no grief, what can we ever know about the wounds of others?

"Maybe I am needed," says the Messiah. This is the voice speaking within each of us, telling us that we, too, have a part to play in healing and consolation. People instinctively recognize the kind of suffering to which experience has sensitized them. Some retreat; the reminder is too powerful and their own wounds too raw. Others draw near. There are, perhaps for all of us, certain kinds of sorrow with which we come to feel at home. They have nested in our heart, and through them we hear God's voice instructing us in the art of compassion. They call us to tasks which are uniquely our own, which someone else could not necessarily do. They show us our part in the process of redemption. Thus for many people an attitude of "Maybe I am needed" becomes the pathway through suffering to purpose and community.

Like many others who have experience of suffering, my mother became a psychotherapist. She enjoys bringing people of different professions and nationalities together to share their understanding of human behavior. She attributes this love of building bridges to her experience of growing up in Nazi Germany and later as a refugee in England. It has motivated her to try to draw people together in valuing differences, rather than letting them divide us. In this way, the very difficulties she encountered became the source of her ideals.

After meeting the Messiah, Rabbi Yehoshua ben Levi went back to Elijah and told him everything that had happened. Then he accused the Messiah of lying. "He said that he would come *this very day*," complained the rabbi, "but he didn't!" What he actually told you, rejoined Elijah, quoting from the Book of Psalms, was, "*Today,* if you will hearken to my voice" (95:7)." In other words, the coming of the Messiah is not some arbitrary event set to happen on a date predetermined by God. On the contrary, it is up to us when the Messiah will come. That will be when each of us listens to God's voice, when each of us fulfills our part in the process of healing and redemption.

Just an Ordinary Person

"There is nothing special about me."

Miep Gies[2]

I was recently privileged to participate in two interfaith encounters. The first was a communal event, when the deacon of the Crailsheim region, near Nuremberg, brought members of his congregation to spend a Shabbat in our synagogue and our homes. It was a brave journey that he undertook, the result of a persistent conviction that Germans should experience Judaism, not only as something which belongs to their past and about which they carry the burden of history, but as a vibrant way of life. All of us were stirred by this visit more deeply than we had anticipated. The second was a series of structured conversations between Jewish, Christian, and Moslem leaders, which drew from us shared concerns as well as sharp differences about how we understood our responsibilities in an aggressive age.

"What is the point of such meetings?" I was challenged. "What have we learned from our time together?" Dekan Pfitzenmeier asked me and the whole group of participants before they returned to Germany.

One might, of course, hope that members of each faith would review the whole history of its relationship with other religions, that there would be a clear change in the perception of the other; that liturgies would be revised, prejudices removed, responsibilities acknowledged, and that not just the lips but the heart would proclaim the long professed truth that God is indeed One. There are such moments in history, Vatican II being an important example, and the changes they herald must be translated into everyday realities. Pluralism, the acknowledgment of the authenticity and value of different paths to God, should he practiced, not just preached.

My answer to what our small, personal, encounters with members of other faiths mean is simple. It is the fox's request to the little prince in Saint Exupery's wonderful novel *Le Petit Prince.* "Please — tame me," says the fox to the child, conveying with those words the trust shared and the responsibility promised when a stranger turns into a friend.[3] Of course, one can still betray friends, but one can't say that one doesn't know them. One can't say of people whom one has tamed, "What are they to me?" Such people no longer have no face and no name; their claim on our conscience is real. That is why we have to meet with those of other faiths: to "tame" one another and to activate that claim.

Tragically, history and hatred can still tear apart even those who have loved each other. I recently heard about two sisters, one married to a Serb and one to a Kosovar, who spent innumerable weekends together with their families. The adults talked while the little cousins, who were all of an age, played merrily; but later the sisters dared not meet lest their husbands kill each other. We can only be astonished at the power of ancient hatreds. But that power is real enough.

So, furthermore, is the temptation to exploit it. A psychological study of the group dynamics of religions is urgently required in order to understand why clerics of all faiths and denominations have at so many critical moments carefully and calculatedly reminded their communities of old enmities, picked the scabs off sores, worked up ancient fabrications, and provoked the most venomous outbursts of hatred.

Against that power is set the simple, fragile trust of *You have tamed me.* Often it is all we have. It is something very frail, merely a thing of the heart. Yet it is the source of the astonishing courage that leads people to risk their lives for others when they could sleep safely in bed with an idle conscience. *You have tamed me* may derive from actual experience, a conscious commitment to the man with whom we once worked, the girl who was in the same class. Or it may symbolize the deeper, universal taming by which it is possible to recognize intuitively the humanity of every person through the awareness of our own. For there are people who, in spite of terrors, live out the meaning of the creed in which the words "love your neighbor as yourself" are followed not by "ifs" and "maybes" but by the eternal demand of "I am the Lord," however inconvenient that command may be, whatever the risk entailed.

The ultimate purpose of encounters with those of other faiths is to help us all recognize the truth that we are children of one God; but that may or may not happen, and few of us are swayed in our daily conduct by such abstractions anyway. I prefer therefore to think of the smaller, less romantic objective of recognizing each other's humanity.

That is why I will never forget listening to Miep Gies. I have often visited Anne Frank's house in Amsterdam and wondered at the courage of the people who provided her and her family with their every need, risking their lives daily for over two years. In her book, Miep describes what happened when Otto Frank asked her to help them go into hiding. She had not a moment's hesitation then, nor did she deviate from her faithfulness for a single moment afterward. What impressed me most was how, nearly fifty years later, she began her talk by saying that she was just an ordinary person. I remember thinking at the time, "If only all ordinary people were like you." If only I could always be ordinary.

Words of Consolation?

Comfort ye, Comfort ye, my people, saith your God,
Speak to the heart of Jerusalem and call to her . . .

Isa. 40:1–2

How do we offer comfort? In the beautiful words of the Bible, how do we speak to someone's heart?

"Do not offer consolation to one whose dead relative lies before him," teaches the Mishnah.[4] The plain meaning of this statement is that it is not the time to speak of comfort before the funeral. The mourners are almost certainly in a state of shock. They may well need practical help with the arrangements for the burial, but offers of consolation are premature. After the funeral, when their loved one lies at rest and the living turn to the future lonely and bereft, then the time to offer comfort has come.

In some sense, do not our dead always lie before us? Sometimes they literally remain unburied. After the destruction of Betar, the stronghold from where Bar Kokhba successfully defied them for three years and proclaimed the independence of Judaea, the Romans reputedly refused to allow the tens of thousands of dead to be buried. Today the desecration of the dead is still considered a mark of particular barbarity.

More significant may be the dead whom we ourselves are unable to lay to rest because they refuse to lie in peace in our memory. For most of us, the inner world is a haunted castle. There are also other kinds of sorrow that do not go away. A little child cannot understand why his father has abandoned him and his mother. Day after day he looks out over the garden gate and waits for his father to come by. One day he does drive past; his son sees with great excitement that his father has seen him, but the man doesn't even slow the car down. Is the pain of such a betrayal ever laid to rest? Does time, healer as it is reputed to be, ever take away the memory or the consequences of our wounds? Harold Kushner, whose son died at the age of fifteen, wrote that there was not a single day in which he did not explore the gap left by his absence, as the tongue examines the space made by a missing tooth.[5]

The heart's pain cannot simply be taken away. How, then, can we ever talk of comfort; how can we speak to the heart?

I often go to houses of mourning. Sometimes I hear people preach to the mourners about God's justice and God's ways and how God knows what he's doing. I try to keep out of it. Often I listen to well-meaning friends telling the mourners what they ought to be thinking and feeling. Perhaps, to be generous, these private sermons may have helped some people to find the faith or the willpower — or the anger — to carry on. But it is more than questionable whether it is wise to inform the bereaved of the theological why and wherefore of their loved one's death, or to instruct them in what they are presumed to be feeling. They know . . . and most of them find the fact that they are talked at just another of the many burdens they have to bear.

Jewish law teaches us not to speak until the mourner breaks the silence. The deeper meaning of this instruction is that our response should be based on listening. We may add a prompt or a question or share a recollection, "Yes, I remember too . . ." "He could be like that, couldn't he. . . ?" We may test out a tentative thought, to see if the mourner feels in tune with it. Then, though we may not directly offer consolation, the mourners will find comfort in the evocation of memory, in sympathetic honesty, and in our openness to what they feel.

Above all, we should speak not *at* life, but *with* life. That is what speaking to the heart means. It means making an opening so that the heart can find its own words. It means allowing the heart an outlet for its sorrow or its courage, its tenderness or despair. It means staying by while it discovers in its own stillness the strength to contain its pain, as the trees grow around the shores of the forest lake. "Speaking to the heart" is not about putting our own words into someone else's heart. It is the art of keeping company while the other person finds his or her own words.

Speaking to the heart means making our own heart accessible. Many of us worry greatly that we will say the wrong thing, but most people will forgive a misplaced word if it is said in the right spirit. It is less what we say than how we say it that matters; it is less our words themselves than where our words come from that counts. For "words that come from the heart enter the heart," and all of us recognize the difference between a clumsy, but affectionate, phrase and a correct, but cold, formulation.

We might also remember that when we try to bring comfort we do not do so alone. Many voices in the world have the capacity to address the heart, especially the wounded heart, at any time. All creation is articulate, and pain can sometimes intensify the capacity to hear. Grief numbs, but it also sensitizes, even intolerably so. "Near is the Lord to the broken hearted," says the psalmist (Ps. 34:19), for the entrance to the heart may then be wretchedly open. I believe that the plants in a beloved garden, the trees in a much-frequented park, speak to us in our sorrow. I think of the many benches that carry a simple dedication, "To John, who cared so much for this place." The birds, the clouds and the reddening sky all speak to the heart. "I, even I, am the One who comforts you," says God (Isa. 51:12). Maybe it's always God's voice that speaks when something brings true consolation, God in the wind, in the trees, in the rushing water of a river, in the moon, and in the stars.

Afterword

I want to end with a story by my late mother.

That is partly because this book is about continuity, the flow of tradition from one generation to another in liturgies and practices by means of the love through which they are transmitted. I was quite small when my mother died, so I am still discovering how deeply she was part of that process.

It is also because this book is about wholeness, and wholeness requires the reconciliation between what we experience, the depth and beauty to which we are exposed through the gift of life, and the knowledge that we must surrender not only that experience, but also our very self, to that same life from which it comes. It is precisely this which my mother addresses here.

The Flower

from *Himmel und Erde*
by Lore Salzberger-Wittenberg

Die junge Blume träumte. Noch war sie eine Knospe und hielt die Blütenblätter nach oben geschlossen wie Finger gefaltet zum Gebet. Im Blüteninnenraum regten sich die Träume. Träume von Licht, von der Sonne, vom Himmelszelt, von dem räuschenden Blumengarten und der Schar der süßen Schmetterlinge. Immer wieder dachte die Blume voll Entzücken, während sich die Spitzen der gefalteten Blütenblätter zu röten begannen: "Ich, ich und die Ewigkeit."

Die Blume öffnete sich. Weit breit-

The young flower was dreaming. She was still a bud and her petals were intertwined like fingers folded in prayer. Dreams were stirring within her: dreams of light, of the sun, of the expanse of the sky, of the whispering flower garden and the host of sweet butterflies. Again and again, as the tips of her petals began to turn red, she thought with delight: "I and all eternity."

The flower opened. Her petals spread out wide toward the light as if they were trying to encompass

eten sich die Blütenblätter dem Licht entgegen, als wollten sie die Welt umspannen. Der strahlende Garten tat sich vor ihr auf, Blumen und Bäume, Sonnenschein, Himmelsbläue, Wolken, Mond und Sterne. Auch die Schmetterlinge kamen, die erträumten; sie wiegten sich auf der Blüte mit seidigen Flügeln und sogen ihren Honig ein. Sie aber trank die Farben und den Duft des Lebens und spendete selbst Farbe und Duft. Sie gewahrte die anderen Blumen rings um sich her, die so wie sie Leben tranken und Leben schenkten. Und sie sah sich inmitten dieser Blumen, eine von Tausenden und Abert-ausenden. Und die Blumen inmitten einer Welt von flügelnden Tieren, und diese wieder inmitten der Welt von Sonne und Wolken, Regen und Sternen. So stand die Blume mit gebreiteten Blättern und blühte viele Tage und Nächte.

Als die Frucht in ihr zu reifen begann, sah sie voll Vertrauen auf zum großen Himmel, und ihr ganzes Pflanzendasein wußte: "Ich und die Vergänglichkeit. Aber die Blumen, aber die Schmetterlinge, die Sonne, der Raum und die Ewigkeit," sie atmete tief, "auch ich bin in der Ewigkeit."

the world. The radiant garden unfolded before her, flowers and trees, sunshine, the blue sky, clouds, moon, and stars. The butterflies of which she had dreamt came too; they swayed on the flower with their silken wings and sucked her honey. She drank in the colors and fragrance of the garden, and added to it her own color and fragrance. She became aware of the other flowers all around her, who, like herself, were drinking in and giving out life. She saw herself in the midst of these flowers, one among thousands and tens of thousands, and the flowers in the midst of a world of winged creatures, and these in turn in a world of sun and clouds, rain and stars. Thus stood the flower with her petals spread wide and bloomed for many days and nights.

When the fruit within her began to ripen, she looked up full of trust to the vast sky above and knew with all her flower-being: "I and all transient things. But, like the flowers, the butterflies, the sun, space and eternity" — she breathed in deeply — "I too am part of eternity."

Translated by Isca Salzberger-Wittenberg and Jonathan Wittenberg

Endnotes

ELUL — THE MONTH OF PREPARATION

1. Rabindranath Tagore, "Gitanjali, Section LXXIX" in *Collected Poems and Plays of Rabindranath Tagore* (New York: Macmillan, 1998), p. 106.
2. Gale Warner, *Dancing at the Edge of Life* (New York: Hyperion, 1998), p. 106.
3. Abraham Joshua Heschel, *Man's Quest for God: Studies in Prayer and Symbolism* (New York: Scribner, 1987), p. 62.
4. M. Rosh Hashanah 1:2; B. Rosh Hashanah 18a.
5. Warner, p. 79.
6. Naḥmanides, *"'Omer 'ani ma'asai lamelekh,"* in *Shirat tor hazahav bisefarad,* ed., Y. Yahalom (Jerusalem: Hebrew University, 5746), pp. 255–7.
7. B. Sanhedrin 106b.
8. Ps. 74:16.
9. Ps. 95:4.
10. Rabbi Shimeon ben Yitzḥak Abun, Prayer for Rosh Hashanah, in *Maḥzor hashalem lerosh hashanah veyom kippur,* ed. Paltiel Birnbaum (New York: Hebrew Publishing Company), p. 231.
11. Olive Fraser, *The Pure Account: Poems of Olive Fraser (1909–1977),* ed. Helena M. Shire (Aberdeen: Aberdeen University Press, 1981), p. 2.
12. L.G. Bolman and T.E. Deal, *Reframing Organizations: Artistry, Choice, and Leadership* (San Francisco: Jossey-Bass, 1997), p. 24.
13. Osip Mandelstam, *Stone,* trans. Robert Tracy (London: Collins Harville, 1991; Princeton: Princeton University Press, 1981), p. 59.

ROSH HASHANAH

1. M. Avot 4:1.
2. Moshe Lieber, *Pirkei Avos Treasury/Artscroll* (New York: Mesorah Publications, Ltd., 1995), p. 211.
3. Howard Schwartz, *Gabriel's Palace: Jewish Mystical Tales* (New York: Oxford University Press, 1993), p. 125.
4. Rachel Naomi Remen, *Kitchen Table Wisdom* (London: Pan Books, Ltd., 1997; New York: Riverhead Books, 1996), p. 271.
5. Ḥayim Naḥman Bialik, *"Yeish li gan,"* in *Shirim* (Tel Aviv: Sifriat Dvir La'am, 5733), pp. 271–3.

6. Sholom Ansky (Sholom Zawill Rappaport), "The Jewish Tragedy in Poland, Galicia, and Bukovina — From The Diaries of 1914–1917," trans. Morton Lang and excerpted as "Choroskow During the First World War," in *Sefer Choroskow*, ed. D. Shtokfish (Tel Aviv: Committee of Former Residents of Chorostkov, Poland, in Israel, 1968), p. 258. Available at www. jewishgen.org/ yizkor/khorostkov.
7. Hannah Senesh, *Halekha lekaesaria, A Wanderer's Prayer* (New York: Transcontinental Music Corporation, 1949).
8. Rebbe Avraham Mordekhai of Ger, following *Likutei Yehuda*, in *Ḥumash peninei haḥasidut, bereshit* (Jerusalem: Hotza'at 'Agudat Peninei Haḥasidut, 5747), p. 11.
9. Janusz Korczak, *Ghetto Diary* (New York: Holocaust Library, 1978), p. 139.
10. Ibid.
11. B. Shabbat 31a.

THE TEN DAYS OF RETURN

1. B. Yoma 86b.
2. Shakespeare, *The Tempest,* Act 5, Scene 1.
3. B. Ḥagigah 15a.
4. E.W. Rollins and H. Zohn, eds., *Men of Dialogue: Martin Buber and Albrecht Goes* (New York: Funk & Wagnalls, 1969), p. 270.
5. Samuel Taylor Coleridge, "The Rime of the Ancient Mariner," in *Wordsworth and Coleridge: Lyrical Ballads,* ed. R.L. Brett and A.R. Jones (London: Methuen and Co., Ltd., 1976), p. 34.

YOM KIPPUR

1. M. Yoma 1:1.
2. M. Yoma 4:2.
3. Vaclav Havel, address to the Polish Parliament on January 21, 1990.
4. *The Times* (London), May, 1985.
5. Rev. Dr. Anthony Phillips, *The Times* (London), June 8, 1985.
6. Rashi commenting on B. Menaḥot 97a.
7. Gerda Weissmann Klein, *All But My Life: A Memoir* (London: Indigo, 1997; Hill & Wang Pub., 1995), p. 86.
8. Rachel Bluwstein, *Shirat Raḥel* (Tel Aviv: Hotza'at Sifriat Davar, 5738), p. 25.
9. Olive Fraser, *The Pure Account: Poems of Olive Fraser (1909–1977),* ed. Helena M. Shire (Aberdeen: Aberdeen University Press, 1981), p. 2.
10. Harold Kushner, *How Good Do We Have To Be?* (Boston: Little, Brown & Co., 1996), pp. 101–2.
11. C. Day Lewis, "Walking Away," in *The Gate and Other Poems* (Jonathan Cape: The Estate of C. Day Lewis, 1962).
12. Vera Gissing, *Pearls of Childhood* (London: Robson, 1988), p. 155.
13. Ruth Picardie, with Matt Seaton and Justine Picardie, *Before I Say Goodbye* (London: Penguin, 1998), p. 103.

14. Rachel Naomi Remen, *Kitchen Table Wisdom* (London: Pan Books, Ltd., 1997; New York: Riverhead Books, 1996), p. 150.
15. William Wordsworth, "Lines Written Above Tintern Abbey," in *Wordsworth and Coleridge: Lyrical Ballads,* ed. R.L. Brett and A.R. Jones (London: Methuen and Co., Ltd., 1976), p. 116.
16. Kadya Molodowsky, "Prayers," in *Paper Bridges: Selected Poems of Kadya Molodowsky,* trans. and ed., Kathryn Hellerstein (Detroit: Wayne State University Press, 1999), p. 145.
17. B. Berakhot 5a.
18. Elie Wiesel, *Souls on Fire* and *Somewhere a Master,* trans. Marion Wiesel (Harmondsworth, England: Penguin, 1984), p. 287.
19. Yehuda Halevi, *"Yah 'Ana 'Emtsa'ekha,"* in *The Penguin Book of Hebrew Verse,* ed. and trans. T. Carmi (Harmonsworth, England: Penguin Books, Ltd., 1981), p. 338.
20. M. Avot 3:10.

SUKKOT

1. Rabbi Yishmael, *Mikhilta deRabbi Yishmael* (Jerusalem: Bamberger & Wahrmann, 1960), Parashat Hashirah, 3.
2. M. Sukkah 5:1.
3. B. Sukkah 11b.
4. John Keats, "Ode to Autumn" in *Keats, Poetical Works,* ed. H.W. Garrod (London: Oxford University Press, 1956, 1970), p. 87.
5. B. Shabbat 22a.
6. Percy Bysshe Shelley, "Ode to the West Wind," in *The Oxford Anthology of English Literature Romantic Poetry and Prose,* eds. Harold Bloom and Lionel Trilling (London: Oxford University Press, 1973), p. 447.
7. Kahlil Gibran, *The Prophet* (London: Heinemann, 1980; New York: Knopf, 1923), pp. 10–11.
8. Eccles. 1:2.
9. B. Sukkah 4bff.
10. Edward Serotta, *Survival in Sarajevo: How a Jewish Community Came to the Aid of Its City* (Vienna: Edition Christian Brandstätter, 1994), p. 13.
11. Reuven Daphni and Yehudit Klaiman, eds., *Final Letters from Victims of the Holocaust* (New York: Paragon House, 1991), p. 18–19.
12. Shelomoh Yosef Zevin, *Sippurei Ḥasidim: Moadim* (Jerusalem: Kol Mevaser, 2000), p. 127.
13. Oscar Wilde, "Lady Windemere's Fan," in *Plays of Oscar Wilde* (New York: Random House, 1980).

ḤANUKKAH

1. Shemot Rabbah 35:1.
2. B. Niddah 30b.
3. *Sefat Emet* (Rebbe Yehudah Aryeh Lev of Ger), *Sefat Emet: Bereshit,* 5634 (Jerusalem, 5731), p. 204.

4. Anne Frank, *The Diary of Anne Frank* (London: Pan Books, Ltd., 1954), pp. 218–9.
5. *Sefat Emet*, op. cit.
6. Nick Naydler, "Like a songbird in its cage" in *For Anne Frank* (Bristol: Loxwood Stoneleigh, 1991).
7. Johann Wolfgang von Goethe, "Zueignung," in *Gedichte* (Munich: Wilhelm Goldmann Verlag, 1964), p. 115.

TU B'SHEVAT

1. Rebbe Avraham Yehoshua Heschel of Apt, *'Imrei Yosef*, in *Ḥumash peninei haḥasidut, bereshit* (Jerusalem: Hotza'at 'Agudat Peninei Haḥasidut, 5747), p. 381.
2. William Wordsworth, "Lines Written Above Tintern Abbey," in *Wordsworth and Coleridge: Lyrical Ballads,* ed. R.L. Brett and A.R. Jones (London: Methuen and Co., Ltd., 1976), p. 114.
3. Viktor Frankl, *Man's Search for Meaning: An Introduction to Logotherapy* (New York: Simon & Schuster, 1984; New York, London: Pocketbooks, 1984), p. 90.
4. John Keats, "Ode to a Nightingale," in *Keats, Poetical Works,* ed. H.W. Garrod (London: Oxford University Press, 1956, 1970), p. 207.
5. Maimonides, *Mishneh Torah*: Laws of Mourning, 14:24, in *Maimonides Reader,* ed. Isadore Twersky (West Orange, New Jersey: Behrman House, 1972).
6. Hugo Gryn, with Naomi Gryn, *Chasing Shadows: Memories of a Vanished World* (London: Viking, 2000), p. 49.
7. Pirkei deRabbi Eliezer, as quoted in *Sefer Ha'aggadah: Legends from the Talmud and Midrash,* ed. H.N. Bialik and Y.H. Ravnitzky, trans. W.G. Braude (New York: Schocken Books, 1992), p. 34
8. Dante Alighieri, *The Divine Comedy 1: Hell,* trans. Dorothy Sayers (London: Penguin, 1949), pp. 149–52.

PURIM

1. B. Berakhot 28a.
2. M. Avot 2:5.
3. B. Megillah 12a.
4. B. Megillah 7b.

PESAḤ

1. Osip Mandelstam, "Voronezh, 19 January 1937," in *Selected Poems*, trans. C. Brown and W.S. Merwin (London: Oxford University Press, 1973), p. 89.
2. Osip Mandelstam, "Tristia," ibid., p. 23.
3. Rabbi Ya'akov Yosef of Polnoye, *Sefer Toldot Ya'akov Yosef, Bereshit 12b* (Brooklyn: 'Ohel Torah, 2000), as quoted in *Sefer Ba'al Shem Tov,* Vol. 1, p. 17.

4. Midrash Tanḥuma, in *At the Threshold: Jewish Meditations on Death*, ed. Michael Swirsky (Northvale, NJ: Jason Aronson, 1996), pp. 27–29.

5. *Maimonides, Mishneh Torah:* Laws of Repentence, 5:2, *Maimonides Reader,* ed. Isadore Twersky (West Orange, NJ: Behrman House, 1972), p. 77.

6. Rabbi Meir HaCohen, *Haggadot Maimoniot,* commentary to Maimonides, *Yad Hahazakah: Hilkhot Teshuvah* 5:2.

7. Ibid.

8. Osip Mandelstam, "Voronezh, 1935," op. cit., p. 78.

9. Shaul Meizelis, *'Ayn shalem milev shavur: 'imrot harebbe mikotsk* (Tel Aviv: Modan, 1988), p. 34.

10. Yosef Ḥayim Yerushalmi, *Haggadah and History* (Philadelphia: Jewish Publication Society, 1975), Plate 58.

11. Noam Zion and David Dishon, *The Family Participation Haggadah: A Different Night* (Jerusalem: Shalom Hartman Institute, 1997), p. 113.

12. Marie de Hennezel, *Intimate Death,* trans. Carol Brown Janeway (Boston, London: Little, Brown & Co., 1998), p. 181.

13. *Shulḥan Arukh, 'Orakh ḥayim* 473:4.

14. *The Passover Anthology,* ed. Philip Goodman (Philadelphia: Jewish Publication Society, 1961), p. 175.

15. Passover Haggadah.

16. Milton Steinberg, *Jewish Reflections on Death,* ed. Jack Riemer (New York: Schocken, 1975), p. 135.

17. Viktor Frankl, *Man's Search for Meaning: An Introduction to Logotherapy* (New York: Washington Square Press, revised and updated, 1986), p. 86.

18. Boris Leonidovich Pasternak, "Parting," in *Doctor Zhivago,* trans. Max Hayward and Manya Harari (London: The Harvill Press, 1996), p. 489.

19. Kadya Molodowsky, "A Letter to Elijah the Prophet," *Paper Bridges: Selected Poems of Kadya Molodowsky,* trans. and ed. Kathryn Hellerstein (Detroit: Wayne State University Press, 1999), p. 357.

20. David Zagier, *Botchki: When Doomsday Was Still Tomorrow* (London: Peter Halban, 2000), p. 198.

21. B. Ta'anit 22a.

22. I heard this story from Rabbi Shlomo Carlebach, of blessed memory.

23. Molodowsky, p. 357.

THE COUNTING OF THE OMER

1. Yehuda Halevi, from *Shirim baharizah mivraḥat lerabbi Yehudah Halevi: Material for seminar study,* ed. Y. Yahalom (Jerusalem, 5735), p. 64.

2. Liturgy for the counting of the *omer.*

3. Shakespeare, *Richard II,* Act 5, Scene 5.

4. Shakespeare, *Hamlet,* Act 2, Scene 2.

5. Rebbe Meshullam Zische of Zhinkhov, "'Or Yehoshua," as quoted in *Ḥumash peninei haḥasidut, vayikra* (Jerusalem: Hotza'at 'Agudat Peninei Haḥasidut, 5747), p. 216.

YOM HA-SHOAH

1. Primo Levi, *Shema: Collected Poems of Primo Levi,* trans. Ruth Feldman and Brian Swann (London: Menard Press, 1976), p. 21.
2. B. Berakhot 6b.
3. Dan Pagis, "Testimony," trans. Stephen Mitchell, in *Voices of Conscience: Poetry from Oppression,* eds. Hume Cronyn, Richard McKane, and Stephen Watts (North Shields: Iron Press, 1995), p. 63.
4. M. Sanhedrin 4:5. The text of this mishnah was altered in the Middle Ages, and the words "of Israel" were inserted after "one life." This marks a response to persecution and shows how a universal vision can become fragmented by oppression.
5. Ibid.
6. Hugo Gryn, with Naomi Gryn, *Chasing Shadows: Memories of a Vanished World* (London: Viking, 2000), p. 253–4.
7. Janusz Korczak, *Ghetto Diary,* and Aaron Zeitlin, *The Last Walk of Janusz Korczak* (New York: Holocaust Library, 1978), p. 7.
8. *Forward,* March 1940, as cited in Nehemia Polen, *The Holy Fire: The Teachings of Rabbi Kalonymus Kalman Shapira, The Rebbe of the Warsaw Ghetto* (Northvale, NJ: Jason Aronson, 1994), p. 12. I am indebted to my teacher, Rabbi Dr. Aryeh Strikovsky, for introducing me to the work of Rabbi Kalonymus Kalman Shapira and, above all, to this remarkable book.
9. Polen, *The Holy Fire,* pp. 25–6.
10. Ibid., pp. 131–2.
11. Ibid., p. 119.
12. Ibid., p. 148.
13. Betty Jean Lifton, *The King of the Children: A Biography of Janusz Korczak* (London: Chatto & Windus, 1988), pp. 9–10.
14. Zeitlin, p. 30.
15. Quoted in Lifton, p. 228–9.
16. Korczak, p. 137.
17. Lifton, p. 320.

YOM HA-ZIKARON AND YOM HA-ATZMA'UT

1. *Letters of Jews Through the Ages: From Biblical Times to the Middle of the 18th Century, Vol. 1,* ed. Franz Kobler (London: East and West Library, 1952), p. 227.
2. Rachel Bluwstein, "'El 'Artzi," in *Shirat Raḥel* (Tel Aviv: Hotza'at Sifriat Davar, 5738), p. 58.
3. Jonathan Wittenberg, "The Well of Rachel's Words," MANNA 19 (Spring 1988), pp. 15–16.
4. Ibid.
5. Ibid.
6. "'Eini kovlah," in Bluwstein, p. 63.
7. "Mineged," ibid., p. 118.

8. Ra'ayah Harnick, *"Uvalailah ba 'elai hayeled shelo nolad,"* in *Shirim leguni* (Tel Aviv: Hotza'at Hakibbutz Hame'uchad, 5743), pp. 31.
9. Zelda, *"Hafugah —* Truce," in *Shenivdelu mikol merḥak: Shirim* (Tel Aviv: Hotza'at Hakibbutz Hame'uchad, 5744), pp. 12–13.
10. Quoted in *The Jerusalem Anthology: A Literary Guide,* ed. Reuven Hammer (Philadelphia: Jewish Publication Society, 1995), p. 313.

SHAVUOT

1. *Sefat Emet* (Rebbe Yehudah Aryeh Lev of Ger), *Sefat Emet: Bemidbar, 5631* (Jerusalem, 5731), p. 23.
2. Rashi on Devarim 5:19.
3. *Sefat Emet,* op. cit.
4. Ibid.
5. Liturgy, *Maḥzor* for *Shalosh Regalim.*
6. R.S. Thomas, "The Bright Field," in *Later Poems: A Selection, 1972–1982* (London: Macmillan, 1983), p. 81.
7. Harold Kushner, *Who Needs God?* (London: Simon & Schuster, 1990; New York: Summit Books, 1989), p. 23.
8. Maimonides, *Hilkhot Yesodei HaTorah* 2:2.
9. Dante Alighieri, *The Divine Comedy 3: Paradise,* trans. Dorothy Sayers and Barbara Reynolds (London: Penguin, 1949), p. 347.
10. Thomas, p. 81.
11. Hugo Gryn, with Naomi Gryn, *Chasing Shadows: Memories of a Vanished World* (London: Viking, 2000), p. 259.
12. Ibid., 142–3.
13. Shakespeare, *King Lear,* Act 4, Scene 6.
14. Rachel Naomi Remen, *Kitchen Table Wisdom* (London: Pan Books, Ltd., 1997; New York: Riverhead Books, 1996, 1997), p. 275.
15. Ibid., p. 156.
16. Book of Ruth, 1:16–17.
17. John Keats, "Ode to a Nightingale" in *Keats, Poetical Works,* ed. H.W. Garrod (London: Oxford University Press, 1956, 1970), p. 209.
18. M. Sanhedrin 4:5.
19. Ibid.
20. Ibid.

TISHAH B'AV

1. Hugo Gryn, with Naomi Gryn, *Chasing Shadows: Memories of a Vanished World* (London: Viking, 2000), opening pages.
2. Reuven Daphni and Yehudit Klaiman, eds., *Final Letters from Victims of the Holocaust* (New York: Paragon House, 1991), p. 18-9.
3. Liturgy, *Musaf* for *ḥagim.*
4. B. Gittin 56b.

5. B. Yoma 69b.

6. B. Berakhot 3a.

7. Yehudah Halevi, *The Jewish Poets of Spain, 900–1250,* trans. David Goldstein (Harmondsworth: Penguin, 1971), p. 136.

8. Etty Hillesum, *Etty, A Diary, 1941–1943,* trans. A.J. Pomerans (London: Cape, 1983), p. 197.

THE SEVEN WEEKS OF CONSOLATION

1. T.S. Eliot, "East Coker," in *Four Quartets* (London: Faber, 1944).

2. Miep Gies, *Anne Frank Remembered: The Story of Miep Gies,* with A.L. Gold (London: Corgi, 1988), p. 11.

3. Antione Saint-Exupéry, *Le Petit Prince,* trans. Katherine Woods (London: Pan Books, Ltd., 1974), p. 67.

4. M. Avot 4:18.

5. Harold Kushner, *Who Needs God?* (London: Simon & Schuster, 1990; New York: Summit Books, 1989), p. 119.